AUTISM – THE EIGHTH COLOUR OF THE RAINBOW

AUTISM – THE EIGHTH COLOUR OF THE RAINBOW

Learn to Speak Autistic

Florica Stone

Jessica Kingsley Publishers
London and Philadelphia

First published in the United Kingdom in 2004
by Jessica Kingsley Publishers
116 Pentonville Road
London N1 9JB, England
and
400 Market Street, Suite 400
Philadelphia, PA 19106, USA

www.jkp.com

Library of Congress Cataloging in Publication Data
Stone, Florica.
Autism : the eighth colour of the rainbow : learn to speak autistic / Florica Stone.
p. cm.
Includes bibliographical references and index.
ISBN 1-84310-182-3 (pbk.)
1. Autistic children--Language. 2. Autistic children--Family relationships. 3. Parents of autistic children. 4. Autistic children--Care. I. Title.
RJ506.A9S765 2004
618.92'89--dc22

2004005450

British Library Cataloguing in Publication Data
A CIP catalogue record for this book is available from the British Library

ISBN 1 84310 182 3

Printed and Bound in Great Britain by
Athenaeum Press, Gateshead, Tyne and Wear

With deepest love to my patient, caring and loving children Sebastian, Alexander and Francesca and to my loving husband Chris who completed our lives with the other seven colours of the rainbow

CONTENTS

Acknowledgements

Without the collective perceptions and the involvement of people from all walks of life, this book would have once again described autism as a behavioural syndrome or perhaps would have tried to promote yet another curative therapy. All the concepts I use in this book – autism, autistic literal learning, literal memory, photographic experience and learning, as well as interaction with the autistic – evolved from understanding that autism is a way of being and that the autistic person deserves respect. He or she must not be subjected to behaviour modification programmes.

A special thank you to David Howkins (the Giant Friend), founder and trustee of Hope–TLC, for his friendship to Alexander, continuous involvement and generosity towards the autistic cause, his words of wisdom and for believing in my dream.

Heartfelt gratitude to our team of volunteer friends, David, Yvonne, Simon 1 and Simon 2, Pat, Ruth, Sarah, Rosie, Illa, Harleene, Norma, Joan, Maggie and Paul, for their patience, imagination and the hundreds of hours they invested in Alexander and me, and to Nadia and Marie for showering Francesca with their love.

My respect and wishes for a fulfilling life go to my autistic friends, Feather, Muskie, Paradox, Seth, Ivo, Elise, Autie, Bexxy, Ian, Naomi, Vic, Alexander, Wolffy, Omy, Waspie and Whilly, for their friendship, patience and extended explanations as I was attempting to make sense of their reality and they tried to make sense of mine.

Thank you to Amanda Baggs, Jim Sinclair, Donna Williams, Temple Grandin and many other autistic people who, through their written work, made it easier for me to visualise the autistic reality and thus empathise through understanding.

I share my hope that this book can facilitate a better quality of life for all the autistic children and their parents in the world, as well as a huge hug for those who shared affection with me. Their affection motivated me throughout my journey of understanding autism.

Unconditional love to my children for their patience during the writing of this book and to my brother Ioan, sister-in-law Aurica and my niece Gabriela for helping me care for Alexander during our year of desperate need and for taking care of us during the writing of this book.

Letter from a loving mother

...I want to build a bridge –
From my world into yours.
Will you meet me half-way?
Maybe one day,
Can it really be that simple?!
To shower you in unconditional love –
Not leave you to flounder,
But inspire you to test the waters
Of this alien land...
From 'Open Your Eyes' by Treasa Granell

In June 1998 we found out that our child, Pierce (aged two and a half), had autism. At the time, we were totally devastated. We were completely ignorant of what autism meant – believing only that he would live in his own 'world' for all the time, and possibly end up in residential care.

In a bid to try to understand our son and find ways to help him, we read anything we could lay our hands on regarding autism and bombarded professionals with questions. We were left more worried than ever. Professionals and books alike seemed to point to our son's future being depressingly bleak – but we simply could not accept this.

Then I attended a talk given by Florica and my beliefs changed. She showed us that we could change the course of our son's life and ease the path ahead of him – by learning to understand him (as much as we were able). Florica is a woman with a depth of understanding and empathy for people with autism who I really warmed to. She cared – and it showed. She spoke from the heart when she explained how people with autism had a different perspective on life from ours. But one thing I'll always remember was her saying that autism doesn't have to be a disability – more of an added ability that we 'normal' people do not have! I liked that. I learned more from her that night than from all the books I have read or from all the unsatisfactory answers given by professionals.

I rang Florica after the meeting and she welcomed Pierce and me into her home with open arms. When we left, Pierce blew her a kiss – I was astounded! And a little jealous – if I am honest – as he hadn't yet shown any affection to me, and I was with him every waking moment. But we learned so much over the following weeks. It wasn't about trying to change Pierce or force him to conform to our ways of doing things. It was more about changing our way of doing things, about changing our attitude towards him, being respectful of him as an individual and hopefully gaining his trust.

Florica helped us to be totally loving and non-judgemental towards Pierce. The love was always there – the being non-judgemental took a little longer.

We set up a playroom for Pierce and enlisted the help of a few trusted and open-minded volunteers, and now spend many hours each day just being with Pierce. We let him know that anything he chooses to do is OK by us – and we saw this by joining him, rather than stopping him doing something deemed 'unsuitable' by society. We are slowly gaining his trust and are definitely reaping the rewards! He is a really happy little boy – and we have finally come to terms with his autism and love him all the more for it, as it makes him the little person he is! We wouldn't want to change that – but we would like for him to be able to function independently in the future in our 'big, bad' world, so we are helping him to learn the tools to get by. Our house is a far happier place these days. Pierce actively seeks our company – which is brilliant – and is allowing us to get a little closer daily. I hope that we are helping Pierce to make sense of our world – so that things are less confusing for him in the future.

We have learned this from Florica, who (from my limited knowledge of autism) is the closest anyone can get to thinking with an autistic mind – and still be considered 'normal'!

PS: I am no longer resentful that Pierce chose Florica to be the first person he bestowed a kiss upon – she deserved it – and I have had countless kisses and hugs since then, so I must be doing something right!

Treasa Granell

Why the eighth colour
of the rainbow?

One evening, very late, Feather, one of my many adult autistic friends, opened her heart and wrote:

> Personally, I don't like the autism term 'Self-driven'. That translates to me 'selfish' or only going through life for himself or herself.
>
> Add that to the lack of empathy in the diagnoses and it adds up to the autistic being selfish, uncaring people, and I have time and time again heard parents say 'My child doesn't *care* about anyone else's feelings'. *That is not right!!!!*
>
> Personally, I would like to change the name of the disorder and the term of 'lacks empathy'. There's too much confusion on the traits and stereotypes happening.
>
> A closer description would be, pursues a self-understanding and lacks picking up on others' feelings but cares and wants to know. (How can you stick that in a nice diagnosis using just a tidy few words?) Does that make sense?
>
> I think it is a very negative description of the people bearing it... I have never known such a kind and considerate bunch of people in my life...but they can't read the emotion and innuendoes so they are labelled as cold and selfish.

These words disturbed me. How should I describe autism to the non-autistic and at the same time maintain respect for my friend's and my son's feelings?

I have heard autism described as the invisible disability, yet after reading autistic people's accounts of their lives it dawned upon me that autism or the autism continuum is only a label for a varied condition which we do not understand and thus find it hard to empathise with. On the other hand autistic describes the essence of a human being (not an alien living in a bubble). For the autistic, autism is not a weed to be pulled out; on the contrary, autism is something to be proud of.

It occurred to me that in the same way as white light is the essence of all colours, so autism is the essence of the autistic person. To reveal the beauty of the rainbow one needs a prism. However, what if we consider the light itself to be in effect the eighth colour – the invisible colour, something to be proud of, something to be valued separately in its own right? Surely this is the metaphor for autism?

We non-autistics can become a stable prism of trust for autistic people and allow them to show us their beauty. We need to find within ourselves the patience to observe and understand what we have in common, not what sets us apart. We need to shower them with the unconditional love and tender loving care that every autistic person deserves; in fact not only deserves but is I believe entitled to.

This book sets out to show that there is no autistic behaviour left to manage when the use of understanding and unconditional love leads to meaningful interaction, shared understanding and friendship. It is, then, that autism relinquishes its role of representing the whole person and becomes just the eighth colour of the rainbow.

The aim of this book

If like us in the past you cannot make sense of your child's behaviour and wonder whether he[1] can make sense of yours, if you would like to enjoy the company of your child more and relax in your own home, but think that autism prevents that from happening, then this book can show how you can assume responsibility[2] regarding the way in which your child is taught and interacted with.

In 1992, as the parent of a newly diagnosed child, Alexander, I had many questions about autism and about what autism was going to do to us as a family. The following represent what I considered core questions:

- Do we understand what autism means?

- Can we relate to it?

- Can we cure autism?

- Do we need to cure it or is it possible to live in harmony without a cure?

- Is autism the same as autistic behaviour?

- Will I ever have a conversation with my child?

- How best can I help my child, my family and myself?

I wanted to find answers for the following reasons:

- My child's behaviour had a negative impact on our home environment and our emotional well-being, and restricted our everyday activities and social life.

- We found ourselves crying because we couldn't relate to Alexander.

- We spent numerous hours asking questions such as 'Why me? Why us? Why him?', including the classic 'What have I done to deserve this?'

As you read through this book you will come across real life stories, some exercises and 'food for thought' ideas and questions. They were designed to help you understand difficult situations or solve specific problems.

A written record of your answers will help you assess your child's progress, your progressive understanding of autism and the changes in your perception of what autism means. By finding answers to your questions you will:

- gather *specific* information about the way in which *your* child's behaviour is affected by his perception of reality

- help yourself to become an effective *translator* of autistic behaviour and autistic communication[3]

- find out what is responsible for his behaviour

- find out how his behaviour affects you emotionally and how your emotions condition your understanding of your child's autism

- develop an *individual plan of action* to teach your child a shared system of significance from which meaningful communication can evolve

- separate *intrinsic aspects*[4] of autism from your child's need for love and acceptance.

It is hoped that your own findings will:

- encourage you to show him your acceptance and understand autism as a way of being

- encourage you to create an autistic-friendly[5] environment for your child and become his best friend, mentor and advocate

- enable you to help him *learn through language*[6] and develop social skills

- show you that autism is not your fault and that it is not your child's fault

- help you empathise with your child and show how you can help him empathise with you

- enable you both to experience mutual joy, which stems from shared understandings.

Notes

1. 'He' and 'him' will be used to refer to both genders.

2. Assuming responsibility means interacting with the child at every opportunity, trying to understand the meaning of his behaviour, teaching him meaningful words and accepting that he has no means of judging his behaviour as right or wrong because his mind dictates it.

3. Autistic communication describes the autistic's attempt to communicate his needs prior to having received help with building a system of shared meanings. Such was Alexander's screaming, pulling me to the fridge, being afraid that his name changed from Alex to Frightened, charging into my stomach to show me that he loves me, etc. This communication can be translated, explained to a willing student and transformed during meaningful interaction.

4. The sensory system with which he was born and his style of learning.

5. See Chapter 7 concerning an autistic-friendly environment.

6. As opposed to only learning in pictures or through experiences.

1

An overview of the autism continuum

Searching for a 'cure'

As a distressed parent, I wished I had a book to guide me towards meaningful interaction with my son and to take away some of my worries. I wished for realistic yet hopeful answers to my daunting questions. The absence of such a book triggered the beginning of what turned out to be nine years of self-funded research. This research was designed to find out the meaning of autism, help my son and, if successful, describe to other parents what they can do to help their child. My research required thousands of hours of interaction. It was and continues to be arbitrated by common sense. Its success is validated and monitored by the willingness of the autistic person to interact with me. My own conduct during interaction stems from empathy and aims to inspire bonding through communication.

As soon as the doctor told me that Alexander had autism and that autism cannot be cured (as in curing an illness), I plunged into a deep feeling of hurt and helplessness. Three days later my question 'Why can it not be cured?' was answered with 'Because we don't know what it is'. I found hope in that answer and decided to challenge the prognosis, not the diagnosis (I was told that there was little that I could do for him and was advised to focus on my normal children).

However, if we don't know what it is, it follows that we don't know why it cannot be cured. Nor do we know if an autistic child could learn to adapt to a non-autistic world without being cured.

If it wasn't for Alex

Since 1992, finding a cure for autism became my overriding goal. During those early years, and believing that the only way I could reach my son was through a cure, I found myself ready to move mountains and, if needed, I was prepared to believe in miracles. I read the latest medical books on this condition. Along the way I searched for a kind and loving therapy that would instil long-lasting change in my son. I wanted a therapy aimed at: teaching him language; stopping him from eating earth and coal; stopping him from screaming and writing on the walls; helping him to hug me; or perhaps motivating him to keep his clothes on. The list is endless. I was willing to learn from anyone who could *show* me what to do, not tell me what I am supposed to do! I wanted to enjoy a hug from my son and I wanted to watch him mix with children of his own age. For many years none of these wishes seemed remotely attainable.

Then, during 1993, I read in our local newspaper a story about a 'revolutionary therapy'. It seemed the most loving approach towards autism I had yet encountered. This approach also claimed to bring about a 'miraculous loving cure'. So, wanting to learn more and in pursuit of a loving cure, my son, my ex-husband and I went to America. As much as I could 'see' my son transform each day, I remained puzzled by many aspects of his 'impossible development'. Every day, before my eyes, my son was changing. Unfortunately, however, those changes were far from long lasting. I left America with three unanswered core questions:

1. How would my being totally non-judgemental 'cure' my son's autism?

2. Why did my son have a need to behave so differently from his brother?

3. Why weren't the changes in his behaviour long lasting? (e.g. Why did he forget newly learned words? Why could he not generalise?)[1]

My questions received the following reply: 'The child does the best he can with what he knows [vague] and for as long as changes occur we don't need to understand *why* they occur.' I found this answer incomplete and fatalistic. Furthermore, if I knew why changes occurred I could have helped bring them along faster as opposed to wondering in the dark.

The answer wasn't the only thing I couldn't quite understand. I was taught that happiness is a choice (I went there to learn how to cure autism) and that I could choose to be happy even if my son was to remain autistic. Furthermore, in choosing to be happy with his autism, I would be doing myself a favour and be helpful to my son. In theory this is a positive thought.

Personally and practically, I found it very hard to feel happy at the time. I could pretend to be happy because I adored Alexander. He could spot from a mile away when I was pretending. My challenge was to find out if this unknown entity called autism continuum or if something else triggered an uncontrollably disruptive and destructive behaviour in my son. Could I change that? Could I find out what that was?

I have yet to meet a parent who readily reached the so-called 'happiness mode' before he or she could communicate with the child or at least be positively reassured that the child is even reachable. Equally, I have yet to meet the autistic adult who didn't feel hurt by their parents' continued search for a 'cure'.

The advice maze

The full implications of autism form the object of various researches.[2] Depending on which philosophical or psychological school of thought people embraced, their advice on how to interact with an autistic person varies from behaviour modification to passive acceptance. Finding my way forward through this maze of advice proved one of my hardest tasks and I wish to make it easier for you. I tried to learn from many people:

- care managers and therapists who claimed to be able to teach me how to manage autistic behaviour – but their 'management techniques' showed little respect for the person who had autism and failed to ask why the autistic person needed to behave autistically[3]

- medics who found themselves fascinated and intrigued by autism and described it in medical terms

- wise people who inspired me to keep an open mind and to continue my search for loving solutions

- documentaries and films about autism – promoting various images of what the condition is about and what life is like for those living with it

- people who wanted to find the cause of autism, who had devoted their lives to attaching blame to the condition

- people who laid claims to a miracle cure for autism through behaviour modification or through love

- people who looked to science for a cure.

My best teachers, however, were the experts in autism – the adult autistic people. They taught me what it feels like to live on the spectrum and how to get closer to my son's reality, heart and soul.[4] They also taught me what we can 'cure', what we cannot cure, and why. I remember starting a conversation with an autistic friend with 'I read in a book that…' Her reply started with 'This is no book baby. This is real life and I am living it!' The successes of the children with whom I played and interacted, my own son included, validated their teaching.

My initial feelings are just a faded memory that has been progressively substituted with joy after I understood:

- Alexander's autism and how he learns

- how it influenced his individual behaviour

- what I could do to help him

- what I could do to help myself

- how to enjoy his company and he enjoyed mine.

Food for thought

Through no fault of his own, my son and your child are living an autistic reality and will continue to. Therefore, I believe that it is within our reach as well as our duty as loving parents to provide them with our loving understanding and a supportive environment.

Traditional clinical definitions of autism – possible causes

> The central problem is a triad of impairments affecting social interaction,[5] social communication[6] and imagination.[7] This triad is always accompanied by a limited, narrow, repetitive pattern of activities.[8] Recent research has shown that the skills of social interaction, communication and imagination are, like other developmental skills, dependent upon aspects of the function of the brain although precise areas involved have not yet been identified. (Wing 1992)

Identifying the existence of such a triad of impairments in a child should be helpful to parents, teachers or care workers. It should remove doubts regarding parenting and warn us about possible behavioural displays that stem from a perception of reality which we, the non-autistics, perceive and interpret differently.

Food for thought

Most important of all, the diagnosis should help the child too. Which means that he should be interacted with patiently and gently. The process of teaching should derive from a process of understanding the meanings of the narrow repetitive patterns of behaviour.

Does repetitive behaviour symbolise lack of imagination? No. Sometimes, in my experience, it acted as my only guide towards a child's level of understanding of social interaction and communication.

The skills of social interaction, communication and imagination are all filtered through our sensory system and you will learn to identify what this means.

> It is generally agreed that autism *is* a behavioural syndrome resulting from a range of aetiological[9] factors and the term 'autistic spectrum disorders' is frequently used in acknowledgement of this. The basic cause in the majority of cases has yet to be ascertained but genetic factors are increasingly implicated. (Stores and Wiggs 1998, p.157)

> ### *Food for thought*
>
> The autistic child's genetic make-up is unique. If autism has genetic origins, it is in no sense the child's 'fault'. This being so, should he be punished for the behaviour dictated by his mind? Should we waste energy modifying the visible aspects just for the sake of 'helping him look normal'? The obvious answer is no. Furthermore, we must consider the following:
>
> - What are the implications of those genetic differences? Are they feeding a 'false reality' to the mind? *Yes.*
>
> - Are those genetic differences causing suffering or confusion in our children? *At a physical level they can.*
>
> - How best can we show our willingness to help a child who thinks differently from ourselves? *Through our interaction.*
>
> - Can a 'normal' mind imagine what the 'autistic' mind is thinking? Yes. How? *Through observing the body language and listening to the autistic's spoken language.*
>
> - Can the two 'minds' relate to each other and can the autistic learn from the non-autistic and vice versa? Yes. How? *Through empathy, literal teaching, and finally shared meanings.*

Uta Frith (1989) concluded that the underlying cause for autistic behaviour stems from the *predisposition of the mind*.[10] Once again I found a reason to hope from her answer. Concluding that a person's mind is predisposed differently from the 'normal' doesn't explain why. Only when we know why that happens can we deliver help or make any predictions (if any!) regarding a person's future ability to make sense of social life. I wanted to know why Alexander's mind was predisposed differently from mine and what that meant in everyday terms.

> ### *Food for thought*
>
> Frith's well-researched answer should, once again, reinforce the fact that the autistic doesn't perceive the world the same way as the non-autistic person. Finding shared meanings with the non-verbal autistic, therefore, can be harder work than if verbal.
>
> In either case directing your energies towards finding how your child perceives the world, how the child learns, and what he or she is trying to communicate through individual behaviour or words will lead you to finding shared understandings and empathy.

Learning from the autistic's perception of autism

All over the world (my own home included) live people who have been diagnosed with 'autism continuum' (from low functioning to high functioning). Whether they were born with it or whether something 'caused' it, these people live in an 'autistic reality',[11] which is the prime cause of their behaviour. People who behave in an autistic way need love, respect and help – in this order. After spending thousands of hours trying to relate to them, I came to believe that the only way in which we can truly understand that reality would be to experience it. Having said that, I also came to experience true friendship, fun and reassuring companionship, unconditional help and acceptance from my autistic friends, as well as enjoying meaningful communication, without actually experiencing the autistic reality.

> ### *Food for thought*
>
> A child who experiences an autistic reality has no recollection of any other. By virtue of his make-up he has no means of comparing one way of being with any other, let alone think about 'punishing the non-autistic behaviour'. What *belief*, and *sold* by whom, compels us to?

Therefore this book sets out to show you how to implement Jim Sinclair's message to parents:

> The autistic child who needs support of adult caretakers and who can form meaningful relationships with those caretakers if given the opportunity... For their own sake and for the sake of their children, I urge parents to make radical changes in their perceptions of what autism means... It takes more work to communicate with someone whose native language isn't the same as yours. And autism goes deeper than language and culture; autistic people are 'foreigners' in any society. You're going to have to give up your assumptions about shared meanings. You're going to have to learn to [go] back to levels more basic than you've probably thought about before, to translate, and to check to make sure your translations are understood. You're going to have to give up the certainty that comes of being on your own familiar territory, of knowing you're in charge, and let your child teach you a little of her language, guide you a little way into his world. (Sinclair 1993)

Talking with, sheltering and finally befriending many autistic people allowed me to witness, decode and enjoy the autistic way of being. This only happened after I learned more about my friends' perceptions of reality. Interacting with them, from a platform of trust and friendship, allowed me both to relate to my own son from a position of understanding and to radically change my perceptions with regard to the skills of social interaction, communication and imagination. This book can guide you – the person who cares – towards what we might term 'an autistic reality'.

Food for thought

Along the way, be prepared to work hard at helping your child distinguish between what we call dreams and what we perceive as reality.

During interactive games or conversations, discover what causes him to experience a distorted reality and find out if and how you can help his sensory system and/or his comprehension of the spoken word.

Once you have achieved this, you will have to teach him the difference between make-believe and true and false; share your imagination and wait for his imagination to unfold.

Once there, you will be able to help your child enjoy social interaction, guide him towards social communication, explain the culturally encoded social rules, and offer a shoulder for support or shelter in your arms or home when life seems overwhelming.

Autism and the family

When a child is diagnosed as having autism we suddenly find ourselves the parents, brothers, sisters or grandparents to what may seem like an alien child. Shattered by the news and confused by various therapies, we stumble through conflicting advice. Motivated by wild and blinding emotions, some of us may feel prepared to do anything to help our children,[12] while others of us may feel too paralysed to try reaching out to the child who needs our long-term love and protection.

Food for thought

If you decide to learn to understand and cater for your child's autistic needs, think up a lifelong strategy. This strategy should be sympathetic towards you, your autistic child and your other children.

Don't be afraid to ask your entire family for help – and by that I mean the autistic child's help too. Be honest and talk with your other children about the difficulties you are experiencing. You will need support and patience to make it work.

As the years go by, some of our non-autistic children may begin to harbour resentment towards a child who monopolises all the attention with seemingly nothing to offer in return. Our non-autistic children soon learn to hate the word autism; either that or they begin wishing for the wrong reasons that they were the autistic ones.

Due to lack of 'normal' communication skills, the autistic child has little input regarding how other people will behave towards him. Whether others will treat him kindly remains at the mercy of our judgement. Grandparents subscribe to several schools of thought. I have met the extremely supportive super-grandparents and I would love to encourage more grandparents to offer their support to their children. If they offered just one babysitting night every two weeks, the parents could rest or enjoy each other's company in peace – thus keeping them united and strong during harsh times. I have heard of 'blame-it-on-someone-else grandparents' and have experienced at first hand the attitude 'I don't think the doctors got it right, your child is normal'.

By the end of this book you will learn that the rewards stemming from meaningful everyday interaction and shared understanding will remove your fear of autism and benefit the entire family.

Notes

1. Generalise = generalisation skills (see Glossary). Common questions from parents like myself are 'Why can't my child learn from experience?' or 'Why can he not generalise?' The answer to the first question comes from understanding your child's sensory system (e.g. the sense of taste). One autistic person said to me: 'I didn't know that I could peel carrots and boil them the same way as I peel potatoes and boil them.'

   I asked, 'Do you like carrots?'
   She replied, 'No.'
   'Do you like parsnips?'
   She replied, 'I do.'
   I asked, 'Did anyone teach you how to cook them?'
   'No. I just did what I had done to the potatoes.'

   I chose this example because it illustrates our motivation to learn generalisation skills when we want to pursue one of our likes or to meet a need. Any autistic person will learn generalisation skills when:

   - he masters a shared system of meaning with you

   - he has a need to resolve

   - his sensory system warns him of danger.

   The answer to 'Why isn't my child talking more?' or 'Why is he not talking more after he spoke his first word?' is 'Because he didn't know that he spoke and how speaking will change his life for the better' – in the literal sense of speaking.

2. Scientific, or any other interventions mainly focused on behaviour modification or behaviour management techniques.

3. Behaviour that puzzles us.

4. The only source of shared emotions present in both autistics and non-autistics.

5. See Chapter 13, 'Interaction: the gateway to shared meanings'.

6. See Chapter 12, 'Premises for social communication'.

7. See Chapter 18, Imagination, p.179.

8.   See Chapter 18, 'Reasons behind repetitive behaviour'.

9.   Study of causes, especially of disease (*Oxford English Dictionary*).

10. How the mind makes judgements and/or thinks.

11. This reality is unique to each child and is determined by the individual's sensory system.

12. From believing in miracles (me) to behaviour modification and/or sending a child to boarding school – a continuum of parental perceptions.

2

Grieving

Before I understood the various meanings of autistic behaviour I used to grieve over it, I was angry at it and I wanted it stopped. If you find yourself grieving over your child's behaviour, I would like to help you overcome your grief by sharing with you what helped me overcome mine.

I am hoping that after you are faced with the diagnosis you can find the needed inner strength to give of yourself before you know what you will receive in return. In the beginning I did not know how important it was for Alexander to live in an autistic-friendly environment. He never asked for it because he could not talk. He did thank me for it years later – after he learned how to talk. His changing behaviour was my only indication that I was doing something right.

Don't mourn for us

In 1993 I read 'Don't mourn for us' by Jim Sinclair (See appendix D). His article is addressed primarily to parents. Some parents react negatively to his article, yet all he is calling for is for us to change our perception of what autism means and asking us to stop showing our grief to our children. I wished I could have read this article before I began my search for a cure. It would have given me an insight into how it felt like for the non-verbal Alexander to experience an atmosphere filled with grief. I know I was guilty of feeling grief. My grief was born out of my inability to understand and relate to my child. The article would have given me the much-needed hope that my child and I could develop a meaningful relationship, but the same article couldn't teach me how to develop it. I learned that the hard way. Jim wrote:

> Some amount of grief is natural as parents adjust to the fact that an event and relationship they've been looking forward to isn't going to materialise. But this grief over a fantasised normal child needs to be separated from the parent's perceptions of the child that they do have: the autistic child who needs the support of adult caretakers and who can form meaningful relationships with those caretakers if given the opportunity. Continuing focus on the child's autism as a source of grief is damaging for both the parent and the child, and precludes the development of an accepting and authentic relationship between them. For their own sake and for the sake of their children, I urge parents to make radical changes in their perceptions of what autism means. (Sinclair 1993)

Substituting my grief and guilt with joy and inner peace took nine long years. Each day seemed like a battle towards:

- helping my son make himself understood – gave me hope

- learning and developing my understanding of the meaning of autism from autistic people (my own son included) – gave me knowledge and ability to empathise with the unknown

- changing my own behaviour – as in becoming more observing and therefore accepting that at times he needs his space

- understanding that autism did not take over, but on the contrary autism caused Alex to communicate his needs through behaviour

- transforming our home into a sanctuary – creating a place where all of us could laugh together.

The battle ended after I began reaping rewards from loving interaction: enjoying Alexander talking with me, then with his siblings, then cracking a joke, then a cuddle, a smile, a small conversation and finally just enjoying his company as it comes.

Food for thought

If your child could ask you to change your perception of what autism means he would find it difficult to explain what he means in non-autistic terms.

Our children can sense our grief but have no idea why we are grieving.

3

Learning and adapting

After nine years of experience, I continue to wish for easier solutions to all the problems associated with autism.[1] However, my adult autistic friends presented their autism as a 'way of being and behaving' that stems from the individual's perception of our world. A way of being cannot be 'cured', which is why some of my friends find the word 'cure' so offensive. This is not to say that the autistic person cannot be helped. An autistic person can be helped in more ways than one and often actively wants to learn to *adapt*. Adapting is not the same as changing from autistic to normal. Adapting means developing and using meaningful communication and social skills whilst remaining autistic.

Food for thought

The autistic person wants you to learn and adapt. Inside this person is a consciousness, a soul that feels pain, joy, belonging and rejection in just the same way you do.

I am in no position to 'predict' how far a child will develop. I am in a position to teach you to inspire development through loving everyday interaction and to make his life on earth more bearable if not happier. The perceptions created by our children about the external environment can be changed to a certain degree. Their perception of our world in general and the perspective on social interaction in particular are strongly linked to how we choose to interact with him.

What you can do

Whilst your love and understanding cannot cure his way of learning, it can prevent your child from feeling lonely, will protect him from physical pain and can inspire him to communicate. It can also inspire you to create an autistic-friendly environment designed to meet his sensory and learning needs and a sanctuary for you. It can motivate you to speak literally[2] with your child until his communication skills are developed enough to have a full conversation.

Unlike what I was led to believe, my love for Alexander did not cure his autism. If I am honest, in 2001 I felt depressed because of it – more depressed than when he was first diagnosed. This depression stemmed out of pressure from social conventions and from having been lied to, not from Alexander's autism.

There are great differences between loving a child and suffering in silence and knowing how best to deliver help. This is where our weaknesses become exploitable. So trust your intuition. Switch off your confusion and pain. Open your mind and become a scholar of life.

Autism doesn't impede your child from developing communication skills and communication doesn't mean that autism is cured. Communication is a ticket to mutual understanding, your child's freedom of expression, self-esteem and a new lease of life. Therefore your efforts to inspire communication will be rewarded in the shape of peace of mind.

Autism doesn't prevent non-verbal communication

Based on my experience, I can assert that every child communicates his needs to you, even if he communicates them through what we perceive as unacceptable, repetitive or senseless behaviour. Providing him with the autistic environment for learning will make it easy for the child to adapt his style of communication to incorporate the non-autistic style.

Meaningful interaction begins when the child (and by using the word 'child' I mean any person of any age and any gender) understands what is wanted. After the child gains confidence around you, further social interaction begins.

Autism doesn't prevent a child from learning language

Perhaps whilst you read this book you are parenting a child who is unable to express his or her needs verbally. I hope that the knowledge shared in this book will help you find your potential to transform yourself to inspire your child to talk with you.

If he talks but his speech is repetitive, this book can show you how to help him learn a large, meaningful vocabulary, thus freeing him from confusion and repetition.

Autism doesn't stop a child from feeling emotions

I also hope that this book will provide some tools to assist you in your quest to communicate your emotions and bond further with an already verbal child. We don't teach emotions, we feel them. Your job is to help your child label them.

Autism is not an impediment to social interaction

The child whom I feared would never make his own friends did make his own friends. The question changed from 'Can he make friends?' to 'What makes a good friend?', 'What makes him miss a friend?' and 'Where can I find more people like the ones whom he really bonds with?'

His sensitive hearing might prevent him from joining in with loud children. Therefore, granting him a silent learning space away from noisy children is within your ability and becomes your token of love to him. Compare this with setting off to change his sensitive hearing or asking, say, 50 children to be quiet because your child cannot cope with the noise. Making allowances for his needs is much easier and more effective.

Autism is not an impediment to social communication or empathy

As my autistic son Alexander approaches 13 years of age, our friendship is blossoming and his communication and social skills are continuing to develop steadily. Autism did not stop them from developing – his comprehension and sensory system slowed them down.

I became his trusted friend, interpreter and translator of autistic communication, teacher of literal language, mentor of non-autistic communication and emotional/human rights advocate.

The child whom I feared would never attend school did attend school. My questions changed from 'Can he go to school?' to 'Is it best for him to be in school?', 'Which school?', 'For how long?' and 'To whose benefit?'

Autism is not an impediment to sharing emotions or imagination

The child whom I feared would never tell me that he loves me did more than tell me, he showed me. His tactile sensitivity might discourage him from hugging or kissing you. If this is your case you will soon learn other ways of expressing and sharing affection.

Autism is not an impediment to meaningful interaction

As you read through this book, you will often come across the word *interaction*. What I am sharing in this book is not a therapy per se because I do not perceive autism as an illness or a disease.[3] Autism is a way of being and learning which requires understanding. Your understanding of your child's way of being evolves with increased *loving positive interaction.*

We and our children interact constantly. It is up to us to change negative and meaningless interaction into its positive meaningful counterpart. In order to apply the principles of interaction, you don't have to be happy with the autistic behaviour. What you have to do is to create a safe physical space where you can observe his behaviour and then make judgements on why it happens and how best you can model your interaction to address his understanding and ability to relate to what you want from him. You don't need language for this, nor do you need a miracle – just patience and knowledge.

It wasn't Alexander's 'autism' that upset me; nor did my 'non-autistic origin' cause my son to be upset. The lack of meaningful interaction between us caused us both a great deal of frustration, weariness and upset. My fear of dying with no one to look after him after my death caused me to cry for hundreds of hours. I believe you are probably reading this book because you are experiencing similar difficulties.

Example

The youngest child with whom I shared the skills of meaningful interaction other than my son was two years old and the oldest was 42. Both needed

TLC. Both needed understanding. Both needed supportive parents. What was different between the two?

Pierce

Pierce (aged two) had supportive and loving parents. Due to their willingness to learn about his autism, coupled with their desire to understand the individuality of their child, Pierce continues to build on his communication skills and to enjoy social interaction. He is learning every day how to deal with the demands of other people as well as making his own demands heard.

FLASHBACK

At the end of our first play session Pierce blew me an affectionate kiss from the car. His gesture should not be interpreted as 'me curing his autism' because autistic people cannot show affection (another myth). His gesture meant that I had gained his attention. He watched me blow him a kiss and because we had had fun he smiled and then copied my behaviour (thus learned through copying in the same way as any 'normal' child does) and blew a kiss back (emotion driven). No miracles, just shared understanding and human bonding.

TWO YEARS ON

Two years after playing with Pierce, his mother[4] told me: 'I couldn't understand you at times. You told me that Pierce needs me to explain everything to him. At the time my son was non-verbal and a whirlwind. I used to wonder how I could explain anything when he wasn't even listening or talking. Two years on I understand. My son asks more questions than I have answers for.'

A strict need for accuracy

The other child (now 45) learned communication skills too. She learned them the hard way and on her own and is less equipped to deal with the demands of other people. We became friends after we met on the #Autism[5] channel in 1998. Gaining her trust was a long journey and I made many mistakes. Eventually she trusted me enough to share her past social experiences.

Throughout the years her behaviour was considered obnoxious, emotionally disturbed and she was eventually diagnosed as schizophrenic. She spent most of her life homeless. At some point she self-diagnosed herself with autism and found a friendly psychologist who supported her.

She holds little faith in the non-autistic population. She lives on her own and feels angry at the lack of proper support for autistics. This extract from a letter offers you an opportunity to take a peek into an inner emotional world that remained unknown for many years, as well as provide you with a simple solution that will help you protect your child from confusion:

> One of the questions whose answer would decide which side of the AS or HFA diagnoses I'd fall could be given by someone who once knew me, and could describe exactly was 'the speech impediment' I remember having once had. I knew I had a speech impediment because I was ridiculed and sometimes punished for it; however, I hadn't any perception of what it was that I was doing 'wrong'. Information from my mother is usually more wishful thinking than memory, so she wasn't the person to ask.
>
> But I'm still in touch with my high school best friend. When I first met her I had been working on my voice for about two years (I wanted to be able to make political speeches), and was speaking much better. But I do know I was still being laughed at occasionally when I spoke in class, and my best friend described me as 'speaking in Ramona (not her real name)'. She told me a number of years ago that I 'spoke in Ramona' until my early 20s.
>
> So today on the phone I asked her what 'speaking in Ramona' was. I was expecting something like 'odd phraseology' or 'peculiar words'. Instead she said (as exactly as I can quote her), 'A lot of gestures and grunting. It was kind of like charades, but not as well organised.' Communicating in a mix of words, gestures and grunts into one's early 20s is not AS.[6]
>
> Okay, so my reaction to this information is irrational. But I am upset. Not about the HFA thing… I was beginning to suspect that given that I seem to function a notch below most online aspies. It's just that I went through a fundamental re-evaluation and re-identification of myself (from 'mysteriously weird' to 'Asperger's Syndrome') and now I need to go back into all the corners of my mind, erase 'Asperger's Syndrome' and replace it with 'Autistic Disorder'. I also, yet again, have a somewhat incorrect diagnosis ('possibly AS, possibly HFA,[7] most likely AS' ought to read at least 'most likely[8] HFA').
>
> This isn't really an 'identity crisis' I guess; it's more like a 'category crisis'. I'm unreasonably attached to categorisation, even meaningless categorisations. I in fact want to continue calling myself an aspie just

in order to not change the labels…but then my urge for strict accuracy objects.

If none of what I wrote makes sense to you, don't worry about it. I'm not being sensible. Lacking anywhere else to post this distressed babble to, I'm posting it to…

There will be times when your child's behaviour might puzzle, annoy or exasperate you because his behaviour just doesn't make sense. I hope that this book will help you make sense and inspire you to keep on trying. As you read it, highlight what applies to your child now.

My quest for Alexander's friendship was long and littered with mistakes. My mistakes stemmed from my lack of understanding and my desire to see him 'normal'. If you wish to save yourself time and unnecessary heartache, please don't repeat my mistakes. Your child can learn to behave 'normal'[9] but the quality of his life is more important than what his behaviour 'looks' like. Alexander's progress could be best described as a 'roller-coaster of changes' and my emotions as a 'roller-coaster ride', taking me from despair to joy, from anger to peace, from lack of knowledge to knowledge and from no hope to equanimity.

The shared triumphs and the blunders in this book are aimed at helping you find a friend in your own child, connect with his soul and become his best friend. Hoping to inspire you to learn how to exchange tears of despair for tears of laughter, I am sharing real life examples. The deliberately repeated examples aim to explain the meaning of medical jargons such as 'triad of impairments', 'pervasive disorder of development', 'predisposition of the mind' or 'autism continuum'. In simple English these mean the same.

Just one aspect of what we call autism, e.g. *sensitive hearing*, can prevent your child from hearing words. Therefore his mind doesn't tell him that he must copy or respond to them. The *first implication* is that social communication is beyond his comprehension, so learning from others is difficult. Therefore, he will engage in some repetitive activities to learn about the environment or to prevent boredom. We interpret repetition to mean lack of imagination. (Another common indication of 'faulty' hearing is our half-belief that our child could be deaf.) The *second implication* is that he will want to protect himself from pain and will cover his ears and/or throw himself on the pavement when a bus passes by or when you are talking to him (or any other repetitive pattern of behaviour). The *third implication* is that he will avoid social interaction with noisy children.

These are all features needed to diagnose the triad of impairments and occur because his mind tells his body to behave and learn according to his senses and to protect himself from what his mind perceives as harm.

Explore this line of thought further. Autism is also described as a behavioural syndrome. Syndrome means condition, disease, pattern, set of symptoms or disorder (frightening!). I believe that the presence of autism is recognised because of a consistent pattern of behaviour. Autism is not the pattern of behaviour. If we take this statement literally, does it mean that my child 'is repetitive' and 'will remain repetitive' because he needs to be repetitive (confusing and scary), or is he repetitive because something causes repetition to happen? The latter statement holds true. Is the behaviour a disorder? Not in my understanding. Is my child's disease the pattern of behaviour? No. It is the only indication of what hurts the child.

Finding an answer to the above questions took ten years of interaction. My explanations and understandings of autism do not stem from quantity, as in meeting hundreds of autistic people and diagnosing them according to their behaviours. They stem from attempted, re-attempted, re-re-attempted, refined and re-refined interaction with 20 people (my son included), to whom I was devoted and did my level best to help assume a rightful dignified place in life. In return, their developments helped me find my own inner peace, which stems from hard-earned understanding and a mutually respectful relationship with my son.

If your child left home and your attempts to understand why have failed, I hope to inspire you to try and bond again. I want this book to seem to you as if it has arms capable of hugging you and calming you down whenever you feel your patience has been pushed to the limits. If you feel angry, commit your thoughts to paper and send them my way. If nothing else, at least you can release some anguish and frustration. Revisit the book after you begin to model your interaction to suit your child's needs and make a habit out of speaking and behaving literally – thus addressing your child's need for preciseness. Use different colours to highlight the changes. Although unequipped to tell you, your child is seeking your love, acceptance, understanding and guidance.

> ### *Food for thought*
>
> Without 'normal' communication, you have no means of knowing how his sensory system tampers with his ability to interact in a 'normal' way. 'Autism' is the only entity validating your child's perceptions of reality.
>
> For example, if your child holds a similar belief to that of my 42-year-old friend, he might *think* that he is talking to you and *expects you to understand his language*. If this is the case, your child remains perplexed at your inability or lack of willingness to communicate back!
>
> Equally important is for you to realise that you cannot feel what it is like living and experiencing the world in the same way as your child does.
>
> *Preciseness* can be achieved through literal talking and lead to your child feeling less confused. Alexander, like many other autistic people, uses it creatively. He creates perfectly interlocking 3-D models, which he imagined. Another friend of mine restores old train carriages for a museum.
>
> Preciseness on your part will help your child develop compensatory skills. I wish we all practised it!

Notes

1. See 'Postscript: an open invitation to better the interaction process', p.253.

2. See Chapter 8, Shaping your language, p.185.

3. See 'Postscript: an open invitation to better the interaction process', p.253.

4. See 'Letter from a loving mother', p.10.

5. An Internet chat channel opened to both parents of autistic children and autistic people.

6. AS short for 'aspie', a term used by autistic people to describe someone diagnosed with Asperger's Syndrome.

7. High functioning autism (HFA). 'What is the difference between high functioning autism and Asperger's Syndrome? At present, the results [of studies] suggest there seems to be no meaningful differences between them. They are more the same than they are different' (Attwood 1998, p.150).

    As I perceive it the only common link between high functioning autism or not so high functioning autism (not that autism functions, the person does!) is the ability of the person to make sense of the spoken word and fit in accordingly.

In October 2001 I was asked 'Are you sure that your child doesn't have Asperger's Syndrome?' because he could speak and make jokes. I was sure. My autistic child had one core 'problem'. He couldn't relate to the spoken word in the same way as my non-autistic children. The only way to overcome the communication problem was to ensure that each spoken word that he uses shares its meaning with the majority of the English-speaking (in his case) population. This process takes time and sheltering from the 'rat race'. When we set off to solve the communication problem we prioritised our action this way:

- his quality of his life – therefore he is more co-operative

- social convention.

8. Any approximation causes confusion in a person who seeks accuracy: e.g. possibly, soon, perhaps, maybe, near enough, etc.

9. See Appendix D, 'Autistic adults and adolescents', p.284.

4

Autism

A way of being

The following visual analogy is designed to introduce you to new meanings of the words *child with autism, autism / autistic* and *communication problems*. Place three identical tablemats on the table. One represents your child at a stage when he feels tense around other people. One represents autism/autistic. The third represents communication problems.

Tense child	Autism/autistic	Communication problems

At this stage, before you learn how to make sense of your child's behaviour and before he can make sense of what you want from him, all tablemats are equal in size. Depending on your understanding of autism in general, you might feel inclined to believe *autism / autistic* as a separable entity from your child's personality.

Place the tablemat representing autism on top of the one representing your child. Try blending in your mind the image of your *child* – his puzzling behaviour, including his perception of our world – with the tablemat representing *autism / autistic*. Therefore your *child* and *autism / autistic* are perceived as one entity.

> Tense child
> Autism/autistic

> Communication
> problems

Before the two of you develop a communication system, his unique perception of our world is a mystery to you and impedes meaningful interaction.

Associate the word *autistic* with a nationality and a system of beliefs and perceptions developed within an autistic culture (e.g. English as in belonging to English culture, or Japanese as in belonging to Japanese culture, and autistic as in belonging to autistic culture).

Make a mental note of the fact that if you were born in England from English parents and have lived in England for most of your life, foreign people can identify you from your *native* origins. Your behaviour, accent and style of interaction all stem from your *Englishness.* When foreign people interact with you, they interact with a human being who happens to be *English.*

In a similar way autism becomes a country in which the natives were born with a sensory system that makes them behave markedly different from the norm and autistic denotes your child's nationality and his *native* belonging to that country. You will learn how to relate to an extremely sensitive human being whose senses and perceptions of reality are radically different from those of your own. With your help he will learn how to relax and relate to your culture. Together you will build bridges of mutual understanding between his and your *native* cultures.

Before I was able to understand the nature of autism, I believed autism to be something that could be removed from my child. My belief made me an easy target for those who sold cures for it. As my understanding of autism grew, I focused my efforts towards overcoming the communication blocks between us. At the time an autistic friend said to me:

> Autism is not a weed that you can pull out and then leave the child cured. Autism is a part of my personality. Something to be proud of and something to be cherished…something that causes me problems and something that makes me unique! I like being called autistic. We have our own culture and our own way of thinking.[1] Autistic culture is precious to me!
>
> I want to understand other people and I want other people to understand me. I want help with understanding other people, but I also want people to stop calling me stupid because I am autistic, bullying

> me for being different, calling me names because I look different!
> Why do you guys need us to show you emotion your way? Does it
> matter if we are different? Why do people make us do things that
> don't make sense to us?

I could relate to what she meant and was already working with autism as opposed to against it.

I hope to inspire you to accept that *child* and *autism/autistic* are an inseparable entity and learn how to work with your child's existing system of learning and way of being. This isn't about terminology or labelling a person. Accepting autistic to mean belonging to a nationality other than ours helped me to understand our differences and our common grounds. From those meaningful communication emerged.

The term *child with autism*[2] might influence you into thinking that without taking away the autism you cannot enjoy communicating with the child. Now consider what some parents asked and/or said to me:

> I want to understand my son. I love him but can't communicate with
> him. How can you talk to these people [autistics]? How do you know
> what to say? Do they understand you? Do you understand them? How
> do you find common topics of conversation? How can you get my son
> to play with you? I hate autism. How can your friends say that autism
> is beautiful when my son cannot communicate with me? His autism
> caused my wife to become depressed. His behaviour and his wants
> rule everything we do or want to do. What is beautiful about autism?
> How can you agree with the statement 'being autistic is beautiful'?

My answers were similar to this one:

> Through interacting and listening to my autistic friends and son, I
> learned to understand the autistic learning style and to decipher the
> various behavioural needs triggered by their individual sensory
> system.
>
> Through punishing the 'autistic behaviour' we are in fact hurting
> another human being as well as preventing the person from learning
> or relaxing.
>
> After hundreds of hours of interaction, I taught myself to speak
> and behave literally. If I used a joke or a figure of speech I told them in
> advance in a format similar to this one:

- This is a joke. *Tell the joke.*
- Do you get it? Did it make sense? *If no, what didn't you understand?*
- Can I explain it? *If yes, then I explain it until it makes sense to him.*

If the child was non-verbal I modelled what I wanted to do. If he liked or understood my idea he came to me. If not he remained preoccupied with his activity.

The beauty my friends are talking about is the beauty of being alive and the beauty of having love to give. I call it the beauty of the soul.

You too can learn to understand your child's needs after you play with him and after he realises that you will not punish his behaviour. Through his play he can show us what is important to him, what he enjoys and what he doesn't, what he understands and what he does not, whom he likes and whom he is afraid of.

Once he perceives us as friends, he will trust us and will seek to interact with us unprompted. Only after he is actively seeking our company can we begin to understand his reality. Equally, only after we begin to understand his reality are we able to offer him help in a way he can make sense of.

Food for thought

Accepting that you and your child are experiencing and learning about the world differently will allow you to focus your energies on unblocking the communication blocks.

Your child will benefit from your acceptance and begin interacting with you.

If your help makes sense to him, the changes in his behaviour become long lasting and your life as a family will begin to change as well. Just as one needs a prism to see the beauty of the rainbow, imagine your understanding of the nature of your child as the prism of friendship from which a relationship of mutual trust may evolve.

Relaxed child Autism/autistic	Individual communication problem

As soon as you and your child enjoy meaningful interaction and develop your personal *communication system*, the tablemat representing joint communication problems reduces in size and is replaced by a matchbox.

> ### *Food for thought*
>
> Autism has not changed nor was it cured.
>
> Your child's nature transformed from tensed to relaxed and from solitary to interactive.
>
> His ability to relate to you and to make sense of your interaction evolved.
>
> Your ability to understand your child has changed too.
>
> You need to remember that you can only get to the matchsticks after you have replaced the tablemat with the matchbox.
>
> It will be your child who willingly opens the matchbox for you because he has learned to trust you.
>
> No one can make him talk about his emotions and problems that stem from his sensory perception of the environment through behaviour modification.
>
> Nor can another person make his working short-term memory work faster through behaviour modification.

The matchbox represents communication problems specific to your child alone. Inside the matchbox there are many matchsticks. Because you can communicate with your child, you can explore each matchstick together – now individual problems. As you solve each problem you burn it and throw it away.

Notes

1. See 'Being a spatial thinker' – Appendix D, p.280.

2. Politically correct term meant to describe autism as a disability or a disorder of development and to separate it from the person.

5

Is my child being aloof?

Amanda Bagg's (1999) article 'Autistic Adults and Adolescents' ends with a powerful injunction to parents: 'We are out there *trying to live.* Remember our existence.' What she means is that they want more than an existence – they want to live with dignity.

As parent to a once non-verbal child I used to think, 'I know you exist. The problem is that we don't understand each other and your behaviour drives us all away.' More than once I looked at Alexander and said, 'Look at me, I am trying to talk to you but you don't hear me. Show me the common ground so that you and I can live a better life.'

On 4 July 2001 I received a letter from a parent who had only just found out that his son had autism and who was in deep despair. Reading it brought tears to my eyes, and memories of my own past despair came flooding back:

Dear Florica,

On June 5th 2001, we were informed that our three year old…has Autism… To say the least we are both devastated by this news. For the last two days I have had moments that have left me weeping and very depressed. My every thought is now directed at my son and his happiness and future. I want to do everything right, and any advice or information that you could provide would be much appreciated. I have read your information provided on your web site Hope–TLC. Thank you so very much for your efforts to help people like myself.

God Bless XX.

My only wish is that this book can transform despair into positive action. A diagnosis of autism has that effect on us parents. We despair because we don't know what to do. We want to see our children happy and don't know how to 'make[1] them happy'. We want to enjoy the parenting of a child with autism but there seems to be no social communication between us. Thus we despair.

If you are weeping, the knowledge you have gathered so far should help you exchange your tears with positive actions. Your actions will help your child communicate. Communication can remove your depressive feelings. If your actions don't allow for your child's way of learning, your loving emotions alone cannot convey your love or your intention to see him happy.

Let your child's behaviour teach you about his needs

If during interactive or just protective moments your efforts are directed towards helping your child within the parameters[2] of his reality, dictated by his sensory system and his ability to make sense of what you want from him, he will learn at his own pace how to adjust to a larger reality.

As for 'getting' everything right, I did not do 'everything right' and I know of no one who was always right. My advice is not to worry if you misinterpret what your child wanted. You can amend and apologise for your actions but you cannot amend inaction. Getting it right is a mixture of attitude, knowledge and desire to learn more:

- If, out of love alone, you don't do to your child what you don't want done to yourself, you have already half 'got it right'.

- Twenty five per cent follows from knowledge.

- And the rest from trials and errors.

With increased interactive times between autistic people and myself I soon realised how easily mistakes are made. Here is one of them. Every time Alexander asked new questions about emotional relationships or just questions about feelings in general, he whispered them or hid behind a chair and spoke from there. His behaviour came across as if he was 'protecting' himself from an unwanted reply. Because I could not hear him, I asked him to repeat his questions. In order to show him that I respected his need for physical distance during such conversations I did not go near him.

All went well (or so I believed) until one day he said to me in a very upset voice, 'I don't think you understand me mother.'

'Why do you say that Alexander?' His comment made me feel hurt. I have done everything humanly possible for him. I had no idea what he would say next.

'Because you ask me the same question twice.'

'What do you mean?'

'I mean you ask me to repeat myself and that makes me think that you don't understand me. What's the point in talking to you if you don't understand me?'

'I do that because sometimes you whisper and I cannot *hear* your words.'

'I see, I thought you didn't *understand* what I was saying.'

'Please don't stop talking to me about what you are feeling. If you stop I would have to guess your thoughts. No one can guess anyone's thoughts. We have a mouth to use. If you tell me what bothers you I can help. If you don't tell me or your brother and sister we don't know.' (I deliberately chose to avoid metaphor.)

Food for thought

During your communication quest, leave nothing to assumptions and speak literally.

Just because your child's question seems insensitive, it doesn't mean that he is insensitive. Once you spot your mistake, make sure your child understands that you did not mean it. This way you continue to build mutual trust.

Talk to your child about your intentions and tell him what he needs to do, to keep the communication channels open.

If your child's words cause you to feel hurt, don't assume that he intended to hurt your feelings.

You might think to yourself, 'All this talk with your child sounds well and good, but my child doesn't talk with me.' In 1993 neither did mine but I wanted to hear him talk with me. I wanted to see him communicate. I started by questioning the definitions of 'aloof' and 'lacks empathy'.

Is my child aloof or is he feeling lonely?

After I had read and re-read Alexander's medical report I felt the world caving in on me. I still did not know what autism meant and what I could do to help my son. The report only highlighted what I already knew about my child's behaviour. In essence that was he did not talk, he was silent, he screamed and he did not play. I wanted to understand why.

During those days I was unable to find information from autistic adults. I remember thinking, 'Where is the adult population of autistics?' I came across a student manual, *Autism: Explaining the Enigma* (Frith 1989), and avidly read it. A picture diagram explained how a child with autism is unable to show friendship (because of lack of empathy) and it introduced a new term that read 'aloof'. I religiously underlined everything that applied to Alexander, hoping that by the end of the book for every 'problem' I could find I would also find a 'solution'. Instead, after I finished reading the book I felt emotionally shattered, as if I had entered a maze without an exit. After all, this was a manual that helped to diagnose a condition, not 'cure' it.

The dictionary definition of the word 'aloof' reads: 'distant, remote, detached, reserved, indifferent, cool and apart'. Can you accept this as a true description of your child? I could not. True enough, Alexander behaved in certain ways:

- He played with my hair and earring but ignored my face.

- He screamed when we tried touching his toys.

- He yelled when we had to go for a ride in the car.

- He laughed when his sister cried.

- He threw himself on the pavement when a bus went by.

- He walked straight past us when we called his name.

- He pushed his way to the front of a queue in the park for a slide.

Although for most of the time his behaviour fitted the definition, there were times when 'aloof' didn't make sense. From time to time Alexander sat on my lap smiling, our eyes met and his 'gurgle of sounds' moved my heart. Tickling his naked body with my hair triggered a healthy laughter as well as enough motivation on Alexander's part to label all the body parts he wanted me to tickle. Therefore I could not accept that nothing could be done.

Although the term 'aloof', as medical jargon, is not meant to insult our children, my heart was aching. I felt this word to be an untrue description of my child's behaviour when he gave me a kiss, when he smiled at me after I gave him a new toy train or when he fell asleep in my arms. Other common words employed to describe 'aloof' are: alien, living in a bubble, shut off in a world of his own, cut off from reality, the lost child, etc.

What do they really want to describe? I had a few unanswered questions:

- What was my child doing when he behaved in an aloof way?

- What is your and my child doing when we catch that lost look in his big eyes?

- Is he lonely or is he happy living in a world of his own? Could I/you enter that world?

- Is he happy inside that world?

- Is that world all that different from our own?

- Did he feel left out?

'Aloof' describes the time needed by our child to 'listen, think, express'

In this section you will learn how to identify the behaviour described in medical jargon as aloof and will be introduced to a new meaning. By the end of it you will be able to:

- substitute the meaning of aloof from 'avoidance of social interaction' with 'the time in which your child is actively seeking information or thinking about it' or 'editing stages'

- learn how to begin to model and adapt your interaction with your child according to his receptivity to further input and his sensory system.

I evolved this perception after observing my son's behaviour during such 'temporary trance-like situations'. Years later, my adult autistic friends were able to confirm that the 'lost' look is an indication of thinking.

A matter of perception – a common dilemma

In 1993 I half-heartedly decided to reject the idea that Alexander was aloof per se. Instead I wanted to know what it was that made Alexander afraid of interactive games or why he perceived them as scary or annoying. My main questions were:

- What was he doing when we believed that he was aloof?
- What attracted him to solitary games?
- Why was he inspecting his toys from every possible angle?
- Why did he scream when a person entered a room in which he was present?
- Why did he lack flexibility during interactive games?

EXAMPLE

One day, an adult friend of Alexander told him a nursery rhyme about frogs jumping in the pond. Alexander responded to this rhyme immediately and they turned the simple telling of it into an interactive game. Every time a frog jumped, Alexander jumped. Radiating with enjoyment and taking in every word she said, he timed his jumps accurately with the word 'jump' and kissed her at the end of each round.

He then indicated that he wanted her to repeat the nursery rhyme over and over again. No problems with that. The problem was that she had to sit in the exact corner of the room where she first sat at the beginning of the game. Why, as she moved away, did he scream and look totally distressed? What did he believe?

THOUGHT

Surely this behaviour did not fit the description of a child who avoided social interaction? It was more like seeking only the types of social interaction with which he felt comfortable. True enough it could be perceived as one-sided interaction, but he wasn't avoiding interaction. So what was he doing?

> ### *Food for thought*
>
> Alexander responded to the nursery rhyme by copying her words and turning it into a game he invented. He chose to jump from the corner of the sofa onto the other sofa. He greeted our suggestion that he could jump on the floor with yet another scream!
>
> Everything that he learned, he learned alone. He behaved as he wanted, when he wanted. Alexander's behaviour was a puzzle and a challenge.

Then again, Alexander's behaviour up to the age of three led me to believe that this 'horrid thing called autism' caused this aloofness. For as long as we left him alone with his toys he seemed happy. Yet sporadically, and before Alexander could share his thoughts verbally with us, he sought some social contact such as chasing or tickling games. He also enjoyed being rocked to sleep. This one-sided interaction could have been perceived as selfishness, but he wasn't selfish. I felt hurt. However, Alexander hardly interacted with me. Therefore, the term aloof did seem to fit.

Furthermore, I was introduced to the idea that his limited and boisterous social contact is not what we call real social contact. I was advised that my son used me to get what he wanted (including a drink from the fridge) and that I should *teach* him that his actions are *inappropriate.*

I wanted to encourage more complex interaction and not to tell him off. I remember wanting to expand on his games and not knowing how. It dawned on me that so far I had not managed to actively engage in *teaching* Alexander anything at all, not even one single word. How then could I teach him acceptable social interaction? Was it that he simply did not want to learn at all or that he did not want to learn from me/us?

I am multilingual and on advice I spoke with my children only in English. This way, I was told, I would prevent confusion in his mind. However, one year on I failed to notice any difference, let alone any enthusiasm, coming from Alexander to learn English. 'Autism goes deeper than language; autistic people are foreigners in every country' (Sinclair 1993).

EXERCISE

Think of a few times when your child enjoyed a game of your suggestion. Did the game have a flow to it or did you notice your child's *lack of flexibility*? His lack of flexibility represents:

- how much he understands the situation

- how comfortable he feels in that situation.

Our children learn 'in pictures' (Baggs 1999; Grandin 1995). The whole set-up of your game is assimilated as one image. If they enjoy it, they want it repeated without any alterations. Perhaps in the beginning they feel afraid of change, or perhaps when a change occurs their understanding of the game changes too. What matters is that *flexibility replaces rigidity*:

- After the child feels relaxed around you, once he trusts you, he will seek further interaction.

- During interactive moments and after presenting him with more experiences, he can identify you as the 'provider of pleasurable experiences' and will relax more. By that I mean that he is not afraid to try new things because you are friendly towards him.

You gain his trust through repetitively playing the game of his choosing until he tells you to stop. This way you are actively passing learning control over to the child. If you deprive the child of the opportunity to make his own decisions, you are depriving him of learning interdependent skills through reasoning.

How could an 'aloof' child seek social interaction?

I was half-afraid that if I did not take Alexander to playgroup I would be denying him the opportunity to form and develop social skills. Equally, I couldn't see how he would make friends in the playgroup set-up when he failed to play with his brother and sister. How could an aloof child seek social interaction? I gave in to my fear and enrolled him in the same playgroup as his elder brother. As I suspected, he made no attempt to make friends. The children who approached him in the beginning soon stopped.

The question about him avoiding social interaction nagged me again. The other children learned to avoid Alexander because he failed to respond to their social overtures. Who was to blame here: Alex for not responding in a friendly way; the children for not persevering? No one really.

OBSERVATION

It was then that the role of the adult play helpers became clear to me. Their aim was not to help Alexander overcome what we suspected to be *avoidance of interaction*, but to help him *make sense of interaction*. The adult play helper could be patient and try reaching out to Alexander when a child of his own age hadn't the patience to make sense of Alexander's behaviour. The adult did not mind if Alexander failed to share his toys whereas other children did and do.

When can I play with my brother, Mummy?

My elder son's constant question was 'When can I play with my brother?'

I really had no answer. At times I muttered, 'Soon.' Other times I would say, 'Wait until he learns how to talk.'

'When will that be, Mummy?' asked my five-year-old son.

'I don't know. I wish I did' was my rather distressed reply.

'But Francesca is younger! Although she doesn't talk she does play with me. She doesn't scream when I go near her. She laughs and giggles. Why is that Mummy?'

'I don't know. They are different.'

My elder son was right. On the rare occasions when they played together, their game failed to last beyond five minutes. The games were lacking laughter and often ended abruptly because of Alexander's screams. I wanted to delight at the sight of my children playing together but ran out of ideas on how to achieve that.

OBSERVE

1. Is your child playing with your other children or children of similar age?

2. Have you noticed him trying to copy or join in the games of those children?

3. Are the other children asking you to intervene and make peace?

4. Can you notice resentment from the other children?

5. Can the autistic child share comfortable silences with his siblings or yourself?

Lack of flexibility during play shows lack of shared understanding

Remember, at an early stage of development, or 'adaptation to our system of communication' as I like to call it, the lack of flexibility is a reflection of lack of shared understanding of a given situation, not lack of willingness to take part. Shared silences are times when your child feels he can bond with you and connect with you. Consider these as 'oases' of belonging.

Examples of 'editing time'

The day Alexander reinforced my belief that what I perceived as aloofness was in fact 'editing time' happened during our holiday in Mexico. Alexander (then ten) dressed up in his suit and joined us at the table, cracking jokes and sharing the day's stories. Each night he took extra time on his own getting ready (perhaps preparing the script?). He went to bed earlier than us but always excused himself before leaving the table. I never deliberately taught him to do that. He learned manners (incidentally) from the other children.

He planned the next day's events with us and shared his perceptions of what was fun to do and what was not. Alexander attended the kids' club for 20 minutes at a time. He left the club when he couldn't cope with further interaction. He told us that he left the club because the children talked too fast or there were too many of them and he couldn't follow all that they said or wanted. So when he informed us about having to go and think about what was being said, Alexander went to do just that. He meant 'I am going to think about it'. He did not mean 'I am going to be aloof'. When he went away from the noise it was because the sound of so many voices interfered with his speed of processing information and not because he deliberately wanted to avoid interaction (central audio processing disorder?). However, he did enjoy the short bouts of interactive games.

OBSERVATIONS

Alexander can't remember not wanting to share time with us (he wasn't aware). He can't remember screaming or the reasons why he chose not to wear clothes (extreme tactile sensitivity). He can't remember the sewing incident, but can remember the drawing on his playroom wall (his gift).

Most children who grow to use language don't remember the early years (or cannot talk about them). This 'forgetfulness' reinforces my belief that at a time when I was worried about him not wanting to interact with us, he was busy learning and not busy avoiding interaction.

> ## Food for thought
>
> Can you identify the times when your child goes through 'editing stages'?
>
> During 'aloof stages' can you reach him or does he object to you getting near him?
>
> Describe at least one repetitive activity that makes you perceive your child as aloof.
>
> If your child copies your other children's games, it means that he wants to play – interact socially.
>
> If the other children don't let him join in, it is because he is too slow at picking up the rules of the game. His shared understanding is not in line with that of the other children. Children generally like playing with other children who show flexibility.
>
> The other children are not saying 'no' to the autistic child. They are saying 'no' to his style of play. This is why an adult play helper is in a better position to play with the autistic child.

Notes

1.   While we cannot mechanically place the feeling of happiness inside our child's soul, we can provide him with the physical environment in which his soul will fill with joy and happiness.

2.   Not to be confused with the 'parameters of autism'. I remember receiving a letter announcing that provision for speech and language therapy was no longer appropriate for Alexander because he will continue to develop within the parameters of his autism. Although he never actually attended speech and language therapy, having this 'provision' as part of his educational needs statement ensured an active acknowledgement regarding his speech impediment. Intrigued and upset, in my reply I asked: 'Please define the parameters of autism, because I don't know what that means.' After a few weeks I received a phone call and was told that 'parameters of autism' was just a term. (How confusing and frustrating!)

6

Creating a shared sanctuary

Your child's behaviour, coupled with his lack of co-operation or communication skills, might lead you towards thinking and/or making comments similar to the following:

- If only my child stopped flapping his arms, screaming, pouring liquids all over the carpet, soiling everywhere, etc., then our lives would be better (true).

- I wish we could play instead of having to constantly tidy up.

- I wish my child wasn't so withdrawn – nothing seems to attract his attention.

- I wish my child had a sense of danger.[1]

- I wish my child would speak to me so I could put an end to guessing games.

- Why can't my child behave like other children of his own age?

- I wish my child were less fussy during shopping trips or visits.

- Why is my child behaving violently?

- I wish my child called me mother/father.

- I wish I had more energy.

- I wish we could visit friends and people could visit us.

- I wish I had a better understanding of what autism is doing to my child and my family.

As a result of your child's destructive behaviour, you may already have made some drastic changes to your home environment, as well as restricting your social life. My suggestion of an adapted or further adapted home should result in your family enjoying peace of mind, increase your autistic child's willingness to co-operate, and experience the benefits of a social life.

What exactly is an adapted home?

An adapted home is a place where your child's autistic way of being can be catered for so you can substitute negative and tiring activities with fun, meaningful and positive interaction. After a few temporary changes it becomes:

- a friendly place where you can prepare your child for further integration

- an emotionally strong place where your child can draw his strength and develop self-esteem

- an accepting place where your child is allowed to behave autistically and not be judged for it

- a learning place where his autistic behaviour can safely unfold under your careful observation, thus allowing you to translate it into meaningful communication

- a sanctuary for both of you where you will notice how, of his own volition, your child replaces some 'repetitive' behaviour with other activities and the violent behaviour vanishes

- a social place where a team of volunteer friends can engage in helping your child interact and develop friendships

- a cherishing place where you and he get to know each other's way of being.

Whether your child behaves like a recluse or has perhaps 'gained' total control over what happens to and in your home, making a few practical changes to your home and creating a play–interaction room could change all your lives for the better.

Exercise

Use the answers to the following questions to help you decide if modifying the interior of your house could benefit all the members of your family.

Revisit these questions monthly after you have decided to modify your home and after you have modelled your interaction to suit your child's understanding of it.

1. List the socially interactive activities (if any) that bring a smile to your child's face. What disruption are they causing?

2. Would you like them to expand into more creative games? What are they?

3. List the activities you suggested to your child which elicited no response.

4. List the dangerous activities invented by your child.

5. Jot down the methods by which you already tried to stop those activities.

6. List the destructive behaviours of your child.

7. List your child's solitary activities.

8. What games can you play with your child?

9. How long can you sustain your child's interest in communicating/interacting with you?

10. Can you go shopping together?

11. Is he screaming when you get in the car?

12. Can you visit a friend's house?

Examples

1. If your child enjoys breaking glass or china, place the remaining intact ornaments/glasses out of harm's way on fitted shelves or perhaps in a box in the attic or in a secure cupboard. This way

you will no longer have to tell him off or feel upset over continued breakages.

2.   If he enjoys pouring liquids over or writing on carpets, or if soiling occurs due to his lack of toileting skills, then why not cover the carpets with heavy-duty polythene sheets or replace them with lino? This way you will not only protect the carpet, but your home will become easier and quicker to clean. The time you gain can be used for positive interaction.

3.   If he likes jumping from heights, make sure you lock all your windows and hide the keys. (Your child might well believe that he is able to fly!) Inside a controlled environment you could join in with his jumping game.

4.   If he likes running into the middle of the road, lock your front door and hide the keys. If you like to go for walks, try and schedule them for late evening or between rush hours when traffic is less heavy. The child runs into the middle of the road because his comprehension of danger is not yet fully formed.

5.   If he likes drawing on the walls, you have a choice. You could decide to live with the drawings until the child develops comprehension skills or until the need for drawing on walls becomes substituted with playful interaction. If, on the other hand, your child understands a fair amount of words, you could begin a *persuasion campaign*. Explain the benefits of drawing on paper as opposed to walls: because you can keep the paper drawings whereas those on the walls have to be regularly erased (stick his paintings on the walls to reinforce and illustrate your message). Involve the child in cleaning or painting the wall. I know of a child who enjoyed this activity so much that what his mother expected to act as a deterrent actually became a motivator.

6.   If he likes turning every room inside out, lock the rooms you use less frequently and only enter them together when you have the time and patience to help him explore. Then again if he has a playroom and people to attend to him, his activity of turning the house inside out ends.

7. If your child spends most of the time *locked away* in a world apart, you need to awaken his interest in people. A child such as this is usually very fragile and needs to be treated like a delicate flower. All these 'orchid children' (as I call them!) whom I have met have had sensitive hearing and shown extreme sensitivity to touch.

8. If he spends numerous hours in front of a TV, thus only assimilating information, the playroom becomes the place where he can output the gathered information.[2]

Everyday household noises could prevent him from interacting with you. A playroom could become his first sanctuary and the rest of the family could again use the living room.

My reasons for adapting our home

I remember the difficult times experienced by our family during my son's early *exploratory* years. Although I loved Alexander just as much as I loved each of my other children, my parenting skills failed to influence his behaviour. When I compared his behaviour with my other two children, I felt overwhelmed with despair. I wanted to achieve a number of goals.

Encouraging Alexander to develop a sense of danger

More than once Alexander ran into the middle of the road. We lived on a busy main street where three accidents a week easily happened. Forgetting to lock the front door meant a ticket to death, as Alexander (age two and a half) would open it in a flash and sprint into the middle of the road. When we left the house for any reason, we had to hold his hands tightly or he would run straight into the middle of the road. Taking Alexander out was exhausting and unsafe. I began wishing that we lived in the middle of nowhere!

Stopping the mess

The contents of each toy box opened by Alexander ended up scattered all over the floor. One other activity that could keep him busy for hours involved taking videotapes out of their boxes. One by one, he carefully inspected each label before throwing the tape on the floor. I remember spending most of my time tidying. (Unknown to me he was teaching himself to read.)

Expanding Alexander's repetitive style of play

Few other toys triggered what seemed to us like a 'fascination'. These were: a garage with spiralled ramps, the marble run, trains and the wheels of any car, which he spun into motion hundreds of times. I watched Alexander mesmerised by a car running down the ramp 100 times or more. I didn't understand his reasons or his joy, but it kept him quiet and relatively happy. At the time I didn't know that he was in fact learning and not playing.

Stopping Alexander from flooding the house

Alexander's love of water kept the bathroom taps running constantly. If our water had been metered, our bills could have easily run into thousands of pounds! The dripping of water through the ceiling pinpointed Alexander's whereabouts. Yet although he loved playing with water, giving him a bath[3] was a one-hour negotiating process. If a raindrop fell on his jumper he would scream and tear it off. I didn't understand why, but badly wanted to. Many years later I read a story about a boy who described raindrops as pins hitting his skin. But the raindrop did not reach Alexander's skin. Why was he afraid of water? What emotion or sensation did a raindrop cause for him to react in such a drastic fashion? I will never know.

Keeping our books intact

Alexander's other main activity was studying train books and tearing the corners from some pages (marking his favourite pages?). In his playroom we gave him books he could rip apart if he so wished. He never did.

Stopping Alexander from writing on our walls

By the time Alexander reached the age of three he was able to draw and write. He wrote numbers and drew trains. I remember wishing to see him drawing and writing on paper, not on our walls. My friends (the few that visited) asked me why I didn't stop him. As if I had a choice! I used to redecorate once a month. But the drawings reappeared faster than I could wash or paint them out. And yes, I did hide the pens, but Alexander could always manage to find one!

Later, after we transformed a bedroom into a playroom, we dedicated one of the walls to his paintings. I wrongly assumed[4] that he would understand the difference between 'Alexander's painting wall' and the other walls.

Food for thought

Alexander drew a fun playground for a cat on the allocated wall. The painting remained unchanged for the following two years. Alexander liked pretending to be a cat.

Meanwhile, Alexander continued to draw a continuous single line throughout the house (save for his playroom). What was so special about this line? I had no solution and desperately wanted one. It became obvious that he wasn't interested in *painting on the wall* and that the continuous line carried a different meaning.

Creating an environment in which Alexander could learn language

I realised that group therapy or a one-hour weekly speech therapy lesson did not address Alexander's individual needs. I felt motivated to build an environment in which I could learn to address them, so I turned one of our bedrooms into his playroom[5] and invited people[6] to befriend him. In this playroom and after many hours of interactive play, the volunteer friends and I used Alexander's love of trains and numbers to inspire him to use language.

FLASHBACK

Before we had a playroom, however, during a group speech therapy class Alexander's love of numbers was the core reason stopping him from playing with other children. His *need*[7] to see numbers in ascending order stopped him from sharing with other children, turning an 'opportunity to enjoy sharing'[8] into 'a situation to be avoided'.

Imagine a friendly room furnished with a sandpit, a table with six chairs, toys stacked out of reach, a large mirror fixed to the wall, six children (around four years of age) each having his own 'autistic interests' and two friendly therapists. Their agenda was to teach the children to sit at the table and play together.

Behind the two way mirror, six loving and anxious mothers, hearts filled with hopes and pains well hidden behind courageous faces, watched the following performance. We couldn't believe our eyes as we watched our children being seated around the table. Our children *actually sat down*! Each child received a cup and looked ready to begin a game of pretend 'having tea'. Within minutes, a completely bizarre picture emerged.

As soon as Alexander noticed the numbers printed on the bottom of each cup, he wanted them! As quickly as he could he grabbed them all, inspected their bottoms and arranged them in ascending order. Another child left the table and begun an intricate, gracious dance in front of the mirror. His mother said, 'Perhaps I am looking at a future ballerina.' Another child went and helped himself to a mouthful of sand (Alexander loved eating sand too).

At this point one of the therapists approached Alexander and asked him to return the other five cups. Alexander realised what she wanted, hugged the cups and began screaming (as in don't take my cups away!). I was so accustomed to this screaming and I so wished to see it changed with language and laughter.

What we had to observe was both depressing and hilarious. In a mixture of kind and hopeless voice, the therapist asked us to stop laughing and talking. She tried to blame the children's lack of co-operation on our behaviour! What she did not realise was that we weren't really laughing out of amusement – just letting off steam – for in our frustrations we felt as if the world had caved in on us. Furthermore the children's behaviour gave no clue that they had heard us. None of them shouted out for his mother. All behaved as they would have in their own home environment.

I left the building thinking that I had to find another, more effective way of reaching my son. I wasn't worried about his lack of co-operation during the pretend play game. Pretend play is an activity during which we copy real-life events that we like or in which we pretend to be people we like. I wondered whether Alexander could play a game of pretend drinking or pretend eating when in real life he never drank out of a cup or joined us for a meal. Alexander liked eating grated cheese and he *pretended* to eat it *like a cat*. He seemed to have fun pretending to be a cat and showed no interest in pretending to be daddy! How could I encourage him to eat like us humans – not like cats?

We shared our first joyful dinner around the table two years after the speech therapy class. If nowadays we talk about the old days, Alexander laughs in dismay, asking 'Did I really do that Mum?' and then, with curiosity, 'What did you do when I did that?'

Providing Alexander with pleasant and meaningful social interaction[9]

For a short while Alexander attended the local playgroup in the hope that he could pick up social skills from the other children. But when he was there he drew and painted numbers. He did not play with children. His accurate and artful replication of numbers gained him much praise from the staff. Everyone was telling me about 'how intelligent' Alexander must be. OK, so he was intelligent. Did his intelligence prevent him from having fun, talking and playing with other children? I did not think so.

Advocating that I was denying Alexander the opportunity to mix with other children, which in turn deprived him of the opportunity to learn social skills, the professional opinion condemned my decision to withdraw Alexander from the playgroup (what a vicious circle!).[10]

Once again I chose to believe otherwise and this is why. As I watched the other children interacting I could see every child – from shy to boisterous – socialising during a day's session. I watched the making of their first little friendships and witnessed some 'falling out arguments'. They decided the people with whom they would make friends and those with whom they would not play. Their development had a flow. Compared with those children, Alexander's behaviour resembled that of 'well-established loner grump'. Alexander was happiest when left alone or when he could play with his favourite toy. His ability to co-operate (nearly non-existent in the first instance) vanished as soon as the Brio trains were displayed. Alexander wanted to build the entire track alone and was unable to cope with other children helping, touching or taking parts of the railway.

All he could hear was 'Share', 'Other children want to play too', 'Wait for your turn' and 'You wouldn't like it if the other children didn't let you play with their toys.' All he replied was a screamed out 'Nooooo!' If Alexander was deprived of anything, he was deprived of quality time and the opportunity to develop his vocabulary. Equally, and assuming that I were the parent of another child who attended the same playgroup, I would resent having to tell off my own child for wanting to play with a toy which Alexander believed he had sole rights to.

Food for thought

So what was it that he needed? Group therapy with other autistic children turned disastrous. Placing him in the middle of a group of 'normal' children in the hope that 'his social behaviour would spontaneously change' turned out to be a waste of time.

What we needed was to create an environment conducive to autistic learning, learn to speak and behave literally, bring in volunteer friends and entice Alexander to play with us.

Other parents' reasons

Just as I needed to find an alternative approach towards getting through to my child, let alone educating him, other parents needed it too. Some parents whose autistic children I played with decided either of the following or both:

- They needed to rethink their attitude and therefore their own actions towards their child's visible symptoms of autism.

- They created a playroom, made the house environment safe and enlisted the help of other people.

They did this in their own time after they realised the distinctive differences between autism and autistic behaviours.

Others found motivation from hearing their child's first word or from enjoying their first shared loving cuddle. Only you can decide what changes are needed to solve your individual problems. The following reasons belong to parents I once met.

I want us to be able to go out without my child approaching every stranger

Your child may be extremely friendly and approach any stranger in an 'inappropriate way'. He or she might call every male on the street 'father' and every lady on the street 'mother'. In this case you need to help him identify the meanings of 'mother' and 'father'. This could be achieved in the comfort of your home, in front of a mirror. With the help of volunteer friends he will also learn to develop the concept of family unit because its core (mum, dad, brother and sister) live in the house.

Volunteer friends go home at the end of the day and although they are friends they are also strangers because we don't meet them every day. Your child can only comprehend the concept of a stranger after he has identified the concept of mother, father, brother or sister.

I want to hear my child talking with me, not at me

Your child might have reached 18 years of age and for as long as you can remember he *spoke at you*[11] as opposed to *talking with you*. Perhaps your child spoke of his own interests and showed little interest in your opinions. Talking at people happens for various reasons such as:

- his lack of understanding of the spoken word

- his lack of ability to figure out the full chain of causes and effects which govern acceptable social situations

- his speed of processing inputted information.

You can help him transform the activity of talking *at* people into talking *with* people through helping him increase his meaningful vocabulary and teaching him to listen and identify various meanings of intonations.[12]

His speed of processing information, in other words the 'listen, think, express'[13] process, increases with practice after your child is actively seeking to converse with you. This is where your role as a parent is to become his best-trusted friend and the role of a volunteer friend is to hold conversations with your child. As one of my autistic friends once said:

> Having a conversation with a friend is not the same as 'social script' therapy. It is all very well going through scripts in class, yet when I talk to you or any other person we seem to get off script. In the beginning I found myself waiting for you to say the right words from the pre-learned script so that I can answer! It was one month later that I realised that you are in fact *interested in me* and that you are *listening to me*. We did not practise 'social script'. We were communicating and you were *helping me in a way that made sense to me*.

I want to see my child going to bed at a reasonable hour

I found that increased interaction will tire your child and he will start going to bed[14] at a more reasonable time.

I want my child to understand that I am his mother and that I love him

If your child is to feel at home, where he has a room, where away from judging eyes he can behave as autistically as he likes, he will experience your care and associate the caring person in you with the words 'mother' and 'father'.

I have met autistic adults who believed that they were adopted or that their real parents were living on another continent. Ask yourself how would you feel and what would you think if the child to whom you gave birth, for whom you cared and did all you could to help, told you that you were not his real parent? Then ignore your emotions and ask yourself 'What makes my child hold such a belief?' 'Could it be my behaviour towards him?'

Food for thought

Because our autistic child's sensory system is different from our own and because he thinks and learns differently from us, some of our parental efforts aimed at showing 'normal or conventional' acts of love and care are interpreted by some of our autistic children as acts of rejection or violence.

I met parents who faced their child saying, 'How would you know how I feel? You are not my real parents!' They were heartbroken, confused and desperate to understand why their child held such beliefs. If you are the parent of such a child:

- tell him that you are his parents
- explain everything in literal terms and leave nothing to intonation or inferred meanings
- tell him that you don't always understand his behaviour but you do love him
- ask him to help you understand his needs and warn him that you may not be able to meet them all
- explain why and be honest
- help him understand your needs
- don't give up trying.

Notes

1. A concept with variable meanings, predetermined by the information sent to the brain by the sensory system.

2. See Chapter 20: Writing, p.203; Reading p.205.

3. Your child could refuse a bath because he feels the water colder or hotter than you do or because he dislikes the feeling of water.

4. See Chapter 20, Reasoning, p.210.

5. See Chapter 7, The play–interaction room, p.69.

6. See Chapter 10, Play helper friends, p.110.

7. See Chapter 3, A strict need for accuracy, p.34.

8. Taking part in a game of pretend and learning turn taking.

9. I wanted him to hear more than just 'Don't do this', 'Don't do that' or 'Stop'.

10. Learning social skills is a personal process. Implicitly they can only be learned by a person who actively seeks social interaction, is unable to make sense of it and wishes to fit in better.

11. See Appendix B, 'Linguistic behaviour assessment table'.

12. See Chapter 14, 'Emotions, language, behaviour and social communication'.

13. 'Listen, think, express': one autistic friend introduced me to this term. It describes the amount of time a person needs to hear the verbal instruction/request, think about it and make sure that he understands the meaning of it, formulate a mental reply and then reply. This time span can vary from one minute to weeks or months. For example, Alexander replied to the question asked on a Monday evening 'Would you like me to bring you some doughnuts?' the next Monday evening with 'Did you bring me some doughnuts?' At that stage he was unable to connect the cause and effect, i.e. if he was to say 'yes' he would get the doughnuts. He told me three years later that he believed that policemen were born policemen and firemen were born firemen. After he understood what training meant, all those beliefs crumbled and freed him from many other confusions.

    Another child copied my words 'Open the window' five hours after I asked him. When I opened the window he failed to see the connection between him saying 'Open the window' and my opening the window.

14. See Chapter 9, Sleeping problems, p.95.

7

The autistic-friendly environment

The autistic-friendly environment stems from a combination of benefits provided through:

- a safe physical place geared towards mutual exploration

- our attentiveness to our child's needs

- our understanding of autistic learning

- our unconditional love for the child

- our ability to speak literally

- no rules imposed by social convention

- our calmness – self-induced (meditation can help).

The play–interaction room (playroom)

The play–interaction room is a sanctuary for both the autistic child and the person who wants to help. By definition a sanctuary is an open and tranquil place, which need not be locked. The atmosphere inside a sanctuary is friendly, inviting and accepting.

Each time your child chooses to leave that room he is exercising a personal choice. Each time you allow the child to leave you are modelling trust. This room is also an autistic place conducive to autistic exploration and style of learning – be it visual, tactile, repetitive or whatever. The physical aspects of the room work hand in hand with the play friend's knowledge of literal learning.

Practical aspect

In 1993 I was introduced to the idea of a specially designed playroom, so I turned Alexander's bedroom into one. If your house is large enough and you can spare a room, I recommend you to do the same. I know of two parents who used a shed-like structure in the garden as a playroom. In this room, volunteers played with Alexander. There were several reasons behind the building of this special environment:

1. It provided Alexander with a simplified and distraction-free environment – no TV, people coming in and out of the house, etc.

2. It created a place where Alexander could do anything he wanted. Because we made it safe, nothing of value could be broken and he would not upset his brother and sister.

3. The flooring consisted of a washable surface – easy to clean up spillages, writing on the floors. (Alexander liked drawing 'noughts and crosses' in the middle of the living room carpet.) Most of the children whom I played with enjoyed spilling a drop of drink and spending hours playing with it. I met parents complaining about their children's habit of pouring the entire content of a bottle onto the carpet whilst laughing. I remember a child inviting me to look at how he poured the contents of a bottle on the floor! In a specially designed playroom, games such as these can be explored and developed further and in time they evolve naturally into more meaningful activities.

4. We dedicated one of the walls to his paintings. I was hoping that he would stop writing on the rest of the walls in the house. That was before I understood *why* he needed to write on walls. It is worth mentioning that Alexander stopped writing the continuous line on the walls when he felt relaxed in the house. Half the wall space in the playroom was covered in mirrors, aimed at helping him develop an image of 'self'. They became a great source of fun. Highly recommended – the more mirrors the better.

5. Inside the room Alexander played with only one person at a time, benefiting from undivided attention. The person was also meant to inspire Alexander to overcome his autism. (Later more than one person stayed with Alexander – because he wanted[1] us to!)

6. The toys we used followed his interests. Therefore we had bricks, marble runs, in excess of 100 marbles, Brio trains, puzzles, books, picture dictionaries, pens, paper, soft toys, a hammock, balls, etc. In essence all his favourite toys.

There is no running away from the fact that I created his playroom because I believed a cure would follow and that cure was the solution to my grieving. Once again I wish to remind you that a playroom is not necessary in order to improve the quality of interaction between you and your child. It doesn't act as a cure catalyst. A playroom is best described as an autistic sanctuary and a place for autistic learning.

Some people looked at the playroom and condemned it. They wanted to know what programme we were following. Was it scientifically evaluated and how would it tie in or better the school curriculum? Others believed that I was denying him the opportunity to develop social skills.[2] Others waited eagerly to see what happened next. I was silently hoping for a miraculous cure. During the day I was smiling, thus showing a strong front, whilst at night I cried for hundreds of hours. As my understanding of autistic learning developed, our whole house turned into a playground, allowing us to find our own sanctuary in it.

After Alexander joined mainstream school life I continued using his playroom for the benefit of other autistic children and helped other parents create a better environment for interaction in their own homes. Here are a few mishaps I encountered.

What could go wrong?

You are happy to build a playroom but cannot find people willing to play with your child

Don't give up searching for them. It is never too late to introduce new people into your child's life. Other people's involvement makes it easier, less tiring and more imaginative for you (which is fantastic), and more exciting for your child. Your child's speed of progress doesn't depend on them. It depends on his sensory system, his working memory,[3] the amount of individual time that he is given when he is in an inquisitive mood, and self-esteem.

His sensory system, fear of abandonment or lack of understanding concepts

If your child cries when he enters the room it could be because:

- the room is too cold – experiment with the temperature

- the room is too dark or too bright – experiment with the amount of light entering the room

- the child is afraid that you are 'abandoning' him in the company of a person with whom he doesn't feel at ease.

You can find out which one of those feelings is the overriding one. Long before the next person is due to enter the room, you tell your child that X is coming. Stick X's picture on the wall and reinforce your verbal statement by pointing at X's picture. Stay with your child in the room until he is happy for you to leave. He will learn in his own time that you are not abandoning him.

PROBLEM 1

Pierce is three years old. He prefers playing with his mother because the two of them could play for hours *without any confrontation*. A volunteer friend arrives and is due to swap places with the mother. David is less in tune with Pierce's needs. Therefore Pierce must work harder at communicating them. The only way David can learn about Pierce's wants is through interacting with him, interpreting his body language and questioning him. Pierce prefers not to be asked but rather to have his wants second-guessed in the way that his mother guesses them. For a period of two months Pierce cried when his mother swapped with David or any other volunteer friend. Pierce's mother becomes distressed and questions her actions.

Solution

Fifteen minutes before David is due to arrive, Pierce's mother tells her son about David's arrival. Pierce's first reaction is 'No David come in, Mummy stay and play'. Mum continues, 'David comes and plays, then Mummy comes back.'

'No Mummy comes back, Mummy stay and play.'

Ten minutes later David arrives, knocks on the door and asks, 'Can I come in?'

'No come in!' replies Pierce.

Five minutes later David asks again, 'Now can I come in?'

Pierce's reply changed. 'Come in.'

David happily enters the room and enthusiastically greets his little friend, 'Hello Pierce!'

Pierce continues in a commanding voice, 'Sit down!'

'Where?' asks David.

Pointing at a corner, Pierce continues, 'There!'

David sits down in a corner and asks every now and then whether it is his turn to play. After another 15 minutes Pierce kisses his mum goodbye and the fun play begins. For the following two hours Pierce becomes engrossed in games without mentioning his mother once.

Possible explanations

1.   Pierce needed time to adjust to his mother leaving.

2.   He needed time to process the next event.

3.   He has not figured out the concept of time.

4.   Pierce realised that everyone was his friend, his mother and David, but preferred playing with mother.

PROBLEM 2

The child cries when he sees mother depart.

Solution

The play helper waves goodbye and teaches the child to wave goodbye to mother. He does this through shouting and smiling 'Come back soon! See you soon! Bring us a sweet! We will be waiting for you!' (or words to this effect). This is done to help the child associate the 'going away' with 'going to get something' that the child can see when the mother comes back.

Soon the child will learn to echo those words, copy the actions (wave at mum/dad) and attribute meanings to them. When the parent returns, the play helper greets the mother in an overemphasised voice. 'You are back! Where are the sweets? We have been waiting for you.' Then facing the child, the play helper continues, 'See Mum is back, she came back to you, she loves you and missed you. She brought us a sweet!' (or words to that effect).

An autistic friend told me how she found it difficult to comprehend the meaning of 'See you later' or 'I'll be back soon'. The words 'later' and 'soon' both fail to represent a concrete quantity that she could relate to. Until your child understands the concept[4] of 'passing of time' and the subjective interpretation of time, substitute the words 'See you soon' with 'See you when *Bob the Builder* is finished' or 'See you when you are reaching the end of your game', or some concrete examples which you know your child comprehends.

You start using the playroom and the child doesn't know it's a play area
Time will solve that.

EXAMPLE

An extremely caring and loving father built a state-of-the-art playroom, heated to the right temperature and stocked with wonderful toys. My children and I fell in love with the room. There was one perplexing problem. The child for whom the room was built refused to enter it so my children and I went in and started having exaggerated fun.

Timid at first, Brandon poked his nose through the door. Wrongly, I quickly closed the door and locked us in (following what I had been taught when I believed in miracles). For the next half-hour, my little friend cried and banged the door, wanting to leave. My attempts to tell him that we were there to have fun failed. I was telling myself that if Brandon were in school he would not be allowed to leave the classroom. There is more than one problem with this line of reasoning:

- My child in 1993 and Brandon in 1997 were unable to attend school.

- The playroom was not a substitute for school. The playroom was meant to prepare them for school.

This was the first time I broke away from my initial teaching. For the following three days I couldn't think of a solution, so each time we went to play I locked us in. Although his crying time decreased each day from 15 minutes to 1 second, I continued to have more than one nagging thought. Why is he crying? Why lock the playroom? What if the room caught fire or if I fainted or something bad happened to his mother or me? What if only the two of us were in the house and the child couldn't let himself out?

Although I brought the child into the room with me, he had no choice in the matter. True enough, if I wanted to play with him in the rest of the house it was harder for me to help him focus on activities of my choice – educational or otherwise. I had to follow him everywhere and could not focus his attention. I still believed that I had to work at increasing his 'eye contact' and at expanding his 'autistic repetitive play' into meaningful play. That aside, can you see how I was the only one exercising choice? I wanted more than that.

My challenge was to motivate Brandon or any other child *to want* to follow me into the playroom, *to choose to stay* with me and feel that he has the *freedom to come and go* as and when he wishes. Instantly my work became harder. I decided to open the playroom door and told Brandon that he could leave. Like an arrow he shot out of the room, but before I could stand up he was back. He pulled a little stool by the door and locked it. Did he copy my previous behaviour? Did I indirectly teach him to lock the door? Most probably! His behaviour exemplifies literal learning, photographic learning or learning in pictures.

His body language also let us know that he wanted his mum and I in the room. This want is emotional, not connected to autistic learning. We don't learn or teach emotions, we feel and share them. A few days later I left the door wide open and waited for Brandon to join me. Driven by his desire to play, Brandon chose to come in. When he wanted the rest of the children out he locked the door – a non-verbal communication meant to say 'I want all the attention!' He wanted all the attention for himself. *He was exercising choice!* Our relationship moved into a *dimension of mutual trust.* I was winning and I liked that.

If his mother or I chose to stop playing before Brandon was ready to stop, he ran to lock the door. We taught him to say 'Stay and play with me' and explained that if he said that we would stay without him having to lock us in.

Food for thought

Are you engaging your child in activities perceived by you as preparation for the times ahead, even if he finds them upsetting?

Can you see why it is important to work with what your child *is* capable of doing at this moment in time, as opposed to working with the image of what your child *should* be capable of doing?

Your child loves the room so much that he doesn't want to leave

In 1999 I met a child with huge sparkling eyes, filled with energy and laughter. Every time he looked at me I felt as if he looked into my soul. We wanted to hear him talk to us.

We managed to bond within seconds. After two hours in my playroom, his mother and I went downstairs for a cup of coffee and a chat. The child remained there, waiting for us to return. His mother had to bribe him to leave the playroom. He joined us at the table and said 'KitKat'. On that occasion he left my home without what I would call really talking.

They returned two weeks later and as soon as he entered my house he ran into the playroom. This child thrived on social interaction. Once again he left my home without talking. One week later I phoned his mother. Her son heard my voice over the phone. His mother told me that he approached her with the car keys and said, 'Go, go, go, see Florica.' *A child could begin talking when you least expected.*

The question of transition

As I mentioned before, interaction is not a therapy, and is practised all day long. Therefore 'transition' is never an issue. The playroom only makes it easier for you to defuse, observe and decode puzzling and sometimes challenging behaviour and offers your child a space where he doesn't have to be 'on guard at all times'.

However, a common parental fear stems from a belief that *allowing* the child to do all he wants inside the playroom might *teach* the child to treat the entire house as a playroom. In my experience I learned that the opposite happens. With the passing of each day, the communication gap between you and your child will close. As a consequence, you will begin to be able to reason with your child.

Example

After using the playroom for less than two weeks we benefited from Brandon's first signs of willingness to compromise. He stopped blocking the television with his body[5] and sat down with us on our lap, or on a corner of the same sofa (at arm's length) when he needed space.

Instead of pouring out the contents of his Battleship Command toy, he brought it to me and we played. We played our own game and followed our own rules. But as opposed to him emptying the contents and his mother and I tidying up the mess, we *played together*. He learned numbers and acquired more meaningful language. When he had had enough, he went to play quietly on his own as opposed to screaming for attention.

Food for thought

Increased interactive time with your child will help you find your own balance between the time you choose to use the playroom and the time you choose to use the rest of the house for interaction.

The difference between a standard therapy or playroom and the play–interaction room

The difference stems from your attitude and your conduct during interaction. Inside a therapy room the therapist decides the length of a session as well as the length of time a child *should* spend on a particular activity. It is the therapist who keeps the room locked and finds ways to teach/impose his agenda to the child. Several factors govern such therapy sessions, the overriding one being, for example, that therapy starts promptly at 10am and finishes at 11am.

Now think about what more than one of my autistic friends have said: 'Although I am awake and my eyes are open, I need two hours before I hear anything that makes sense.' They managed to reinforce in my mind that when our children behave in a non-responsive way, it has nothing to do with 'not wanting to respond' or that the therapist isn't skilled. It is more likely that they did not hear us or that what we said meant nothing to them. Therefore your child might be present in a room but non-responsive because he is not fully awake.

On the other hand where therapy starts at 10 and finishes at 11, your child might find himself confused over why he has to leave when he is enjoying himself and just began learning something new. Either way the child is missing out on opportunities to expand his own knowledge.

Another factor to consider when assessing the benefits of any therapeutic intervention is the length of that child's *shared attention*. I will explain what I mean by this term. Successful teaching happens when the teacher uses his pupil's attention. The teacher shares knowledge and his attention is directed towards making sure that the student understands the meaning of what he is teaching. The student's attention is naturally directed towards acquiring that knowledge and asking questions when in doubt. The process of *teaching–learning* happens during such shared attention periods of time.

Furthermore shared attention is an *act of will* during which our learning occurs naturally. We recognise it as curiosity. I have never heard of anyone who could enforce curiosity upon a child through restraining his behaviour or confining him within a teaching environment. This is why the interaction room is always open and the volunteer friend follows the child's agenda. When the child leaves the room his friend leaves with him (if invited) or waits for the child to return. Whoever enters the interaction room (parent, therapist or volunteer helper) carries the intention of *sharing and building a relationship based on friendship*.

When we follow the child's agenda, we are in fact working with the child's interests, curiosity and attention. Autism as a vague entity is of no relevance in this context. The interaction play friend joins in with the autistic play because the child's attention is focused on something. The friend's job is to translate that something into words and encourage the child to repeat those words. The greatest hurdles experienced by therapists working against autism are:

- 'getting' a child's attention

- directing his attention towards an activity introduced by the therapist, especially if that activity makes no sense to the child.

In comparison, because the friend is constantly observing the child, he notices those natural 'shared attention' moments, acknowledges them and chooses activities which will increase the duration of shared attention. Every child connects with you, even if for one second!

I have a re-occurring tearful memory of a young child who I met in a therapy room. The therapist left the room and the child pulled me towards the toy shelf. He pointed at a farm toy and smiled. As I reached to bring it down the therapist returned and said, 'X, your time is up. You had time to play with it but chose not to. Next time play with it when it is given to you.' The child continued to look into my eyes and tears fell as his grip on my hand grew stronger. I had his attention. His eye connected with mine. His body language showed me his willingness to explore a new toy, yet I couldn't do anything to help him. When I think of it, I couldn't do anything to help myself either. If this child had been non-autistic and verbal, he could have voiced his needs and reasons, but he wasn't. This is just one other reason why a friend follows the child.

Food for thought

If your house is danger free and you have made it 'boring', your child will seek your company and return to you or call you somewhere else.

Television can be a best friend or a great enemy. Some children are happy spending hours in front of the same TV programme or just watching the flickering of the screen. You could control the visual input by choosing to play video recordings of you and your child at play, Makaton videos and Sesame Street videos. Your child will learn only positive things from them. If and when he decides to copy the contents of such programmes, you will be the one who reaps the rewards.

The role of a friend

1. Invites the child into the playroom and waits for him to respond to the invitation.

2. Follows the child's interest and offers assistance.

3. May leave the room when he feels uneasy. Remembers that he is there to inspire change, not to frown upon the child who needs help.

4. Observes, copies in front of a mirror and describes to the child his autistic activities[6] (spinning objects, flapping limbs, watching a car running down a ramp 100 times).

5. Joins in with an identical game and expands on it. If the child spins around, the friend spins too and offers to spin the child. Nine out of ten children will understand what you are suggesting and come to you of their own accord. The child might enjoy your game so much that he wants you to continue for as long as one hour. Stick to that activity even if you find it boring. Such interactive games become your first steps towards a trusting relationship. The child could feel overwhelmed by such pleasant experience and when you pause the game he runs away to hide. If that happens, wait for him to return to you and spin him in a gentle way. If he doesn't return it could mean that he did not enjoy the sensation. Therefore you need to find a different game.

6. Discovers activities that trigger fun interaction.[7]

7. Aims to spend as much time as the child allows or the friend can sustain on any shared activity and observes the child's responsiveness.

8. Uses the child's motivation and asks him to repeat the words which describe the activities they are doing.

9. Spends peaceful times with the child when he is silent.

10. Introduces and labels a variety of toys and helps the child to explore them.

11. When a child is finished with a toy or a book, the friend tells/shows the child where the toy will be placed before he removes it.

12. If the child wants the toy back (even for one second), the friend lets him have it.

13. Models the way in which we play with a toy and invites the child to copy those actions.

14. Invites the child to join in and asks for his assistance when the child looks towards him.

15. Never removes a toy without telling the child first.

16. Never removes a toy from a child because in his opinion the child has spent too much time on a repetitive activity.

17. Introduces songs, nursery rhymes, books and fun games.

18. When the child shows an interest in a book, the friend explores the content of that book with the child at a pace set by the child.

19. Verbally labels the child's body language and visible emotions.

Example

Before Alexander looked towards us, we had to wait until he finished writing all the numbers from 1 to 1000. Before another child looked towards me for a brief moment, I held him on my lap and watched him play with the marbles on the marble run for four hours.

Autistic behaviour – can we encourage it?

The answer to this question is a resounding *no*. Our ability to encourage autistic behaviour is just as redundant as thinking that we could teach it! As well as being asked by parents 'Why should I change the physical environment of our house?', they shared a common source of fear and upset:

- Am I encouraging my child's autistic behaviour if I copy autistic behaviour or if I allow my child to behave in an autistic way?

- Why can't my child learn to follow our rules and respect our boundaries?

You are not encouraging autistic behaviour if you allow your child to behave in an autistic way or if you copy his behaviour. *You are not responsible for the autistic behaviour.* You did not teach it or model it to your child. To all intents your child *invented* it; that behaviour is unique to each child. It can mean any of the following:

- his style of learning

- a means of exploring the environment

- a means of relaxation

- a way of communication
- an insight into how he might feel.

You will also learn to identify which behaviour means what and, where feasible, help transform it. For example, one single child will do the following:

1. Stop hitting people if his personal space is respected – an emotional need.

2. Continue to 'inspect' objects because this is a visual need.

3. Eat earth, sand or washing powder (known as pica) because his sense of taste is different from yours – sensory mis-wiring.

4. Stop hurting himself if you don't make him do something that he doesn't feel comfortable doing – emotional communication.

5. He will continue to write in a 'photographic'[8] way – literal learning – until you help him develop flexibility of thought through increased meaningful vocabulary.

6. Learn words after he hears them – auditory problem that prevents the mind from hearing words.

7. He will stop touching dangerous objects and respond to verbal requests after he understands that 'danger' is a concept, not the name of the object. A mother told me how her child picked up an object to which she had previously told her son, 'Don't pick this up, it is dangerous.' Minutes later, the child ran to her and while holding the object he said, 'Mum, look, dangerous.'

8. In extreme cases, if the child's pain threshold is higher than yours, he will wash with scalding water because he is unable to feel the pain. The skin will burn but the sensation of pain fails to reach his mind in time to warn the body about the dangers. You can teach him to regulate the temperature by using a thermometer.

9. Your child could scream because he has a toothache. Because he is not telling you, you might think that he screams for a different reason. He doesn't tell you about his toothache because he hasn't 'worked out' that telling you means that you can help end the

pain. Furthermore, by the time he experiences the pain his tooth may be beyond repair and has to be extracted.

10. If your child's hearing were hypersensitive, then he would throw himself on the pavement covering his ears at the sound of heavy traffic or he might run across a busy road. He would do this to protect his hearing, not to cause embarrassment or to place himself in danger.

Over the years, I copied autistic behaviour because I wanted to:

- understand what it meant – playing detective

- show the child/adult that I don't judge their behaviour. As I copied it I also made a habit of asking, 'What are we doing? What does this mean to you?'

- relate to the person 'hiding' behind the unusual behaviour and wanted to find out various reasons for that behaviour

- find a way to interact with it in a way that causes minimum or if at possible no upset to that person.

I sincerely encourage you to do the same.

Food for thought

The word *danger* is a concept with varied meanings. The sensory system, the feedback of information to the brain and the working memory of a person, prevents the ability of an autistic person to relate to the non-autistic system of common meanings. Personal accounts of adult autistics tell us that.

We follow rules or reject them because we understand the implications of our actions. As a result of everyday interaction the non-autistic child learns to categorise acceptable and non-acceptable activities.

The autistic child needs more time to assimilate the surrounding environment before he can examine and understand the implication of rules.

If the child's sensory system is damaged, then the meaning of danger will not exist or it will signify something different from the norm.

Reminder

The autistic child will conform to our rules, from simple house rules (such as do not play with a sharp knife) to more general unwritten rules (such as not taking crisps belonging to a complete stranger), after he's understood about the concept of rules.

Notes

1. This was another breakaway from my initial teaching. I realised that children are more relaxed (adults too) when their parents are present during play sessions. All the children looked at their parents for reassurance and wanted their parents to understand them. They had fun playing with me and kissed *their* mother for a reward! Fantastic! If they didn't like what I did, they hid behind their mother or father for comfort. Even better! I call this human bonding and communication! True empathy.

2. Unfortunately, the belief that keeping a child at home denies him the opportunity to develop social skills continues to be circulated. After I withdrew Alexander from school, I received a letter stating: 'Keeping him away is not the best way to address his social needs.' What social needs? Being bullied? Being told off for not playing? Being laughed at for not talking fast enough or having to start his sentence from the beginning if interrupted?

3. How fast he can listen, think, express.

4. See Chapter 8, Shaping your language, p.185.

5. Meaning 'Play with me right now!'

6. See answer to 'Does autism mean the same as autistic behaviour?' in Appendix A: Frequently asked questions, p.255.

7. As perceived by the child.

8. See Chapter 20, Writing, p.203.

8

Sensory 'mis-wiring' and behaviour

Autism creates as many individual[1] ways of behaving and being as there are autistic people. This way of being stems from a genetic make-up that tampers with the sensory system. Because the sensory system feeds the brain 'false' information, the body responds in an unnatural way. You can recognise which of your child's senses are most affected from the unnatural behaviour.

What could it do to your child?

Hearing

1. He could feel dizzy from the sound of the vacuum cleaner and refuse to use it or even to enter the room when the cleaner is in use. If you are unaware of this you might think that he is lazy.

2. He might panic when cutlery is thrown in the sink or refuse to do the washing up.

3. If the sound is too loud he would cover his ears or panic, rock himself or hurt someone.

4. The sound of another person's voice could sound piercing and he will cover his ears or go and hide.

5. He might not distinguish the sound of words from the rest of the sounds and therefore will not repeat them or will not understand verbal requests.

6. He could hear sounds that we cannot and, for example, become distracted, annoyed or unable to fall asleep because of the sound of a transformer.

7. He could be unable to cut out the 'background noise' in a room filled with people and focus his attention towards the speaker. Therefore he will not enjoy social gatherings or will be unable to make sense of a teacher's words.

8. He would be unable to decode intonation – thus the intention of the speaker.

9. He could hear perfect pitches and compose beautiful music.

10. He could hear music as a cacophony of sounds and would hate listening to it.

11. He could impersonate any voice to perfection.

I had a friend for whom everyday sounds caused her to feel pain in her ears. The sound she reacted most negatively to was the TV transformer. The sound preventing her from sleeping came from the dimmer switch. Another friend told me that he could hear a piece a paper 'hitting' the floor from three floors up. I watched another friend becoming 'instantly confused and lost' after we entered a noisy pub. She experienced too much stimuli or *sound overload*. She asked for us to leave[2] and we did.

I took another friend to a Chinese restaurant. For approximately two hours the place was pleasantly quiet and we enjoyed our conversation. However, two hours later a group of merry people entered the restaurant. In front of my eyes, my friend transformed. Her smile vanished. She moved her hands under the table and her body looked as if 'crushed by 100 tonnes of sheer weight'. I recognised the symptoms and asked, 'Too much noise?' She replied with a smile, 'Is it OK if we leave?' It was more than OK if we left. What was the point in staying when the atmosphere did not allow her to have fun? Once again we did not leave *to avoid social interaction*; we left because the restaurant was *noisy*.

Tactile insensitivity or hypersensitivity

The brain helps us feel pain and identifies it as pain. This is why we drop an overheated object before it can cause extensive damage to our body. If as a reaction to pain we were to see colour, we would be unable to link the cause of pain with its source:

1. Your child could begin crying hours after he got hurt because it took hours for the sensation of pain to reach the brain.

2. If he burns his hand he might continue holding on to the hot object, causing extensive damage.

3. He might cut open a wound only to look at the blood trickling.

4. He could chew a sharp object and cut the inside of his mouth because he cannot feel the pain when it happens.

5. He might not know where his body ends and will therefore bump into walls.

6. Rain could feel like pins hitting his skin.

7. He could swallow hot food because he cannot feel the burning in his mouth.

8. He could be able to 'feel' the gravitational axes of objects and will therefore spin them for fun.

9. He would play with our hair as opposed to physical games.

10. He would scream when given a bath because he feels the water too cold or too hot.

11. He might refuse to dress because the clothes are hurting his skin.

Papillary

1. He could eat washing powder, sand or earth because his sense of taste and smell fails to warn him not to.

2. He would eat only foods of a certain texture.

Visual

1. He would be unable to recognise the face of a friend in a crowd or his own face in the mirror.

2. He cannot see the difference between a boy and a girl and will call a girl 'boy' and vice versa.

3. He might look directly at a source of light because it doesn't hurt his eyes.

4. He would look at a room from every possible angle before entering it.

5. His eyes could be able to see the detail as opposed to the whole, e.g. toy train, the whole toy car, the whole person. This in turn leads towards him inspecting the same toy over and over until he can see the whole picture. He could examine our earrings as opposed to looking at our face.

6. He would have to jump over cracks in the pavement.

7. He could feel dizzy when looking at a tiled floor and fear stepping on it.

8. He could draw like Steven Wiltshire because his photographic memory is infinitely better than ours.

The difference between eye contact and connection

You may believe or were led into believing that your child is deliberately avoiding eye contact. He refuses to look at you. I used to believe that too and for many years my first aim was directed towards *getting Alexander to look at me.* On numerous occasions I placed my body in front of him, my eyes below his eye level and asked him to look at me. I even waved my arms in front of his eyes and yelled, 'Alexander, look at me.' All this came to an end the day he shouted at me, 'No look at me, play now!' I sensed that what I was doing was wrong. Although I knew instinctively that he didn't like me asking him to look at me, I knew of no other alternative which would direct his visual attention towards me.

I was taught to constantly ask Alexander to look at me. If he looked at me I was meant to thank him for looking at me, show him and tell him that I liked that very much. The teachers meant well and I meant well. Every now and then Alexander looked at me. When he did, I believed he was *working on his eye contact*. Many years later I watched an interview with an adult autistic lady. She explained how she finds it hard to focus on two things at once. By that she meant looking at you and talking with you at the same time. I believed her because I remembered my son's reaction. I tried to imagine how difficult it must be to be her and I found myself asking:

- How would I like it if other people ignored my problem?

- How would I be able to distinguish between what I am asked to do?

- Am I being asked to look at them?

- Are people asking me a question or are they asking me to look at them?

- Is looking at them more important than answering the question?

Nine years on, Alexander has reached the ability to do two or three things at once. By three things at once, I mean that he is able to effortlessly listen to a question, process the reply, reply and ask his own follow-up question/s. The length of such interactive communicative times varies and could be interrupted by one or more intervening factors. We all know when we have lost his attention. His behaviour lets us know. We also know that if Alexander says 'Never mind' it means 'I need time to think' or 'I am not sure I understand your question'.

Visual stimuli – gazing

I asked Paradox (a friend who loved gazing at lights), 'Assuming that both of us are looking at the same tree in the garden, I see a tree. What do you see?'

'A tree. Why do you ask?'

'I ask because I read somewhere that we might not see the same thing. Perhaps that might explain why I am "looking at the tree" and you "are gazing at the tree".'

'What do you mean by gazing?'

'By gazing I mean that you look towards the tree for two hours and seem to me as if you are somewhere else.'

'I see what you mean. When I do what you call "gazing", I am looking at the rays of light flickering through the leaves. All my life I loved lights.

Lights make me feel comfortable. I might even talk to the lights, don't know. I want to show you my favourite toy.'

She opened her backpack and showed me a CAD light; a light that flickers rapidly and changes colour from white to red and back. 'Would you like to see it work?'

'Please show me.' I wasn't prepared for the pain that hit the back of my eyes, as if someone had set fire to them. That was my last attempt to look at her toy whilst turned on. She laughed at my reaction, yet our little experiment and her willingness to communicate with me shed light over our visual interpretation of stimuli.

I learned to accommodate my friend's needs. I had to accept that some of my friends' activities will not be pleasurable for me and they understood that. If you catch your child 'gazing' at the tablecloth or a painting or just a plain coloured wall, don't automatically assume that your child is 'gazing'. I will use the word *gaze* to represent our perception and the word *investigating* to represent our children's perceptions. I met the mother of a child who loved investigating pictures of birthday cakes. His mother told me how she believed that by introducing her son to a variety of books she was hoping to help her son overcome his obsession with cakes. What became evident however was the fact that her son combed every book and left each book open at the page where he could see a birthday cake. Although his mother felt frustrated, she became aware of her son's ability to sort out visual images.

What could we learn from this example?

1.   We don't know why this child liked the look of cakes.

2.   We do know that he knew what he was looking for in his books.

What could we do with these findings?

I suggested that as a sign of friendship she cuts out birthday cake pictures and sticks them on his bedroom wall. She was afraid to follow my advice just in case this course of action would reinforce autistic behaviour.

In a diary of 'behaviours and thoughts', write your answers to the following questions. Revisit them monthly after you spend more time observing and shadowing your child.

1. Make a list of your emotions (e.g. anger, upset, confusion).

2. List the activities that you wish to stop your child from doing (e.g. spinning, flapping his arms, talking to himself).

3. List *your* reasons.

4. Could you empathise with *your child's need* for that activity?

5. Could you accept that your child doesn't know why you want him to stop?

Pointer

During a conversation with a parent he voiced his confusion. 'What do you mean accept that my child needs to flood my bathroom? Are you implying that I should just sit there and watch him do it?' By accepting that a child needs to do an activity, I mean that the child likes to play with the water. Hence he becomes totally absorbed by water. The child's intention is not to flood the bathroom but to have fun with the water.

The child who liked spotting cakes in books wasn't obsessed with cakes. He found something in them that we don't see and/or understand. If we choose to explore his interest, we can help him translate his visual thoughts into words and stop the guessing game.

The trouble with toys

I am convinced that you too have noticed how your child plays 'oddly' with toys. The trouble with toys is that you and I perceive them in one way and our children perceive them in another. My friend Paradox told me, 'Your house is full of autistic-friendly toys. Can I have some of them after you move?'

'What do you mean?' I asked.

'Take "Connect a Straw" – my friend likes chewing the soft straws as well as building almost anything out of them. K'nex is great too because together we can build the perfect spinning toys out of them; the marble run because we both love the marbles and the loops; the Brio is perfect for building ramps and the tracks don't fall apart; Lego is hard for me. It lacks flexibility and curves, but my friend likes it.'

Now read what a parent (myself included) said: 'I hate the marble run! My child can spend hours staring at one marble. The house is filled with marbles! Brio is so expensive and building a perfect track takes up too much space. K'nex is a good toy but *I lose* my child to it. His play becomes *exclusive!*

I ended up buying 100 toy cars for Alexander. He lined them all up! A dear friend of mine shared her perception on what we call 'lining up toys'. My son stopped lining them at the age of eight. She was 21. As she was my guest over Christmas she had free use of Alexander's playroom. To my surprise I went into the room and found 30 cars perfectly lined and sorted by colours. I asked her why she did that. She replied, 'It gives me a sense of order.' Her reply is one possible answer. Her answer may mean nothing to the exasperated parent, yet to her it meant:

- the truth

- a comforter

- fun play

- inner peace during this activity.

Notes

1. Hence the diagnosis reads 'autism continuum'.
2. She did not ask to avoid social interaction.

9

Other behaviours

Some behaviour cannot be pinned down to only one function of a 'sensory stem'. It happens as a result of his perception of reality, personality and personal experiences; for example:

- If he suffers from what Paradox described as 'inertia', he would take a long time to leave his bed, wake up in the morning or compile an answer. By inertia she meant 'I know that I have to do something or say something. I want to do it. I am not lazy (that is different) but I can't get my mouth to open or my body to move.' By that she did not mean 'I am afraid to talk or move'. She meant that for reasons unknown to her she couldn't move or talk.

- He could lie on the pavement without considering how other people might interpret his behaviour.

Each less natural behaviour exhibited by your child has a good reason. No one child experiences all of the above. Every child can benefit from your help. I don't know how Alexander developed the ability to look at us and talk to us at the same time. I can share how it developed, what helped and what did not.

Visual appreciation

At the age of four, Alexander insisted on having his food presented to him cut into eight pieces. As much as this need upset me sometimes, I continued to find it intriguing. One day I brought his Kit-Kat on a large carving plate with the eight pieces of biscuit arranged in the shape of a heart. Alexander glanced at the plate, then quickly looked straight into my eyes and smiled. *That look was what I call a connection.* My next step was to invent more activities that incorporated Alexander's need. My course of action was aimed at showing unconditional love.

In 1999 a mother described the style in which her three-year-old child ate his Smarties. She told me that he ate them in a specific colour order. Should it happen that one was lost, he would scream as well as refuse to eat the others. I suggested that next time she offers some Smarties, she placed them on a tray in the exact order that the child liked eating them. Then she was meant to present them as if she was serving in a silver service restaurant. She phoned to let me know that her child behaved the same way as Alexander did. Her son smiled, looked at her and pushed his body into her in a 'hug-like' bodily contact.

As soon as you know your own child's routine and can bring yourself to join with him, your child will connect with you. To verify my belief I sat on the pavement with another child when he decided to throw himself down. He used to throw himself down so often that his mother dreaded the next shopping trip. He was well accustomed to being picked up and dragged to the car. His mother had learnt to become oblivious to the looks and/or comments made by the local people. Well, we all experience their looks! So when my little five-year-old friend threw himself on the cold and dirty pavement during a return trip from the shops, I sat down next to him and told his mother to go ahead without us. His big eyes grew even bigger and stared straight into mine. Instead of a screaming child I witnessed a happy and curious child. The passers-by had their own beliefs, but these are irrelevant here. I asked him, 'Why did we sit down?'

'Me tired now,' replied my little friend before placing his head on his lap pretending to snore.

'We could go home and sleep. Home is very near,' I suggested. 'See, mummy went home. We could do that too. We could go home and play trucks.'

'No trucks, me tired, me sleepy.'

'OK, I will sit with you for a little while.' After five minutes I stood up and invited him to come home with me. Unsure, he held my hand and we skipped and hopped for the next 30 metres. I thought we would make it all the way home.

We had ten more metres to go when my little friend decided to stop once more. This time he gave me a one-second verbal warning and shouted, 'I am running that way!'

Before I could do anything he was off. I had to run after him and turn the running away into a game. My little friend and my son had no sense of danger. Neither of them would have thought about the dangers associated with running across the road.

I am not asking anyone to go out and sit on the pavements with their children. I have done it because I wanted to find an alternative to having to pick up a screaming child. I wanted to *reason* with my friend and we did. After I sat down with him he stopped throwing himself on the floor.

Sleeping problems – what could they mean?

Donna Williams (1992) describes her *inability to distinguish between dream and reality*. I tried to imagine what it would be like not knowing if my nightmare was real or not. Scary thought! You could be the fortunate parent of a child who sleeps at bedtime. Alexander, like many children and adults, does not. Some adults I spoke with shared their reasons for not sleeping, as well as what would help them to relax.

Talking to oneself

At the age of 11, Alexander enjoyed going to bed at the same time as us. However, we were asleep long before him. He used to spend hours whispering to himself before he actually fell asleep. Sometimes he was willing to share his thoughts. Most times he denied whispering to himself. If I asked him 'What are you doing?' he would reply, 'I am not doing anything. 'If I asked 'What is happening?' he would reply in a staccato-sounding voice, 'Nothing is happening, g-o-o-d n-i-g-h-t Mummyyyy.' If I enquired 'Could I hear your story?' he would reply, 'I am not telling any story. Good night Mummy, kiss, kiss.' If he felt distressed his whispers turned into loud 'mouse-like squeaks' interrupted by coughs and spits. When Alexander is talking to himself he is repeating previous conversations or new sets of sentences he learned that day. It is his way of 'storing' information. *He is not deliberately keeping awake.*

Better mental performance

As described to me by 18-year-old Bexxy: 'I love nights. There is less noise and light in the night and *I can concentrate better.* During the day, in my boarding school, I used to blank out my bedroom windows and study. However, the staff took them down every time and told me that this is not the right behaviour.'

'What do you mean?'

'Well I used my duvet to cover the window because the curtains were too thin. Then I blanked out my door because I couldn't stand hearing the noise coming from the hall. The staff told me that I couldn't do that because they can't watch me and took them off. After that incident I felt tired and angry. I refused to go to class and went to bed.'

'Did you ever tell them what you are telling me now?'

'No.'

'Why?'

'They never asked me.'

'Would you tell them now?'

'I don't know if I would. I don't know if they would believe me. Anyhow I have no intentions of returning to *that* boarding school. I learn better during the proper night. Perhaps I should study long distance and take only one course a year? My own mum is upset with me when I stay up late and sleep in the day. I wish she understood that days tire me. Nights don't.'

Nightmares

Four nights out of seven Alexander woke up in the middle of the night, crying or screaming. Someone suggested that I lock his bedroom door and stop attending to him when he woke up. I could not do that. Alexander was experiencing nightmares and more than once I found him in the middle of the bed, sweat pouring from his body and with his eyes wide open screaming, 'Take them away!' Whatever those things were, to Alexander's mind they were real. They were crawling towards him, scared him and had to be taken away. I tried to bring him out of the nightmare and said, 'This is Mummy. Look at me. Do you know who I am?'

'You are Mummy!' screamed Alexander. 'Now take them away!'

I pretended to pick up a fistful of 'creatures' and then threw them on the floor.

Alexander yelled, 'Not on the floor! Open the window and throw them out!'

As soon as I followed his instruction he began relaxing. Pointing at another corner of the bed he said, 'There is one more over there!' I threw the last one out the window and Alexander went back to sleep.

Food for thought

Imagine experiencing the same nightmare, stuck in the middle of the bed with your whole being paralysed by fear and no one there to help you. Would you like it? How would you survive until sunrise?

According to many personal accounts, an autistic person has difficulty separating events that are real from the dreamed ones. If your child experiences the dream state as an identical reality to that of being awake then the concept of a nightmare is not formed. Imagine having to live with that and having no one to reassure you when you most need it.

Unnatural fear of abandonment

Verbal or physical reassurance is the answer to abandonment fears. For brief moments my adult autistic guests woke me up. I felt glad that they felt comfortable waking me up and that I could provide them with emotional support.

Up to the age of eight Alexander fell asleep only if I kept him company. As soon as he fell asleep I left his bed. However, if I left too soon he woke up and screamed. He needed two further hours before he could fall asleep again. His body language conveyed fear of being left alone. Because he was unable to talk about his emotions I was only guessing.

I met a young lady who could not fall asleep until her parents returned from an evening out.

Fear of death

Another friend told me that she used to wake her mother at various hours of the night because she was afraid that her mother had died. So I asked her, 'Do you dream?'

'I do. I have dreams and nightmares.'

'Do you have recurring nightmares?'

'Only one. I dream that our house is on fire and that my parents, my sister and brothers are stuck inside. I try saving them but I can't fight my way through the flames. When I wake up I am afraid to fall asleep again. I miss my mother badly. After a dream such as this I want to wake her up to reassure myself that she is alive. She doesn't like me doing that though.'

The mother confirmed the story and told me that she was unaware of her daughter's dreams.

A need for reassurance

A personal account: 'I never woke my parents up. However, I did wake up in the night and gaze at them. It made me feel good. They don't know this. I did this because I loved them. However, if I were to approach them during the day they would have hugged me and I hated that.'

Suggestions

If your child is naturally more alert at night, it could be that he is sensitive to light, sound or both. Reducing the level of lighting or noise in his room could change your child's behaviour instantly for the better.

If your child wakes up in the middle of the night drenched in sweat and looking frightened, it is very likely that he has had a nightmare. Fitting nightlights in his room might reduce some of his fears.

Temper tantrums

The following examples act as pointers. The content of this list is as individual as a child:

- verbal disagreement – stemming from lack of shared meanings of the words being used

- hugging a child against his will

- making him sit down and perform an activity that fails to make sense to him

- moving a toy without his knowledge and consent

- changing the furniture around without his knowledge and involvement

- a toy that doesn't 'behave' the way he wants it to.

Loving solution for one temper tantrum

It was bath and bedtime, but my little friend Pierce, then three and a half years, had no intention of parting with the wooden train set. I tried the friendly 'We play five more minutes, put the train in the box and then go for a bath.' My suggestion was greeted with a scream. After a few minutes I presented him with a different suggestion. 'Let's give the train a bath!' It worked. The train went into the bathroom, waited for my friend to jump in the bath and dived in with him. The train brought the soap, the shampoo and sometimes tickled him. As the water began to cool it was time to get out. Well that was my opinion and once again not shared. Therefore the train brought the towel, the train complained about feeling cold and sleepy and the train asked my friend to take him to bed. I brought another towel for the train and a small cushion. Pierce sniggered, ran into the bedroom, placed his train on the cushion and then giggling snuggled under the covers.

Repetitive behaviour stems from delayed reactions

If your child experiences a delay in processing the information[1] fed by the sensory input you will observe a repetitive behaviour, which could lead you to believe that he is deliberately hurting himself. His linguistic behaviour[2] is also affected by his hearing. Normal at a cognitive level or normal in terms of suggested action–reaction through feedback from the brain describes each of the following situations:

1. If I bump my head into a hard object, I immediately connect the source of pain with the bump. I don't need to repetitively re-bump my head to help myself understand the connection between bumping into a wall and feeling pain. Therefore I stop

doing it. I don't do that because I feel the pain immediately and my brain sends me the needed signals that will make me stop.

2. I understand that the scars left behind after self-mutilation will influence what other people think about my emotional stability. Also I would feel pain. If my pain threshold were higher than the norm, I would not feel it and thus perhaps not feel motivated to stop.

3. I don't need help to realise that language is an information-conveying tool and that I must learn how to use it, not just repeat it.

4. My learning ability is in line with most other people. I don't learn in pictures.

5. My literal interpretation of words disappears with my growing age and life experiences.

6. I don't call a stranger 'father' because I am able to distinguish and identify his facial features within a crowd of people and I understand the meaning of the word 'father'.

7. If I were to ask people in the room to speak quietly, I would not shout out my request because I am able to hear the level of sound of my projected voice in relation to others.

8. I know the implications and meanings of intonation and volume.

Food for thought

These examples are here to demonstrate the amount of havoc that autism could cause. Assuming that you were to experience this autistic reality, then you would not know what was wrong with your behaviour!

Furthermore, it would be very easy for you to assume that 'If people want to cure my autism, they don't like me the human being', as opposed to realising that 'You the carer feel hurt when I the autistic bash my head against the wall, scald myself because I can't feel the temperature of the water, and scream every time you talk because my ears are hurting'.

Fascination with fire

Face your fear and use it

If your child has discovered fire and plays with it in a dangerous way, become involved with his fascination until he can hear you and understand the concept of danger. I have met only two children who held such fascination. The older child was 22 years old and started a small fire inside the ashtray. As I walked into my living room I found him hiding under the cushions whilst watching the little fire with amazement and fascination. I told him that it was dangerous and as I removed the fire he said, 'Why are you taking it away? It is beautiful to watch. I can take care of it.'

I explained that if he wanted to have fun with fire he would have to do it in a controlled environment. I explained that having a fire on a wooden table inside the living room is not safe. He then asked me why. I continued explaining that the ashtray was made of glass and that glass could crack when heated. If the ashtray cracked he could panic and if he panicked he might not know what to do. Fire could kill us as well as burn the house down. My friend thanked me for the explanation and promised not to start a fire again. He also apologised for starting this game.

You might think that my explanations were too obvious. Three years ago I would have agreed with you. However, after three years of sheltering various autistic friends I learned from them about the need to be guided through the entire chain of causes and effects. The length of such chains differs from person to person and is unique to your child.

You can only explain and/or share reasoning through teaching cause and effect to a person who is willing to listen. Explaining is not the same as 'telling off' (see shared attention, p.78). By the time these children used my home as a shelter they were tired of being told off. They wanted explanations and they wanted friendship.

The other child who liked fire was nine years old. Terrified that their child could set the house ablaze, the parents locked every room and kept the matches and lighters well hidden. However, just like Alexander who was able to find a pen to draw on the walls, this child found lighters and matches. In my living room I turned on the gas log fire and we sat by it together. I wanted to teach him the link between fire and danger. I wish you could picture his beautiful face totally excited to sit by the fire. As we sat next to each other he pointed at the flames, smiled and then looking at me said, 'See...*casle!*'[3]

His parents clarified it. He meant *candle*. I told him that this was a log fire, not a candle. He didn't like my explanation and shouted at me, 'See…CASLE!' I brought a little candle and said, 'This is a candle, that is a log fire.' His face turned brighter than the sun. Looking at the candle twice as excited as when he previously looked at the log fire, he came close to it. Yet before the candle could develop a flame he blew it out. He watched the smoke fizzle away, flapped his arms and smiling with great anticipation exclaimed again, 'Casle!'

He also ran to the door, shut it and blocked it with an armchair. His mum and dad said, 'No, don't do it, we are not at home.' I wanted to show him that he could feel as if my home was his home and lent him a hand. He looked puzzled at first. He then jumped up and down with excitement, smiled and gave me a hug. I became an instant friend!

His reactions made me wonder. After all, he did not seem to be interested in fire as much as he was interested in smoke. I turned off the log fire and switched my attention to the candle. I chose to ask him to say 'candle' whilst I lit the candle. At first he responded to my request through nervously jumping up and down and hitting his stomach. I chose to jump too and to continue to ask for the word 'candle' as well as lighting it – even though he did not say the word. It wasn't my intention to condition the lighting of the candle on his willingness to respond to my request.

Three hours of perseverance paid off when we heard a clear 'candle' and watched his face light up realising what he had just done! Afterwards little sentences such as 'Light the candle' or 'Light the candle again' followed effortlessly. It was now his father's turn to play with his son. Together they came up with a deal on how many times the father would light the candle before they stopped that game. Father and son experienced their first meaningful interaction.

Food for thought

Making a habit of giving extended explanations will provide a necessary tool for your child when he needs to exercise and respond to reason.

Modelling clear enunciation of words and encouraging the child to repeat them pays off in the long run.

Violence means 'help me'

At this point I would like to emphasise the simple meaning of *helping a child overcome his need for violence*. Help means building on your child's understanding of cause and effect. You can only do this when the child is willing to interact with you and learn from you.

In time, some of my adult friends allowed me to see their self-inflicted scars and shared their stories on past suicide attempts. In time I met some of their parents. The act of self-inflicting injuries caused pain to both parties. For many years these parents were unable to understand why their children behaved that way. Because their children spoke fluently (Asperger's Syndrome) the parents/carers assumed that their children knew the implication of their actions (implied meaning again). Through our extended and repetitive dialogues I was able to find out the extent of their reasoning. Here are some reasons behind the actions of my friends and what the parents assumed had happened.

Tactile enjoyment coupled with a lack of feeling pain

'I first used a razor blade on my arm because I liked the look of my blood trickling down my arm.'

'Did you not feel pain?'

'Not at first, much later.'

'How about your parents? What did they think?'

'I don't know. They never asked anything.'

A cry for help copied from movies

'I began cutting my wrists when I thought that nobody cared for me any more. I watched a movie and decided to copy the actions of a girl.'

'Did it work?'

'No. I gained the attention but my father threw me on the floor, restricted my movements and called the ambulance.'

'Do you know why he did that?'

'I guess because he *didn't care!*'

Parent: I had to call for assistance. I didn't want her to die. I was feeling really tired of this kind of behaviour.

A cry for shelter

'I knew that if I threaten my parents to overdose they would let me stay with them one more night.'

Parents: We were tired of listening to the same threats. Besides it was a bad influence on the other children. We just wanted our child to behave in a normal way.

'I had no place to go. So I took enough pills to make the hospital take me in, not enough to commit suicide. I don't want to die. I want to belong but no one seems to want me.'

Parents: We were unaware of such behaviour. There are better ways to communicate. Our child is old enough to care for himself. His sister needs our time now.

A threat acting as a cry for help because he felt unable to admit that he was seeking help

'I told you that I am going to jump off a bridge because I wanted your help. I thought you wouldn't help me if I didn't sound dramatic.'

'What made you think that? I helped you so far.'

'Yes but you were upset with me and before I left I wrote that note saying that you should stop caring for me.'

'What did you think when I told you that if you want to jump you can?'

'At first I thought that you didn't care. Then I realised that you would not have offered me a return ticket to your home if you didn't care.'

Communicating the need to be loved

'I carved the girl's name on my arm because I wanted to show her that I am in love with her.'

'There are better ways of showing your love.'

'I know that, but she uses razor blades quite a lot. I thought I can stop her if I tell her that I am doing it to myself.'

'Would you let me use cream on your arm? If we start using it now the scar might become invisible.'

'The scar doesn't bother me.'

'When it does will you let me help?'

'I don't think that this scar will ever bother me.'

'What if you fall in love with another girl?'

'I never thought of that.'

'More than once I threatened my parents that I would jump out of the window.'

'Why?'

'Because I wanted them to stop me.'

'What would it have meant to you if they stopped you from jumping?'

'It would have meant that they love me.'

'Did they stop you?'

'They did, but they also threw me on the floor, called the doctor and I was taken away.'

'Do you know why they did that?'

'No.'

'They didn't know your *intention*, they assumed that you wanted to die.'

'I never thought of that.'

Parent: I was afraid when she sat there on the windowsill. I was embarrassed in front of the neighbours too. I loved her but her behaviour drove me mad. I never understood her.

Communicating despair

'Why are you burning your hands with the cigarette end?'

'It doesn't hurt. Did you not feel the need to burn your hands?'

'No. Why do you do it?'

'Are you not going to stop me?'

'No. I would rather you stopped because you wanted to stop. I guess other people stopped you before.'

'How do you know?'

'I don't know, I am guessing.'

'They did.'

'Why do you do it?'

'Sometimes I do it to feel that I am alive.'

'I hope one day you stop.'

'Why should I?'

'Because you have beautiful hands.'

'No one called my hands beautiful before and the people whom I want to spend my life with don't care about my hands.'

'What made you run away from school?'

'The reasons changed all the time but mainly I wished I could live at home with my mum.'

'Tell me more if you can.'

'Well, when she told me about this last school I was really excited… I thought to myself … At last a normal school! Then when I went into my class and was unable to communicate with anyone I despaired again. How can I possibly learn anything from a kid who has the same problems as I do? Why did she place me in a special needs unit?'

'Did you ask her?'

'No.'

'It felt as if I was there because I was considered weird.'

'How about home? What was the atmosphere when you visited?'

'Nice in the beginning. However, I remember that every time I entered my brothers' room an atmosphere of ice developed. I never knew why. Perhaps they thought that I was weird, I don't know.'

'Did you always go to a special needs school?'

'No. In my early years I went to a normal school.'

'Did you like it?'

'I did, but I don't think that the children liked me much.'

'Why do you think that?'

'Because I wore glasses. I hate my glasses. I used to leave them at home so that I had an excuse to leave the classroom when things got tough.'

'Do you think that you could cope in mainstream school now?'

'I don't know. I find it so hard to concentrate in the day.'

Parent: I tried very hard making sense of my daughter's behaviour. When she was born I hoped that she would become a missionary and spread the good news in Africa. She was such a beautiful baby. She was very shy and very frightened most of her life. Then, as she turned into a teenager, she changed again. I became so tired.

I wanted to find a cure for all this, a way out. I wanted us to have a happy family. Her behaviour did not help. We tried medication and had no luck. When the doctor suggested this last school I thought that we had found a solution to our problems. But she continued running home. Why? And when she was at home she stayed up late, cried and asked far too many questions.

How can you understand her so well? I tried for most of my life and failed. All the things that I am learning about her inner emotional world were a secret to me. If only I had known sooner. But as you said, it is never too late to start.

Notes

1. Through cognition.
2. See Appendix B, 'Linguistic behaviour assessment table'.
3. There are two reasons for him saying 'casle': (a) He was hearing casle, thus repeated casle. (b) He could not form the sound made by the letters *nd*.

Real friendship

Why is it difficult to form relationships with age peers?

Age peers and our children look alike. Hence autism is also known as the invisible disability. Both our special children and age peers seek the company of other children. This is where the resemblance ends. Age peers relate to and interact with us in a way we can understand and are able to relate to:

- They readily approach us for more knowledge and varied interaction.

- They continuously and actively seek the company of other children.

- They show *flexibility* during play and learn without having to be taught to value the *need for flexibility*.

- Their literal interpretation of language disappears *without your help* with their growing up.

Our autistic children, for reasons you will learn to appreciate, lack flexibility during interaction, need your help to overcome literal interpretation of language and feel overwhelmed by many aspects of interaction with other children. Age peers, from an incredibly young age, become aware of our children's lack of flexibility and avoid further interaction.

What made other children avoid playing with Alexander?

In essence it was his *lack of flexibility and responsiveness.* The children reacted by avoiding further interaction. At the age of four-and-a-half, Alexander used some words but possessed no social communication skills. At the time Alexander didn't seem to want to learn words. The little language he knew he used only to ask for the toys he wanted; for example, 'I want the *red* car', or 'I want the *red* tractor.' The helpers decided that he had an *obsession* with red.

From time to time, children would come up to him and ask 'Would you like to play with me?' or 'Can I play with you?' Alexander failed to respond to such invitations. He remained preoccupied with his car, train, or painting numbers. On the rare occasions when he heard the sound of another child's voice and realised that the approaching child wanted his toy, Alexander screamed.

If we are lucky enough, our autistic child becomes extremely fond of at least one interactive game and wants to play the same game repetitively.[1] I don't know many age peers who are happy to repeat the same sentence 100 times without changing it.

Is there a solution?

Yes, there is a solution. Together with adult volunteer play helpers you can help your child develop flexibility through interactive games in the privacy of your own home. Protected from judgements stemming from social conventions, your child will flourish. The following story is meant to show you that your child wants to make friends, but for a friendship to evolve *the friend* has to be flexible about autism.

'How do I make a real friend Florica?' asked my 21-year-old autistic friend. After a short pause he continued, 'I often wondered, what makes a real friend? I know that my mother meant well when she told me, "Go and play with the children, make some friends." However, once I gathered enough courage and *took my body* in the middle of the crowd I didn't know what to do.

'I was useless at playing any ball game. The ball moved faster than I could follow it with my eyes. Other games – like chase – were worst. Worse than a ball game I mean. I couldn't stand people bumping into me and their shouting hurt my ears. So I sat there, in the corner of the playground, and watched a mass of children. I wished I could play with them but their games meant nothing to me.

'When I felt lonely, I pretended that all of the children were my friends… My first real friend was a neighbour of mine. We met when I was 18. I don't know how he came to our house. Perhaps my mother tried to help me 'make friends' and brought him along. I like this guy. He likes the same music as I do. He likes staying up late and I like that too. He doesn't seem bothered about my autism. I wish I could meet more people like him.'

Your child, too, is seeking non-judgemental[2] friends.

Play helper friends – the alternative to age peers

What makes a good play helper and why would a total stranger want to help you and your child? In my experience, play helpers are ordinary people turned extraordinary. None of our volunteers knew anything about autism before they approached Alexander with their love and willingness to help. Everyone wanted to see Alexander flourish and they wanted to see it happen in *a fun* way. As the years went by, the initial so-called 'volunteers' became our only friends. I found out that every person had his own story to share and personal reasons to share their care. At some point in their own lives they had made a promise to return a good deed.

A completely different group of people came forward because they were studying a course about 'autism'. None of these stayed longer than three months. You choose whom you want to allow into your home and near the child who is not a 'project' and needs your protection and love. They divided into two subgroups:

- Group A: people who studied autism with the intent of understanding it and becoming involved in future issues. Find out what those issues are.

- Group B: people who have to finish a project and put their skills to the test with your child's responses.

Then there were retired people who wished to spend time with a child because their grandchildren lived far away (extremely loving, wise and accepting). Also there were students with an incredible zest for life who wished to share it with a young child (imaginative, energetic, wild and accepting); not forgetting mothers of grown-up children (they acted as second mothers with plenty of love to give).

> **Food for thought**
>
> The people who come forward from the goodness of their hearts become the best play helpers.

Why consider bringing volunteers into your home?

To replace the 'impatient non-autistic' age peers with patient and flexible adult play friends

As Alexander reached three years of age, I wanted to see him playing with children of his own age, his own brother and sister included. My wish remained a hope for five more years. The volunteers became Alexander's friends and prepared him for further social interaction.

To free some of your time

Every one of my three children wanted my time. Looking after Alexander *ate* time. Not being able to share a smile with Alexander did depress me at times. Sometimes you just need to go out alone, smell a flower, feel the rain smile at the sunshine and remind yourself about the beauty of being alive and having love to give.

To provide your child with friendly people who will help him socialise

As well as needing more time for Alexander, I had a nagging thought. I had read in a book that *although a child may communicate with one person, the same child will not communicate with a different person.* Bringing a variety of people into our home was my attempt to provide Alexander with an opportunity of talking to people other than myself.

To help him develop generalisation skills

At the time, Donna Williams's (1992) book *Nobody Nowhere*, medical books and the US-taught 'Option Philosophy®' heavily influenced my perception and approach to autism. On the one hand, Donna Williams helped me become aware of the existence of a 'different reality',[3] but I had no means of imagining it, let alone empathise with it. On the other I wanted to believe in a miraculous cure. In the middle, I continued to read medical research in the hope of finding a scientific solution for Alexander's problems. According to the medical books my son found it hard to communicate with other people (e.g. even after he was able to ask me for a drink, he did not ask a volunteer. Why?). His behaviours matched those described by the medical books. The ability to ask anyone for a drink followed after he understood the meaning of 'Can I have a drink?'

To give you emotional support

As well as Alexander needing help, I too needed help. The play helpers made me feel less isolated. At times of despair they listened to my crying. At times of success we celebrated together. When one of us ran out of ideas on how to play with Alexander, someone else would come up with a game. We were a team.

To test your child's readiness to play/interact with other children

Some mothers brought their children to our house with the intention of helping Alexander relate to his peers. Occasionally Alexander greeted them, but continued to play on his own.

To introduce an age peer friend

I will dearly remember a young boy with a heart of gold. He was naturally patient with Alexander and happy to share and wait for Alexander to talk to him. This child became my benchmark for 'normal' behaviour and helped me monitor Alexander's progress. The same child became Alexander's *rock* during his first school years. Such children I regard as true gifts of life and love. *Lloyd, thank you.*

Finding volunteers

You could do what I did and approach your local paper, asking them to write an article appealing for volunteer friends. The reporter listened to me and wrote a most empathising article: 'Play Helper Plan Aids Autistic Boy'. Fifteen people came forward, all willing to share their time, love of life and children with my son. The volunteers were made up from a mixture of 16-year-old school students, housewives and retired people.

Some were scared at first because for a period of three years Alexander hated keeping his clothes on.[4] His nudity created unease. Soon they became accustomed to ignoring it and got on with playing games. Imagining that we lived in a jungle helped our mind set. All of us tried to encourage Alexander to at least keep his pants on. If you were a visitor you would have been able to spot at least three pairs of pants in every room. The trouble was that as soon as we put them on him, he ran to hide and took them off. I remember wondering if he would ever keep any clothes on. The day he did was the first of many thousands of days that followed. He was able to keep them on after he had conquered his sensory hypersensitivity.

The role of a volunteer friend

Inviting volunteers into our home was the best present I could have given my son. It was a gift of love and future social skills. Thanks to their time, effort and understanding, Alexander transformed into a child who enjoys interaction. Unlike age peers, volunteer helpers could model what friendship is all about:

- They had time to listen to every word Alexander said.

- They helped him learn every word they could think of.

- They had time to tickle him and run after him.

- When building train tracks they could model for Alexander every word that he could learn by association (e.g. train, engine, steam train, red train, small train, bridge, under, over, in, around, wait, stop, green, yellow). This list is endless. At the end of our first year of play and by the time we held Alexander's fifth birthday party, he knew every volunteer by name and greeted everyone with a hug, a smile and a kiss.

- They did not *steal* parts of the track he needed! Instead they offered them to him.

These people had patience with Alexander – age peers need patience too.

As every volunteer became his friend, Alexander's vocabulary soon included words such as 'friend', 'fun' and 'play with me'. He began voicing his first questions: 'How old are you?' 'Where do you live?' 'Do you have children?' Two months after we started our play programme, Alexander named all the parts of his body, greeted his friends with a great big smile, screamed less and slept longer. I called that progress.

How did the play helpers know how to play?

Unlike you, having read this book, we had no knowledge regarding autistic learning, so we guessed. It would be accurate to say that, even after you know more about autistic learning, guessing continues to play an active role in helping you *understand your child's perception of reality.*

We chose to play the same games as with any other child, but followed Alexander's pace and imposed no rules; by that I mean play any game that he wanted from those we introduced. We played the same game 100 times (be prepared to do it). We played no games if he didn't want to play.

If Alexander wanted to play in the playroom we played in the playroom. If he wanted to play in the bathroom, dining room or garden we followed him. Our whole house became a playground. Interaction is not a therapy that happens only in a playroom. You and your child are interacting constantly and by following him everywhere you will provide the right environment and support for a photographic and literal learning.

In other respects we played with Alexander differently. Being aware that he was non-verbal, we wrongly assumed that:

- if he acquired language his autism was cured

- we had to teach him *how to learn.*

We addressed him with single words as well as fully formed sentences, just in case he heard us. *While we had no expectations of Alexander, we had many goals.*

Years later after we finished our home-based programme and Alexander went to school, I dared to ask everyone who helped me: 'Did you believe that Alexander would learn how to talk to us?'

Unanimously they replied no. Each person had his or her own reason, but they all agreed on one common denominator. 'Why did you help *me, us?*' I asked in dismay. The general gist of the answer was that they had a conviction and a belief. They wanted to become part of it as well as helping Alexander.

I will remain eternally grateful for their unflinching support. Without them, our lives during Alexander's early learning years would have been unbearable. Personally, I feel indebted to the people who stepped forward and listened to my cries for help and tears of despair. At times they coped with my exasperating moods, supported my dream, invited my son into their homes, extended their love to incorporate my family, allowed me to catch up with sleep and, most importantly, made us feel less of an outcast family.

For a brief moment I wish to switch your attention towards the soul of your child. I described the concepts of autistic, interaction and a shared system of meanings. Forget all the terms for a minute and all the riddles of autism. Think about the times when *you* could not communicate what you wanted. How did that feel? You were able to talk but couldn't. You might have been afraid or just thought that there was no point in trying. The person you are trying to address is not listening. Magnify that emotion 100 times over and you might just begin feeling the emotion felt by your child when you cannot understand him. You are caring for the child that you gave life to. He can give *you* love and *he* needs your love. You are the 'big guy', the compassionate giant who can offer comfort. He is the little guy who has no idea that you find his behaviour hard and frustrating. Your child needs you to develop more patience than you have ever had and perhaps more love than you ever experienced yourself.

Exercise

Jot the names of a few people you like and trust right here.

1.	6.
2.	7.
3.	8.
4.	9.
5.	10.

Give them a call and ask them to help you help your child to play. Describe their role as that of a friend and that the patience required matches that of a fisherman. Once you have a few people committed to help, you can tell them to read this guide. If they cannot come and play with your child, ask them to recommend you someone who would be interested to learn how to relate to a different mind.

> ### *Food for thought*
>
> Finding people to help you may prove an emotionally daunting task (e.g. admitting to yourself that you and your child need help – pride driven, forget it).
>
> A child who's capable of making sounds can learn to pronounce words and then converse. You don't need conviction, nor do you need to believe in miracles – just patience and interactive games.

Notes

1. This time repetition means enjoyment and not an 'autistic' pattern of behaviour; similar to playing and replaying a favourite song.

2. Not to be confused with passive acceptance. The friend must observe, interpret and then model his action in response to the body language.

3. Described as a prison without walls where no one prevents you from leaving but you cannot find the key.

4. Tactile sensitivity, which is more than not enjoying a hug. One friend told me that he preferred not wearing any clothes. However, if he did he would bump into walls because he doesn't know where his body ends. Scary reality!

Life before verbal communication

Just deciding to believe that my child can form a meaningful relationship with me seemed impossible. Here are some reasons. Alexander liked eating grated cheese and his style of eating mirrored that of a cat. I remember his reactions when I smiled at him and when I frowned at him. I also remember my feelings. Sometimes they were accepting and other times my smile covered my pain. Each time my smile was fake, Alexander removed his plate from the table and hid in a corner, where he continued his experiment. If I frowned at him, he left the food untouched. I could have stopped him. I chose not to. Instead I wondered why he needed to eat this way.

We had more writing paper in the house than the corner shop, yet Alexander chose to draw on the walls. Why? Alexander's drawings on the walls were harmless compared with other expensive or dangerous activities. An unsupervised tube of toothpaste turned into an *invasion of snakes* and a tube of shaving foam was instantly transformed into *mountains or floating islands*. It was like watching £3 pouring down the drain. I had to learn not to leave anything within reach. My computer disk drive became *the best hiding place for a lollypop* and £60 to fix.

The trail of tarmac left on the pavement by the cable company became instant railways for Alexander-turned-steam-train. Those railways danger-ously crossed main roads. When I came to realise that Alexander played 'steam trains' during our walks, I shouted out 'red' and he stopped. I had to accept that he would respond better if I addressed him as a train. Before that I was afraid to go walking with him. Alexander didn't respond to stop and always ran faster than I could.

Apart from covering the walls with drawings of my earrings, trains and buses Alexander also drew a continuous line. Try to picture this. We returned from our two-week holiday and I was unloading the car. After I finished and locked the front door my eyes fell on a newly drawn continuous line. I thought he had outgrown his need to write on the walls. I was wrong. It took him less than three minutes to draw a line that started at the front door and continued over the radiators, the door, the TV, the sofa, all the way up the stairs into the bathroom, bedroom, beds – everything that was against the wall. I reached for the cleaning solution and tearfully cleaned the soaking fibre pen marks. Why on earth did he need to draw this line?

I found Alexander in the middle of his playroom in a pool of sweat. His heart was racing but his face was smiling. Could it be that he used the line to mark the borders of a familiar and friendly territory? Could it be that when the line was on the walls he could see the walls, thus not bump into them? Donna Williams described her autism as 'a prison without walls' that you are allowed to leave but you cannot find the key. Could it be that those lines marked a territory outside such 'prison'? I will never know the true meaning of that line. I will always know that for five years it was Alexander's best friend. After every dangerous object was safely locked away I decided to keep the paintings and lines on the wall. I thought that we had achieved the perfect mutually comfortable environment. I was in for a surprise. Alexander climbed on the arms of the sofa, squeezed his tiny foot underneath the metal bar that keeps the lampshade in place and stepped onto the light bulb – burning his foot. Compared with the writing on the wall this was cata-strophic. *My question was 'How can we interact and have fun?'*

Grains of hope

Examples of non-verbal social communication

EXAMPLE 1

Alexander and I shared our first non-verbal, meaningful, quiet and non-boisterous time together around the sewing kit. In that kit there was a circular pin holder with which he liked to play. One day, Alexander walked into the kitchen looking for me. Realising what I was doing, he quickly and happily grabbed a chair and sat next to me. Pointing at the sewing box he looked straight at me and drew a quick circle in the air. Bursting into laughter I exclaimed, 'I know what you want! You want the bold-pins holder.' He laughed with an infectious laugh and nodded *yes*.

I was so delighted that he had shown me what he wanted by drawing a circle in the air that I gazed at him with tears of joy in my eyes. He could have screamed instead and I would still have known what he wanted. However, this time he did not scream, he communicated. We sat together until I finished and kept glancing at each other, giggling.[1] He took all the bold-pins out of their circular holder and carefully rearranged them – sorted by the colour of their heads. He proudly showed it to me and placed it back in its box. This was the first time when I actually *felt* that:

- he wanted to spend time around me

- he did enjoy keeping me company

- I could connect with him

- he would learn to substitute screaming with a kinder style of communication.

One year later he wanted a particular toy for Christmas but still didn't know enough words to describe this toy. He called it 'Yellow!'. I gave him a piece of paper and a yellow pen and asked him to draw it (non-verbal communication) for me. It was a marble maze.

Exercise

Remind yourself of a shared event between you and your child when he was comfortable around you. Perhaps you watched a video together, had a bath together, walked in the garden and gazed at the same thing. The source of common enjoyments is irrelevant. Feeling the magic of such connection is what matters. *If you felt it, then your child felt it too.* You would know if he felt it by the way in which he leaned on you, looked at you or smiled at you.

If you have experienced such connecting moments, your objective is to recreate an environment to allow them to be repeated. During such moments you entered a *mutually comfortable world*. You don't have to (not that we can!) teach connection, just create an environment where it can take place.

EXAMPLE 2

A non-verbal child aged three loved his Smarties. His mother described to me how he ate them in a certain order. I suggested that next time she gives him Smarties she should place them on a tray in the exact order that she observed her child doing it. She phoned me to say, 'You were right. He did look amazed and smiled at me. He also pushed his body into mine, in a hug-like fashion.'

Exercise

Observe one of your child's routines. He might like having his food cut into eight pieces (like Alexander) or he might like lining up his cars. Perform that routine for him and then show him what you have done and observe his reaction:

- Is he happy that you are accepting his routine?
- Is he showing his gratitude in an observable way?

If he is, then continue to show your acceptance of his needs this way. If he doesn't react from the beginning, persevere until he notices your efforts.

Grains of communication

Motivated by Alexander's love of trains, I found a little train station where he could watch the trains go by and ride his little toy train on the platform. His face lit up with anticipation every time I placed his toy train in the boot of the car. He knew where we were going, yet he could not tell me his emotion. I could see it on his face. I could tell that he looked excited and I knew that he was going willingly because he did not scream as I strapped him in his chair. On the platform he rode his toy train and learned to count[2] from the changing numbers of the clock. His first words were: 'train, train is coming, train left, happy carriage and sad carriage' (describing the posters on the station's walls). If money were no object I would have bought him a train station and a train only to hear him say more words, laugh the way he did and co-operate so easily.

FLASHBACK

During our learning trip to America, I told my mentors about Alexander's increased receptivity to language in the railway station. I was advised to use this interest to teach him language at home in the playroom (positive conditioning). For example, we were meant to pretend play going to the station. I was meant to hear Alexander ask 'Mum, can we go to the train station?' Then I was meant to ask him why he wanted to go there, to which he was meant to reply 'Because I like it there' or something along those lines. The suggestion seemed plausible but I had a nagging thought regarding pretend play or pretend anything in particular (see photographic learning, p.204). My thought was that if Alexander had the ability to express his needs he would have done so. How could he learn to ask for a trip to the train station before he could ask for a drink? I was the one who noticed his change in moods at the railway station and I was the one who wanted to see him happy and receptive more often. What made him so incredibly co-operative there? This was the premise for further thoughts:

- The language that he learned in the station was meaningful language.

- He enjoyed being there.

- Whilst there, he was happy and co-operative.

- Why didn't he ask me to go there? His younger sister by two years was already asking for things.

- The only thing that Alexander could pretend play was being a train, not a driver or a passenger.

- Before he could ask me for anything we needed a shared meaningful communication system. Within such a system he would have had to:
    - use language or sign language to make his needs/wants known
    - know that I could answer yes or no
    - know that I can do what he wants me to do.

One of my friends told me how she couldn't paint from memory, visualise future events or ask for something that she wanted. Perhaps Alexander, like her, couldn't see the link between 'If I tell Mum I want to go to see the trains' Mum would 'get in the car and take me there'. Yet he was able to link the toy train, car, Mum and him with the destination of our journey. So some reasoning went on in his mind and I was grabbing on to the little that he showed me. I concluded that conditioning a trip to the railway station on his verbal request was pointless and cruel. I am glad I reached that conclusion.

Time is not of the essence – quality of life is

Autism is a lifelong way of being and therefore the biological school age of our children[3] should be less of a priority over the quality of their lives:

- Our child's spatial thinking and photographic memory will stay with him for life. Is the school teaching in a way that addresses our child's thinking skills?

- Is he expected to 'act normal'?

- Teaching a child shared meanings takes *individually tailored interaction and time.* Is the school equipped to observe a child for the entire amount of time that he is there? Is the school equipped to use every opportunity to instil interaction?

- Our child's sensory system is unique to him. Can he relax in a classroom filled with children? If he becomes distressed his behaviour will become 'markedly autistic'. Will he be punished for that?

I was inspired by many true-life stories of autistic individuals and secretly wished for a prosperous life for my child. However, not all our children will become doctors, like Temple Grandin, nor will all our children crack codes like the child in the film *Mercury Rising*. This doesn't mean that they don't deserve to experience quality of life.

Should you decide to bring in volunteers to help your child communicate, try not to worry about 'How long will this take?' or 'What will become of my child?' Your efforts are aimed at helping him enjoy his life on earth. The amount of time required by a child to realise the purpose of language – what people are trying to do for him, the fact that those people, you included, cannot readily understand his reality – varies from child to child. Equally, the amount of time your child requires to feel free to talk to you about his needs as well as the amount of time he needs to translate his visual thoughts into verbal thoughts varies from child to child.

Notes

1.   Non-requested and meaningful eye contact.

2.   Visual learning.

3.   A social convention which varies from country to country, culture to culture and educationalists' beliefs.

12

Premises for social communication

Willingness to please and the sensory system

The success of any social interaction depends on the individual's interdependent skills. At the most basic levels *interdependent skills are a mixture of language and behaviour.* Both language and behaviour are governed by our *sensory system.* The sensory system feeds information to the brain, which in turn processes that information and 'tells' the body how to behave/react through a process named feedback. The ability to make full sense of language is a blend of:

- hearing language

- understanding language

- talking

- understanding what we are saying

- feeling confident to voice our opinion

- feeling comfortable to ask for help.

Learning behaviours from others stems from the following:

1.   Learning social behaviour through observing others (e.g. turn taking, passing a plate, waving goodbye).

2.   During any given situation being able to model our behaviour according to the general mood. We can guess the general mood before we understand language because we can see it (e.g. people are smiling) as well as hear it (e.g. people are laughing, silent or whispering).

3.   We are born with our sensory system that feeds us information through:

   - hearing – audio
   - seeing – visual
   - smelling – olfactory
   - tasting – papillary
   - touching – tactile.

In a person diagnosed with autism those senses are 'mis-wired' to varying degrees, thus causing confusion. Your child's *linguistic behaviour and body language* will direct you towards the areas where help is needed. Your child will use his social skills and enjoy social interaction after he has mastered a large, literal, non-confusing vocabulary; has begun using expressive language; and has begun moulding his behaviour after yours.

Experience taught me that a child *willingly learns* to adapt his behaviour even if he cannot feel/experience the surrounding environment in the same way as we do. He does this because he was born with the same *willingness to please* as you and because he wants to fit in.

Food for thought

If the brain receives wrong information it will tell the body to behave in the wrong way. The child doesn't behave autistically to displease or to avoid social interaction and communication. He behaves according to his senses and makes judgements on what is appropriate or not according to those.

Interdependent skills

Chapter 6 helped you to assess whether making physical changes to your home environment and enlisting the help of volunteer play helpers would be beneficial to your relationship with your child, as well as increase his ability to interact and relax around people. Assuming that your home environment is in peak condition and that you found volunteers to befriend your child, your remaining steps are:

- to assess your child's understanding of language and to guide him through its use

- getting to know his sensory system and helping him relax and adapt.

Linguistic behaviour assessment form

Run through the Linguistic behaviour assessment table in Appendix B. Where applicable fill in the blank boxes. For example, if your child has never pronounced one single word (such as bye, hi, food, drink, etc.) but you have heard him making sounds during solitary play (eee, aaa, bebeb, tititic, etc.), then write those sounds in the first box.

If your child uses language, but for some unknown reason your conversation ends with him asking you the same question over and over again, then write his question or statement *exactly as he is asking/telling it*. Make a note of your answer/s. Your child's linguistic behaviour gives you an insight into how much he understands the spoken word. His ability to enjoy social communication is closely linked to his understanding of language. The processes of thinking in words, expressing his needs through language and feeling confident using language can be supported through your choice of actions. If your child's behaviour doesn't fit either description, describe his behaviour and contact us via our website.

Appendix C reproduces a snapshot of Pierce's language development over eight months. His vocabulary began in October 1998 with 'tc, tc, tc', meaning the face of the man on a box of Pringles crisps. After three years of home play he began attending playgroup and now goes to mainstream school with support. His linguistic skills range from continuous language acquisition to questioning everything that he can think of. Just as his mother, father, brothers and team of volunteer friends encouraged him to perfect his linguistic skills, I believe that you can do the same. Before he developed language, Pierce behaved in a way that could have easily been perceived as self-centred.

Food for thought

A child willingly participates in social communication and enjoys social interaction when he can hear, understand and contribute to the conversation or the common project; in other words when *he can function interdependently*.

Exploring social communication

In essence we engage in the act of social communication:

- to make our needs known to our mother as babies – a need to survive

- to understand our baby's needs before he can voice them – a need to protect

- to make and maintain friends – a need to have fun and relax

- for getting and keeping a job – a need to thrive

- for just making our needs understood in a foreign country while using the native's language – social pleasure or an entertaining need.

No matter why social communication happens, it fulfils a *personal need*. This need is no more self-driven in an autistic than it is in a non-autistic. The way in which this need becomes apparent through behaviour – an area of social skill – sets us apart. Some of us are better communicators than others, but in essence we all share the need to interact with each other. Thus we communicate – the human is a social animal.

During my life I have adapted to three different cultures and countries (autism included if we consider autism a culture), so I came to believe that *social communication* is something that 'just happens'. I would like to describe it as an *act of will*. For social communication to happen, *you must want it to happen* and *your child must want it to happen*. Pleasurable social communication stems from positive interaction, never from behaviour management techniques.

Please explore in depth the premises from which social communication happens. Thus realise the difficulties encountered by your child and see for yourself that just exposing a child to interaction with age peers is not going to teach him social skills. It will show him activities that he could copy, but it will not modify his sensory system. Contrary to popular belief, the autistic child does not deliberately avoid social communication. He communicates the best way he can with what *his own mind helped him to learn[1] alone.* I believe that your child communicates with you too. Therefore his *will* exists.

Even self-inflicted injuries, hitting other people, spitting, screaming, being totally silent, sniffing toys or people, refusing to wear clothes, flapping his arms, not responding when you call out his name, eating only certain foods, running after people with a knife in his hands, hiding under the table, and talking to himself in many different voices or just in one voice are all forms of 'telling' something. The main questions that need answering are:

- What does this behaviour want to communicate?

- Why is the child using this type of behaviour and not language to communicate his wants or emotions?

- How can it be transformed?

During 'play times' your role is to help the child relax enough and learn to substitute a non-co-operative or violent behaviour with a co-operative one. Every autistic child and adult I have met have resorted to some of the above-mentioned behaviours when they wanted to express an emotion. My role was to help them substitute this 'telling about emotions through behaviour' into communication so we could find a mutually acceptable solution. *I have done this when they found enough courage to discuss the reasons[2] behind such behaviour and after we had found enough common vocabulary.* They then used the newly acquired communication skills to better their own lives.

Communication skills

You can help your child turn the act of 'telling of something' into communication if you remember a few key points about communication as a two way street:

1. Communication skills, as well as 'the role of communication', can be taught to a *willing student* during *joint activities*, where the student and the teacher show *shared attention*.

2. Shared attention is the foundation from which *shared understanding* evolves. Joint activities such as social interaction stem from *shared motivation*.

3. Personally, I do not believe that communication needs to be taught or that it can be taught. We are born knowing that we must communicate (e.g. the non-verbal child *pulls you* towards the fridge to get his drink. *You know* what he wants – communication happened). The blind child responds to your teaching him Braille because he wants to communicate and because he realises that Braille would set him free from dependency.

4. Hearing your child scream when you do something makes you realise that he doesn't like that. However, although you realise he's upset, because he cannot communicate you don't know *why he is upset*.

5. We were born knowing that language makes our lives easier – therefore we began using it. Imagine communication as an act of personal will *that is exercised during interactive times*. Ask yourself what would happen if you did not hear language and identified it as such. Would you know that you have to use it?

6. The emotion of wanting to please can be employed to direct the autistic child's attention towards the fact that using language leads to immediate gratification (cause and effect).

7. A willing student is a child that actively *seeks your company* and *asks questions*. He does that when *he realises that you care*.

8. A willing teacher is *a friend that empathises* with his student's current ability to learn and helps him adapt.

9. Communication stemming from empathy is pleasurable and has *a natural flow and development* to it.

10. Teaching words to a child through any 'programme' could eventually lead to that child pronouncing a string of words. That in itself doesn't mean that the child communicates.

11. Communication can be verbal or non-verbal.

Autism does not destroy your child's ability to participate in acts of social communication and the skills of social communication can be taught. However, his level of shared understanding and pleasure governs the length of the social communication and interaction. The observed 'aloofness' happens because your child's sensory system is not the same as yours. Therefore he will 'avoid' some forms of interaction (peer play included). This is why interaction should be modelled to suit that child's sensory system, *what he feels comfortable doing* and his understanding of what is wanted from him – *comprehension*.

In most cases, I found that a child understands more than he can tell and he expresses his understanding through body language. This is why you need to carefully observe your child's responses to your everyday requests. Non-co-operative behaviour shows the areas where your child needs assistance. You need to find out what might trigger him to behave like a 'recluse'.

Your child readily empathises with you but his body language and spoken language[3] do not convey emotions[4] in ways that are easily recognisable by you. Therefore you feel confused by some of his responses. If your child doesn't use language for communicative purposes you can inspire him to do so. Your child uses less facial expressions than yourself. After prolonged interaction he will begin using them – thus making communication easier. His facial expressions may not be identical to yours but you will learn what each means.

Exercise

Here are five repetitive steps towards meaningful social communication:

1. Create a unique environment for 'visual, spatial, olfactory, tactile, papillary and literal learning'. There model your acceptance of your child's autistic play by asking him to let you take part in his games (including the lining up of toys). Copy his play to help yourself understand your child's thinking. Offer to assist him with difficult tasks and only give your assistance when he asks for and accepts it. If he doesn't allow your participation, observe him and offer assistance when he seeks it.

2. Use every interactive moment to your advantage and model the use of *functional / concrete language* (open, on, off, run, stop, spin, laugh, blow, empty, etc.).

3.   Throughout the day use every opportunity to model positive and reassuring *social language* (e.g. I love you, I like you, Let me make you laugh, Let me help you, Come and help me, Come sit with me, Let's play, I need a silent moment, I see, you need a silent moment, etc.).

4.   Behave in a *predictable* way for your child. Do what you say and only say what you intend doing. In other words *behave in a literal way*. Fun and interactive play lead towards him showing 'social interest' and prolonged shared attention moments. Use them to teach anything that comes to mind. Teach him the role of a question. After he is using questions, his comprehension of the spoken word and acceptable social behaviour will grow. When that happens you can explain rules regarding social interaction, but not before.

5.   Enjoy social communication with a child whose sensory system is affected by what we know as autism and discover his imagination and perception of your interaction.

Medical jargon made simple

Assuming that your child was diagnosed to be on the autism continuum, your medical report might read similarly to my own son's. But what is it trying to tell us and how do we implement all those recommendations when our child *lacks the motivation* to talk or co-operate with us or just simply seek to play with us?

The following extract is from Alexander's medical report dated 15 April 1993. He was then 3 years 8 months old. I have changed the key words to italic. The numbers in brackets call for the actions listed under the previous heading until such time when your child co-operates with you.

Alexander is very serious, interested in the activities, and concentrates and attends very well. On the Symbolic Play, Alexander scores towards the ceiling, which is at a 3-year-old level. He had good *simple understanding of functional play* [1], although he does *not elaborate his play to imaginative sequences yet* [5]. In contrast, Alexander's *language development* [2] is at a 2- to 2-and-a-half-year level, which is two standard deviations below the mean for his age. He is a very *silent* [2] child and although *he has some simple understanding of language* [3] and uses occasional words and phrases, *he makes very little communicative use of his language* [1, 4]. Similarly, he shows *very little social interest* [1, 2, 3, 4]. Alexander *lines up little objects* [1] and has some rigidities, but not very many at this stage.

Alexander will have special needs when he starts school and indeed requires nursery education now. In this placement he should have *skilled support* [1, 2, 3, 4]. The emphasis should be helping his *speech and language development* [1, 2, 3, 4], and, in particular, to enable him to *use language communicatively* [1, 2, 3, 4]. In addition, he requires *help with understanding social rules and situations* [4, 5]. He also needs *help with developing peer relationships* [5]. In addition *his interest and talents should be fostered* [1, 2, 3, 4, 5]. His needs at the time of entering school should be reviewed nearer that time. It is likely that he will need skilled support within the ordinary setting or in a language unit.

Behaviour

Alexander settled well and worked with interest especially on the non-verbal tasks. He made *very little eye contact* and shared little of his pleasure… Alexander seemed to *understand all simple instructions in context* [2, 3]. He was very silent but occasionally came out with an odd phrase, e.g. 'go to bed', when asked to identify the bed in the Reynell[5] Test. However, *he did not use language communicatively* [3, 4, 5].

Summary and conclusions

Alexander shows wide discrepancies in his *cognitive functioning* [4]. He is a bright little boy in the non-verbal areas and has good understanding of small toys and functional play. His *language is well behind for his age* [1, 2, 3, 4]. He shows very little social interest in others and *does not use much gesture for communication* [1, 2, 3, 4]. His social interaction shows many characteristics of autism.

Alexander would benefit from nursery attendance with extra help to enable him to *develop his language and social interactive skills* [1, 2, 3, 4, 5].

In reality, at the local level, Alexander's behaviour was considered 'too autistic' and disruptive, so he was never placed in the existing language unit. Nursery school, with its many children, sounds and rules, confused Alexander as opposed to enabling him to develop his language and social interactive skills. His interests and talents could not be fostered in a formal environment either. His 'interests' were very autistic. They seemed 'selfish' and his behaviour was non-co-operative. The reasons stemmed from his sensory perception of our world. Without his 15 volunteer friends, his brother, sister and me, Alexander would have remained unable to express himself today.

We worked with Alexander's ability to relate to what we wanted of him and he worked hard at understanding what we wanted. In time he searched for, rejected or accepted his own 'peer friends' and the social communication skills followed. You too can do the same for your child. Almost every report ends with the emphasis on *skilled help*. You might like to add to it *loving and autistic-friendly skilled help*.

Notes

1. If you remember, I was told that *a child does the best he can with what he knows*. I finally found out what that really meant. If an autistic child is left to learn alone (or flounder) he will learn some of the right things and some of the wrong things – but because of his sensory system he has no way of knowing which is which.

2. See Chapter 20, Reasoning, p.210.

3. See Chapter 9, 'Other behaviours'.

4. See Chapter 20, Literal emotional communication, p.207.

5. One nagging thought that fails to leave me alone: any person that designed a test reasoned with a normal mind. How can we test an autistic mind with tests designed by a normal mind?

1 3

Interaction

The gateway to shared meanings

The role of playful interaction is that of helping a child to assimilate a shared system of meaning so that he may communicate and interact with society at large. It is your friendly way into your child's perception of this world; it is your road towards discovering his way of being. I was often asked the following questions:

- What makes you think that my child will play with you?

- Don't you think I tried?

- What do you do to make him play?

- Are you a magician?

- Are you a miracle worker?

- My child knows at least 500 words but is not using any of them. What makes you think that he will communicate[1] with you?

The loving parents asking me these questions felt as if they had lost all hope that they could successfully communicate with their child. Others felt as if they had reached the end of their patience. All these emotions stemmed from not knowing how to relate to the 'autistic system of learning' and not from not loving their child. If *you* feel guilty, please stop. Start again. I have seen enough parents who found the strength to start again:

1. *You can learn how to inspire your child to communicate with you and then talk with you:*

    - You don't need to be a miracle worker.
    - You don't need to be a magician.
    - You do need more patience than you already have.
    - You need to further develop your observation skills.
    - You must gain your child's co-operation.
    - Your efforts should solely be aimed at increasing his will to interact with you.

2. *What do you mean by his will? How do you do it?* In a nutshell, coax him into friendly interaction, respect his boundaries and he will automatically increase his willingness to interact more often.

3. *Then what?* Use interactive moments to teach him to copy the words that represent what we want. In the beginning he is using body language or screaming to indicate his wants.

4. *How do you get him to trust you?* Through behaving towards him during interactive moments in an extreme literal way.

5. *What does behaving in a literal way mean?* When he tells you to stop, you freeze. When you ask him 'Would you like this toy?' and he walks away after you show it to him, you say 'You don't want it, I see' and put the toy away. If he tells you that he wants three carrots on his plate, you place three carrots on his plate.

Through behaving in a literal way you are in fact modelling cause and effect as well as true meanings of words. Your child becomes aware of your predictable behaviour and learns to relax around you. He soon realises that you will not physically manipulate him or force him to play a game he doesn't want.

You are modelling unconditional acceptance and love. A child who has learned to repeat words but doesn't use them for communicative purposes is the child who learned them out of context and/or being a spatial thinker[2] he is unaware of why we talk.

The purpose of this chapter is to help you find a style of play that becomes attractive enough for your child to wish to take part in your games and to spark his understanding of *why* we are using words.

Interacting with solitary boisterous behaviour

Personally I found it easier to turn boisterous behaviour into playful interaction because *the child is doing something that I am able to join in with.* If the child runs around aimlessly, I can catch him. If, as a response to my chasing him, he giggles, I know that he wants me to chase him. I stop chasing and turn it into an anticipation game. Because the child wants to be caught, the child waits for me. If I don't appear, he looks for me and comes back for me. We have achieved positive interaction and connection. If this child is non-verbal, his first words could well be 'catch me', 'run', 'stop' or 'chase'.

If the child spins around, I can offer him a spin. I can spin him fast or slow. When I do it I can stop and ask him to indicate which type of spinning he requires. If he cannot translate his wants into words, his giggles or the arching of his body towards a particular direction show me his choice.

Examples

My own child could spend half an hour spinning on his own. I chose to spin him round and he liked that. During a half-day interaction in the garden he learned to say: 'Spin!' 'Spin me again!' 'Spin me clockwise! 'Spin me!' 'To the left!' 'Spin me anti-clockwise!' 'Spin me faster!' 'Spin me to the left!' 'Spin me three times!' 'Stop!!' 'Spin me to the right!' 'Spin me four times!'

Because he learned the words clockwise, anti-clockwise, left, right, slow, fast and the number of times in context, he was able to generalise the use of those words. What this meant was that he was able to say unprompted,[3] 'I was spinning my red car clockwise and it crashed.'

I met a child who possessed the incredible ability to 'feel the gravitational axis' of an object of any shape, from a table to a chair, from a ball to a stool. Mesmerised, I watched him feeling/searching for it. It was like watching a magician at work. I tried to copy him and join in with his game. Each time, I failed miserably. Whilst he was silently watching my attempts I looked at him and exclaimed, 'I can't do this, teach me!' He came over and showed me.

This child had reached nine years of age and used no words but understood most verbal communication. Apart from wanting to show him that I cared for him, my aim during interaction was to spark his understanding that he must pronounce the words he already understood. I wanted to help him pronounce his first word because it would make his mother happier.

We began a frenetic game of chase until he was tired out, jumped behind his mother and sat there looking at me. I asked and mimed 'Time out?' Smiling and looking straight into my eyes he nodded.[4] My two-hour attempt had failed to inspire him to pronounce the one word that would have helped his mother feel better. If you feel disheartened please don't give up trying. Time is not of the essence, but perseverance is. I was celebrating the fact that this beautiful boy honoured me with a connecting gaze and our hug. I never needed to ask him to look at me. We were connecting.

Another child who liked dancing entered my playroom. The base of one wall was covered with mirrors. He soon discovered the reflection of his moving legs and became fascinated by their motion. I began dancing with him. We walked up and down parallel with each other at least 30 times. As I was walking I offered my hand. The thirty-first time he held my hand and we walked together. The thirty-second time he looked at me, held my hand and smiled. As we stopped I reached for a ball and began bouncing it. I invited him to try bouncing it. After two seconds he toddled over, hit it once, watched it bounce, looked into my eyes, smiled, giggled and ran to the corner of the bed. From the corner of the bed he looked back for me, smiled and stretched out his hand as if inviting me to hold it. I reached out, held his hand[5] and the second round of dance began.

Shouting and screaming

During my first meeting with Pierce, then two years old, we played with a puzzle toy clock. He tipped out the numbers from the clock and on his own struggled to replace the numbers. He had trouble replacing the numbers six and nine in the clock. I could see and hear him getting angrier and angrier. Lying next to him, I offered my hand and kept repeating 'Can I help you?' He replied to my suggestion with a scream and continued to struggle alone (just like Alexander used to). Anticipating a temper tantrum, his mother watched silently. She had seen Pierce breaking many clocks in anger before. Five minutes on I continued to offer my help, but I did not take or touch either of the two numbers. I only sat close to him, with my hand out, waiting and smiling. To his mother's surprise, Pierce placed the numbers in my hand. I placed one of the numbers in its hole and offered him the other. He placed the other and gave me the clock. His mother whispered, 'I have never seen him co-operate before. We had to hide all the clocks in the house because he would smash them.'

What prompted Pierce to accept my help? It was the non-intrusive yet persuasive way in which I delivered my help. An offer of help forms part of *social communication*. His mother adored him and every time he showed signs of upset she stepped in to help and did it for him. However, it could be that Pierce wanted to finish the puzzle alone but was unable to say it.

What you should remember is that after I stood there in front of him for five minutes with my hand opened, waiting, *he was the one who placed the number in my hand*. I did not take the number from him. He was relaxed and waiting. He had control and I gained his trust and shared attention.

They left my home that day and on my porch I waved excessively, jumped up and down smiling, and called out 'See you soon Pierce!' I also blew him many many kisses in a row. His face lit up, he smiled and blew his first kiss – showing yet another *sign of social communication* in the same day. Months later his mother wrote an article for the Hope–TLC homepage (see 'Letter from a loving mother', p.10).

Interacting with solitary passive behaviour

I describe the following behaviour as passive:

- staring at a wall, light, toy, tree, traffic, and/or blank television screen

- non-responsive to tickles

- hiding in a corner or under the table

- leaving a room when a strange person enters.

The activities in which you engage with children such as these aim to reduce their hypersensitivity. Through careful interaction:

- you gauge their attention towards you as a provider of fun

- help them see/experience how your actions could provide them with equal if not more pleasure

- remove any reasons that they might have to fear you.

Staring at a wall

What we call 'staring at a wall' means something else to our children. I read a personal account in which a girl explained how she could 'become totally lost in the texture of the colour of a wall'. I find it impossible to experience and relate to such a concept. The nearest experience to which I could compare it would be a meditative state during which the person experiences various shades of the same colour. One must assume that the only thought one is able to hold at that time is curiosity regarding the possible numbers of shades, so the thoughts are entirely focused on searching for shades.

Assuming that your child stares at the wall, you could change the colour of the wall once a week and wait for a reaction. Watch the wall together and talk about it. Involve your child in painting the wall in different colours. Offer the child a set of paints and plenty of paper. His reaction might positively surprise you.

Staring at a marble

Imagine meeting an incredibly withdrawn child; a child who has no wants; a child who silently shadows you, yet if you showed him a bar of chocolate he would shy away; a child who would stop breathing if he could do just that. The marble run is the only toy that brings a smile to his eyes. He can spend four hours at a time watching the marbles rolling down the ramps. He wants you to help him build the run, yet if you ask him for anything in return he chooses to give up seeking help and instead chases a rolling marble.

I once met a child just like that. If we removed the marble run and left one marble on the floor, he would engage in a *chasing and examining game* with it. I watched him happily giggling to himself as he followed the rolling marble on the floor. I wished I could transform myself into the most exciting marble so that he could play with me. We played together for three days. On the third day, I blew a marble into motion and accidentally blew on his fingers. It was the first time that my actions had managed to trigger a snigger. Daringly, the child looked at me and placed his hand near my mouth and waited for me to blow on it again. I dared suggest that he copied the word 'blow'. Within a fraction of a second I had lost his attention and he withdrew his hand. It was as if talking was too much hard work. Just the same, I chose to blow on his hand again – anything to encourage this beautiful little boy to enjoy my company.

Later that night I enlisted Feather's aid. I wanted her to help me understand why this child didn't seem to want anything. She told me how, in her early years, 'wanting' anything felt like an unbearable pain. If someone made her feel that she wanted something she would refuse to take it. The pain of being discovered to 'want' *something* was far greater than the pleasure of actually receiving what she wanted. Influenced by my friend's story, I decided not to ask for anything from this child, but to continue to give and to play with him. At the end of the fifth day he asked to be spun round by making a sound. As he was making the sound he was looking into my eyes and laughing. I felt as if half the battle were already over.

Staring at a light source or examining a ray of light

I have met more than one person who drew an incredible amount of pleasure from gazing at lights (fibre optics, lightbulbs, flickering lights). The explanations were that 'It calms me down' or 'It makes me feel good'.

I continued, 'Looking straight into a lightbulb gives me headaches and makes me close my eyes. Aren't your eyes hurting? Don't you see a red spot when you look away?'

'I don't see a red spot when I look away from the lightbulb and I don't get headaches either.'

Once again I cannot relate to such experiences but I have played a positive part in ensuring fun interaction. I was holding a child in my arms under a tree. The sun was shining and he was happily smiling at the rays of light slipping through the leaves. I observed that every time the wind blew he smiled to himself with delight. When the wind stopped I blew the leaves into motion. Excited, he looked at them and flapped his hands. When they stopped he looked at me and then at the leaves. I blew again and he played again. When the movement stopped he looked at me again. I chose to play silly and pretend not to know what he wanted. He pushed my face toward the leaves.[6] I asked, 'Do you want me to blow?' His back arched with excitement. I blew the leaves once more and the child honoured my efforts with a smile before he redirected his intense attention to the leaves, flapped his arms and giggled to himself. Within half an hour I reached a state of near hyperventilation, but the child's attention was with me. Each time I pretended to be the wind, he honoured my efforts with a smile, a touch, a hug or a giggle.

Six months later, in his playroom, he pronounced his first word. One year later he ran towards me on the street and was ready to climb into my car through the opened window. Yet again, this 'orchid child's' action proved that he could identify a friend (me in this case) in a crowd, in his home, in the playroom or in the garden. He might not be able to say hello but running towards you for a hug means just that: 'Hello, I am so glad to see you.'

> ### Food for thought
>
> Could you become the wind? Or can you see yourself playing in the dark with a torch to help your child smile – perhaps teach him his first word?
>
> Are you prepared to accept that the first word may not be 'Mum' or 'Dad', and that instead it may be 'torch' or 'wind' or 'blow'?
>
> Are you prepared to patiently reach out for one month before your efforts are rewarded?

A child who becomes totally absorbed in a toy

If one toy and one toy alone fascinates your child, then you could either explore his toy together or, if that is impossible, shop for an identical toy. This new toy is yours. If you cannot find an identical toy, look for a similar one. Sitting next to your child while he is playing, engage in a parallel play. You are playing with *your toy*. Nine times out of ten your child will reach out for your toy. He or she will do it in his or her own style. Some will grab it from you. Some will ask for it. Others will look at it and others might just glance at it. As soon as that happens, *give your toy to your child*. Please do not tease. You are there to show your child that he can use you and that you can make things happen. You are interesting and reliable. You are there to model sharing.

Feel free to ask for his toy in return. Be prepared for your child to notice differences between the two identical toys that you are unable to notice. Our children's ability to pay attention to detail[7] is greater than ours. Be prepared for your child to want them both. Let him have your toy and sit there and wait. Don't pretend to cry and don't tell him that you are upset in the hope that he might 'feel sorry for you' and thus feel motivated to share. Sharing comes naturally after many more hours of play.

At these early stages, you are the one seeking to interact with your child. Denying him *your toy* carries little meaning for him since he was perfectly happy without it in the first place. Remember that you are working at increasing the *motivation to want your involvement*. Only after someone wants something badly can you begin placing conditions. Be prepared for a child to stop wanting as soon as you place conditions on your shared games. If that is the case, rethink your conditions but don't give up trying.

EXAMPLE CONDITION

If you let me hold your toy I will tickle you once. If you let me play with it I will tickle you twice. If you want my toy you must tickle me first (or some similar conditions).

Fascination with the traffic

There is room for improvement here because I have not cracked it yet. I watched and joined a child watching the traffic. If I spoke or tried naming the cars going by, he pulled his body away from me or covered his ears. I understood that my input wasn't welcomed so I stopped talking. Half-an-hour later, he looked at me, smiled, waited for my smile and returned his attention to the traffic. I'd never seen him so peaceful before. I forgot to mention that he sat on top of my dining room table and looked as if he were a king.

In another corner of the same room, a 22-year-old autistic friend made the following remark: 'He looks so cool and peaceful. I wish my mum allowed me to take time out and do my own thing from time to time.' Perhaps my little friend shared something with me when he looked at me. Perhaps they were looks of appreciation for allowing him personal space. Perhaps it was my imagination. Either way, he looked peaceful and my eyes filled with tears of joy.

Non-responsive to tickles

Some children *hate* being tickled, or run a mile when you just tell them of your intention to tickle them. I am a firm promoter of physical contact with your child. I am also well aware that some of our special children cannot cope with the sensation that a tickle leaves behind. Is there an alternative? Yes. You need to experiment and find out what type of physical contact is most acceptable to your child.

A gentle massage can feel just as rewarding as a tickle. A squeezing massage can replace the gentle massage. Long before I met my 23-year-old friend who explained how she was terrified of tickles, I played 'a squeezing game with a young child'. We became best buddies in seconds and his first word was 'squeee' for 'squeeze'. In my older friend's case, she was able to tell me how hard I could squeeze her leg and this squeezing massage substituted a 'friendly hug'. Here is someone's personal account:

I used to dread the bus journey to school. The children realised how terrified I was of tickles. So they chose to tickle me until I screamed and peed my pants. My body became paralysed by this hard-to-explain emotion and I felt embarrassed and ashamed. My feelings did not seem to matter to them. They had fun at my expense and I had no means of stopping them. The day I chose to strangle the leader of the gang – only to frighten him – I was labelled violent, mad and out of order. Why can't people respect our boundaries?

Hiding in a corner or under the table

When my friend hid under the table and started playing with a small ball, I assumed she wanted time out. Perhaps she was tired. Five months later she wrote in a letter:

> There were times when you could have played with me but didn't. Perhaps you didn't know or perhaps you didn't want to play. Perhaps you wanted to give me my own space, which is good, but if you waited a little bit longer for me to respond then you would have seen that I wanted to play, like the time when I hid under the table and passed you the ball. You passed it back and then left the room. I don't know why.

I left the room because after I passed her the ball she held it tight. I *assumed*[8] the game was over. If the same situation arose again I would check and double-check my assumptions with the child. If the child did not answer my question, I would sit in a corner waiting for him to leave first or perhaps turn his head away from me, thus showing me that he wants to be left alone.

Notes

1. Most human communication is non-verbal.

2. The opposite of thinking and learning from words.

3. Expressive language.

4. Non-verbal communication.

5. A child development documentary introduced three types of hand holding: (1) grabbing, the parent *holds on* to the child's hand but the child's hand is open; (2) grabbing, the child *holds on* to the parent's hand but the parent's hand is open; (3) they both hold hands together. I use this knowledge to judge if a child is willing to join in with me. Therefore, if a child holds my hand, I deliberately keep my hands on a very light hold so that he can free his hand when he wants to – passing total control.

6.   Meaning 'Yes I want you to'.

7.   See 'Open your eyes', Appendix D, p.290.

8.   There are times when the same body language doesn't carry the same meaning.

1 4

Emotions, language, behaviour and social communication

Unblocking the communication blocks

During interactive moments with autistic people I have had the following wonderful experiences:

1. I have helped non-verbal children utter their first word.

2. I have helped children say their first meaningful words in context.

3. I have helped them accumulate words.

4. I have shown them how to build a sentence.

5. I have shown them that by using language life becomes easier.

6. I have watched them further developing the use of language unaided.

7. I have enjoyed their own realisation that they are talking.

8. I have helped them re-allocate correct meanings to some of the words (sentences) which they learned alone.

9. I have removed their fears of the written or spoken word –
    including those they read in the Bible because of their literal
    interpretation (such as burning in hell).

10. I have unlocked their own potential to use language for
    communicative purposes.

11. I have helped them reopen communication channels with their
    own parents.

12. I have watched them share a first hug with their own parents
    (where I couldn't do that I continued to act as a 'protective eye'
    while they were fighting for their own new lease of life, a new
    job, friendship or flat to live in).

13. I have helped remove the fear that some people had of certain
    words or phrases such as:

    - *Can I help you?* Because to them *help* translated as me
      offering to restrain them.
    - *How can I help you?* Because they were *never* asked to voice
      their opinion before.
    - *Will you let me help you?* Because they thought I would
      behave towards them in the same way as others did before.
    - *Do you understand me?* Because they thought *understand* means
      that I believed them to be stupid.
    - *I love you.* Because they associated the meaning of love with
      being sent away from home or being punished for not being
      'normal'.
    - *What are the problems?* Because they thought that *problems*
      means being autistic is a problem.
    - *Emotional pain.* Because no one helped them identify and
      label their emotions.
    - *Being in love.* Because they were afraid that their relationship
      would not last.

Above all I have enjoyed a hug from each and every one of them, the kind of
hug where the whole of their body became heavy and was leaning against
mine. It was in that moment I knew we were friends and that the person was
beginning to relax.

You can do all this for your child and your child needs you to do it for him. Throughout these activities my role was to initiate and motivate interaction as well as 'guess' what I was doing wrong. I relied on the body language of the person with whom I interacted to warn me if and when my actions were too overwhelming.

The myth about teaching language

For three consecutive years I searched for non-verbal children, wanting to know if I could help them 'learn' language in the same way I had helped Alexander. To my surprise, all the children copied my body language within minutes of play. Eighteen out of twenty spoke their first word straight away (faster than my own son in the past). One child spoke after six months and another did not form a recognisable word during our play sessions. However, this child did understand verbal instructions. I was puzzled.

What did I do to trigger the use of language in these children? What determined the speed of their responsiveness? I discovered years later that it was the combination of their hearing coupled with the level of sound of my projected voice. I began to believe that every autistic child was born with the ability to learn language. They repeat words when they hear them and when they realise that language is a communication tool.

Is your child able to repeat words?

I remember the times when Alexander repetitively watched *Thomas the Tank Engine*. He was two and a half years old. At the time I was afraid that Alexander might be mute or deaf (a common parental belief or puzzle prior to a diagnosis of autism). As we lay together, I heard him *talking to himself*. What I heard were not words, just the intonation of the story line. Every five minutes or so he would say 'Pooh-Pooh', just like a steam engine, and then continued chanting what sounded like unarticulated speech. In disbelief I whispered to him, 'Are you telling the story of Thomas the Tank Engine?' He smiled and pushed his body against me. This was our first exchange of words that I dared call *communication*. I knew he could hear me and that he understood my question because he pushed himself against me and smiled at me. I also had a feeling that if he could say 'Pooh-Pooh' then he could also learn to say other words. The question was why he only said 'Pooh-Pooh' and not the rest of the words.

Food for thought

If your child likes Thomas the Tank Engine, Bob the Builder or Tom and Jerry, etc., he is likely to repeat words from the cartoons. If he can repeat those words, then with your support he can expand his vocabulary.

It is easier to teach the meaning of words such as tickle because the child can experience it.

After meeting Tom (an autistic adult) I understood why Alexander didn't talk. He did not know that he was supposed to learn words, pay attention to them and then try to copy them. In Tom's own words:

> Words were just like every other sound, I could hear them but did not think of them as anything. When I was very young, sounds were simply sounds. I could hear them but never gave any conscious thought that I was hearing a sound. Some sounds were more interesting to me. These were the things that were special to me as an interest, whereas words were of no interest.
>
> When I was nine years old I can clearly remember associating the word 'thunder' with the experience of 'thunder'. Things that I experienced sensationally had been my life, whereas words with their conceptual values were beyond me.

Tom's account also reminded me about how much fun Alexander (then age four) and I had with the same word. During a stormy night Alexander heard the sound of thunder. We turned the bed cover into a tent and listened for the thunder. As soon as it stopped I tried to repeat the sound. He pulled the cover down and yelled 'Thunder!' and I covered him in a 'thunder of tickles' and laughter.

We kept this simple 'repetitive' game going for at least half an hour. He was there with me! I felt as if we were connected and happy in each other's company. At the end of the half-hour game Alexander was able to say 'more thunder' as well as reproduce the sound of thunder.

> ### *Food for thought*
>
> I repeated the word 'thunder' because Alexander wanted me to repeat it as part of a game. I did not repeat the word because *autistic children learn through repetition* (another myth).
>
> Similarly an adult friend asked me to repeat a whole sentence because he found the conversation interesting. He wanted to 'embed it' into his mind before thinking about what was said. He did not ask me to repeat it so he could learn it 'parrot fashion' and store it into memory. He asked for repetition for time to make sense and compile an answer.

There were and are times when Alexander asks me a question but doesn't hear my answer. I know when his mind is somewhere else because the light in his eyes seems covered by a veil. I have seen that 'veil' in the eyes of many other children and adults, even if they were not autistic. It is important therefore that you give as much eye contact as you wish to receive from your child. This is a part of observational skills. There is no point in feeling upset that you can't get through to your child during the times when his senses are too tired.

Decoding immediate or delayed echolalia

Without Alexander's diagnosis I would have never known that 'echolalia' means a parrot-like repetition of words the child had just heard. All Alexander's spoken words were in fact echolalia. Is there anything wrong with echolalia? Not really. After giving it some thought I realised that all of us learn through repeating the words that we hear. The difference between Alexander and myself was that I was instinctively attributing the right meaning to the words I repeated (well most of them). Alexander was attributing meaning only to some of the words. Most of his vocabulary was just 'a repetition of words'. I wanted to know why.

I read that 'autistic people remember whole conversations for no apparent reason'. This statement made no sense to me. Many years later, with the help of my autistic friends, I realised that 'stored' conversations are a sign of confusion. It happens because 'the meaning' of those words or conversations is missing. Similar to delayed echolalia there are 'delayed reactions' or actions that we might perceive as repetitive or 'echolalic'. What should we learn from this?

- The positive thing about our children repeating words is the fact that they have reached the stage in their development where they can single out the sounds of words from the rest of the sounds.

- We are reassured that our children can talk.

- By listening to their words we can help them attribute meaning to them.

- Echolalia constitutes *proof* that your child *learns incidentally* from his environment. You don't need to *repetitively drum words* into his ears.

- The words spoken by your child during 'echolalic' moments direct your attention towards the area where your child needs help to make sense.

Language acquisition – a natural process

According to one linguist, a child doesn't 'learn' to learn language more than he learns puberty. He moves on to describe the ability of learning language as a 'virtual organ' and that language acquisition is a process that just happens. I liked this description because it explained why the children who began talking in my playroom used more words than I introduced within a play session. It also helped me realise I wasn't teaching a child how to learn. I was teaching a child to voice the words that he is able to hear (Alexander included).

I was modelling the use of language and through my choice of actions I was teaching 'shared meaning' to both language they already knew and to new words. This discovery reinforced in my mind that *every parent can teach shared meanings* to their child after they find ways to sustain their child's interest to interact.

This short lesson in language system is meant to help you place 'expressive language' under the microscope. Every child whom I have met knew some language. He knew it because he acquired it incidentally[1] from hearing it. Because of that he allocated wrong meanings to some words and right meanings to others. In order to avoid creating more confusion in a child's mind, assume the worst. Speak in a literal fashion and only use metaphor after he communicates with you. The way in which your child expresses himself will help you identify which of the words that he knows hold a shared meaning and which words he needs help with to clarify their meanings.

How do we learn shared meanings?

Shared meanings are learned through non-verbal communication (body language), social communication and language – all of which are learned during interaction. Within each culture, native language is the fastest yet sometimes confusing information exchange tool. Most of us work our way through our native language without many difficulties but the autistic child needs more help.

Talk to him about the use of language and model it daily

1.   Language works hand in hand with *intonation*.

2.   When it comes to social communication, *spoken language* and *body language* work hand in hand. Body language aids spoken language and is used as a powerful visual tool. Through our body language we are reinforcing our spoken words.

3.   At times we choose to use only body language.

4.   As well as intonation, body language conveys the *intention* behind the spoken word, possibly reducing the *double interpretation of the spoken word*.

5.   The meaning of crude body language is recognised and understood internationally (smiling, hugging, pointing, waving).

6.   Some styles of body language are culturally embedded and only practised within that culture, such as styles of greeting.

Observe what motivates you to communicate and discover your child's current sources of motivation

1.   We like to socialise, a very self-driven[2] reason!

2.   Before entering into a conversation/social communication we need a *reason*.

3. The reason could be personal to us. We might want to find out something, need something, we are feeling bored and want someone to help us find an activity, we want to share a story or we are seeking help from someone.

4. Other reasons for entering a conversation could be triggered by the other party. A few examples are:

   - the teacher asking us to answer a question or our participation in a group conversation
   - our parents wanting to know if we enjoyed the birthday party or questioning our bad behaviour
   - our boss calling us into his office for questioning or for praise
   - a person sharing their desire to become our close friend
   - our parents needing advice.

Compare your behaviour during social conversation with that of your child

1. Our *motivation* to participate in a conversation governs its length and style. By style I mean choice of words, intonation and body language.

2. The motivation is influenced by many factors. At an oversimplified level, *motivation is killed by boredom.* Boredom arises from lack of interest in the subject of conversation, lack of understanding of the subject, lack of willingness to pay attention, or a poor speaker.

3. A poor speaker is a person that either cannot convey meaningful information in an easy to follow format or lacks charisma.

4. A poor listener could be the person that cannot make sense of the conveyed information.

Your steps towards making social communication attractive to your child

1. *Shared attention:* you start by becoming *interested* in what he is doing.

2. *Shared understanding of meaning of words*: use only concrete words, words which you can model. Show him their meaning in picture, help him experience the meaning of the word you are teaching and avoid using words with double meanings.

3. *Shared understanding of the intention behind words*: as your child progressively builds a large concrete vocabulary and after he is using questions, teach him about the double meaning of words.

4. *Shared understanding of body language*: you start with the simple goodbye wave. Mirrors are very useful for 'acting out' body language and labelling it.

5. *Shared use of body language*: this comes with practice (see Chapter 20, Literal emotional communication, p.207).

6. *Shared understanding of intonation*: follows after the child knows the meaning of the word without intonation.

7. *Shared use of intonation*: he learns it through interactive games.

8. *Shared motivation*: the greatest source is willingness to please.

9. *Use of questions for clarifying purposes*: examples throughout the book.

10. *Use of praise for reward*: this can be anything from a kiss to a tickle, from a sweet to a new toy, etc.

11. *Mutual respect.*

12. *A desire to learn and to please.*

13. *The ability to understand reason and respond to reason.*

14. *The ability to agree or disagree.*

The last four behaviours rely heavily on empathy, although love seems to be the only driving force.

Notes

1. Alone, without the help of his parents or a therapist.
2. 'Self-driven' is the translation of autism: aut = driven and ism = self.

Why perceive the language of autism as a foreign language?

Thinking in words or learning from words is not in your child's nature. The following comparisons will cover some differences in how we learn. The following questions frequently occur:

- How do I understand what an autistic person is communicating to me?

- How do I know if my message was understood?

- How do I find common ground?

I wish to share how I change my 'mind set' when I communicate with an autistic person.

1. I imagine autism to be a foreign culture. Therefore the autistic language is a foreign language.

2. I look to identify our common body language.

3. I am motivated to talk to autistic people because I have an autistic son whom I wish to understand and relate to.

4. When I don't understand him I ask questions.

5. When the answer doesn't make sense I ask again.

6.   If my style of questioning upsets the other person, I change my style.

7.   If I am asked to stop talking or asking, I stop for a while.

8.   I declare my intentions in advance and make sure that my intentions are understood.

9.   I ask if I am understood.

10. Through asking if I am understood, I've learned that some people (for cumulative personal reasons) hate the question 'Do you understand?'

11. Because I wished to be respectful, I have learned to substitute 'Do you understand me?' with 'Am I making sense?' or 'Is this concept making sense to you the way it makes sense to me?'

12. The common ground came from learning to love and respect a 'nation' that doesn't perceive my world the same as I do.

13. I interact with respect and willingness to learn more.

14. I do not impose my system of beliefs on what is right or wrong. I am only trying to make sense and then let him make his own judgement (e.g. I do not conclude that repetition is an obsession or a bad activity because normal people don't behave that way).

15. During interaction I make mistakes, not deliberate ones.

16. When I realise my mistake, I try to correct it.

17. I ask the person who feels wrongly done by me what I have done wrong. I leave nothing to assumption.

18. We share most body language with autistic people. Body language helps me identify the emotional well-being of the person with whom I am interacting. It also helps me identify if we share the attention, motivation, understanding and pleasure. It helps me see when I have said the 'wrong' word.

19. I don't give up.

20. If I lose their attention I know that we have lost shared meaning and shared understanding, or I know that my friend wants a rest, so I stop interacting.

How can you help your child expand on echolalia?

Listen to your child's words and help him allocate meaning to them. This can be done through interactive play or just by talking to him. The process of teaching and learning shared meanings varies in length from child to child and parent to parent.

Example

Alexander was 12 years old when he approached me giggling and said, 'I thought that policemen were born policemen. I didn't know that you become one by training.' He also said, 'I thought that there was only one school in the whole of England. I was angry that we lived in the area where there was a school. I was also hoping that if we moved there would be no school nearby.'

Perhaps because a child feels embarrassed by some of his previous beliefs it will be some time before he can talk about them. However, the point I am making here is that a child remains a 'literal speaker' only until he realises for himself that one word could have more than one meaning and he is not afraid to use it. After that he will build his own sentences and entertain you with his wit.

The development of expressive vocabulary stems from interactive games between you and your child. Literal learning and literal vocabulary acquisition stem from:

- associative learning (*Sesame Street* programmes are one good example because of the way in which they teach concepts)

- shared learning (e.g. watching his favourite video and television programmes and helping him make sense of them and/or encouraging him to talk about them)

- learning the meaning of words through experience (e.g. tickle, run, stop, go).

Brandon

I first met the adorable and friendly Brandon when he was four years old. His vocabulary was made up of three phrases: 'Hi', 'Bye' and 'What's this?' If

Brandon walked past us 100 times a day he would say 'Hi' and smile 100 times. He also *needed* us to reply 'Hi!' or else he showed great signs of distress. After a few days of play he trusted me and began shadowing me everywhere, so his mother and I set off:

- to teach him by association that 'Hi' stood for hello

- to teach through modelling that one 'Hi' a day is enough

- to expand on it: e.g. 'Hi, where are you going?' or 'Hi, what shall we play next?' It was important to use only words which he showed full understanding of.

- to help Brandon understand that 'Bye' meant a greeting directed to somebody leaving the house. Every time he said 'Bye' I put my coat on and left the house saying, 'Bye Brandon, see you later.' He would pull me back so I said, 'I see, you don't want me to go. You want me to stay and play. OK, I will stay and play.'

- to answer what something was every time he asked 'What's this?' We asked him to repeat the word. At times he did and at times he did not. However, through our actions we made it easy for him to learn every time he asked a question.

Within a month, Brandon's vocabulary grew to 1000 meaningful words and he replied to all the practical questions:

Q: Where is the truck?

A: In the garden.

Q: Where is Mum?

A: Sleeping [or watching telly or whatever she was doing at that time].

Q: Do you want to come with me for a walk?

A: Wait, I go get my shoes and coat [and he did].

One late night the other children rode their bikes in the garden and he wanted to join in but he could not ride a bike yet. So he picked up a bike and walked alongside it, following the same trail (echolalic play?). It showed his mother and me that Brandon wanted to play with the other children. Brandon learned incidentally from the other children and enjoyed being around them, even when he couldn't actively take part.

As children ourselves, didn't we all learn games from watching other children and copying them? Our autistic children do the same as us. By the time Brandon returned to his home, his echolalic way of addressing me stopped. He called me Florica and his mother Mum. I know that initially Cathy felt the pain when Brandon addressed me as Mum, but remember that when Brandon called me Mum he copied my children and used echolalia. As his understanding of language grew, he *understood* that I was my children's mother and Cathy was his mother. Big difference! Your child can do the same and more.

Exercise

List your child's echolalic words and think of an activity that would successfully teach him their meanings. If you cannot come up with a solution, post his words to us and we will send you some suggestions.

1 6

Receptive language disorder

As a token of friendship, in 1998 I funded the birth of an organisation called autistics.org, where an internet chat channel symbolically named #AutFriends was operated. There I met my many autistic adult friends who subsequently helped me with fine-tuning my understanding of autism. If it wasn't for them, this book could not have been written today and its title would not include *The Eighth Colour of the Rainbow*. I would have continued to wander aimlessly in search of a cure without understanding what *I am supposed to cure.*

The website (www.autistics.org) continues to remain a space where the autistics can voice their emotions and beliefs without fear. The articles in their library will supply you with plenty of 'research material'. 'Autistic adults and adolescents' (Appendix D) is just one of many. As you read it, I am asking of you to filter it through your heart and thus feel the anger and frustration. Imagine that you are autistic. Parts of your autism do not allow you to show your emotions and your language is unintelligible. Therefore no one can understand what you are going through. The author of the article, Amanda Baggs, was also diagnosed with Central Auditory Processing Disorder (CAPD). CAPD is described as a receptive language disorder that makes it difficult to process sounds, particularly speech sounds. I have more than one reason for wanting you to read this article:

- In real life, because of her CAPD, Amanda would find conversation hard going (so would your child).

- Although she knows that she has difficulties conversing, she cannot experience the frustration of the listener (nor could your child).

- Also she is working on her linguistic skills. Therefore she is doing something to help herself.

- Your child is silently doing something too. Do you understand his behaviour well enough to recognise what he is doing to improve his communication skills?

- Just because Amanda cannot converse with ease, it doesn't mean that she doesn't have a message to give. Autism doesn't affect the ability to think and make judgements. However, the mind makes judgements on what a person's sensory system feeds it and perceives as reality.

- The 'reality' is fed to the mind through the sensory system.

- Your child is likely to suffer from CAPD if his behaviour fits any of the examples in this chapter.

At three years of age Alexander's communication skills were in their infancy. The extract from his medical report gives an overview of his abilities:

> Alex made his first attempt to speak at 18 months. He used certain words but this was not sustained and he stopped using words he appeared to have known previously. In retrospect it is likely that he did not understand the use of these words and therefore he did not make the appropriate association with the right situation in which to use them. Now he is repeating phrases but these are repetitive and frequently 'echoed'. He counts by rote but without any indication that he understands the significance of number. (14/12/1992)

Expressive language

> Some name confusions were noted, e.g. called 'cow' a 'horse', 'helicopter' became 'aeroplane'. He was heard to use stereotype phrases whilst playing, e.g. 'see you', 'bye-bye'.[1] He did not use language interactively with adults or children in the group other than to express displeasure… Alex's speech system is on occasions immature, i.e.

spoon-boon, he does not always give polysyllabic words the correct number of syllables, e.g. Television-tevision, tractor-trac. (15/04/1993)

It was impossible for me to imagine that Alexander and I could ever have a 'real conversation' or that he would ever play and derive pleasure from playing with other children. I felt devastated. If I were to think about it, both cow and horse are farm animals, have four legs and eat grass. A helicopter and an aeroplane both fly. One could say that Alexander's language was 'nearly there'. What stopped him from using the correct labels? Perhaps he failed to see the need for preciseness? No. Unknown to us he suffered from CAPD.

Parallel realities

Helping your child to compensate

For reasons stemming from CAPD combined with one or more of the following (missing link, e.g. the unlearned behaviour of knowing that we must use language; a small verbal working memory; difficulties recognising facial detail), your child could behave in any of a number of ways:

1. If he is asking you to repeat your questions or verbal instruction (What did you say? Say that again. What? I did not hear you. I can't remember. I have to think), and if when asking for repetition you detect an 'absentee' look on his face, then it is likely that he is experiencing difficulty focusing on your spoken word. He can hear all the other background noises and your words 'get lost'. Discriminating between what sound is important consumes much energy and most of your child's attention. Therefore a silent environment where only the spoken word is heard will help your child hear your voice and words. A classroom filled with many sounds makes it hard for your child to focus on the teacher's spoken word. By the time he focuses on her words she has probably finished talking.

2. If he is using echolalia (he repeats words but doesn't use them for communicative purposes), then he can hear the sounds that make up speech and reproduces them, but those words still make no sense to him. Therefore away from a crowded room you must

constantly interact with him so that he can repeat more and more words. *You want him to realise for himself that he is talking.*

3.   If his speech sounds immature (childlike) or he is 'shouting' when he means to whisper, then it is likely that he hears your speech distorted or he cannot hear the volume of his own voice. Therefore you have to model the whispering voice (or any other intonation) and ask him to repeat it. In time he will make his own log of that voice.

4.   If he responds incorrectly to verbal instruction, then he probably cannot hear them, hears only half of them, or hears something that doesn't make sense. Thus his responses will not match your expectations. Therefore his first need is to build his meaningful vocabulary before he is punished for not following rules.

5.   If he apparently hears you and seems to ignore you, then he is experiencing a delay or 'lag time' in processing speech; as in hearing what was said, thinking about it, formulating a reply and voicing that reply. Therefore in a one-to-one situation, he can take all the time he needs to understand what is required of him. Within a formal environment he must behave according to the clock.

6.   If he doesn't talk at all, then he can't recognise speech as speech. Therefore within a silent environment you need to talk to him until he hears it so that he may repeat it.

7.   If he is talking *at* you as opposed to *with* you, then he doesn't feel confident around people, feels afraid of being interrupted and/or not remembering where he was interrupted. Therefore your first call to action is to help him relax around you.

8.   If he cannot remember the right names for the right people, then he cannot see those faces and/or cannot hear the intonation that belongs to those people (a combination of audio and visual sensory input). Therefore he has no means of recognising that person. The input from the surrounding environment is overwhelming. One-on-one play is the first call to action.

9.   If your child talks in more than one voice, then he is using them to take care of himself. Those voices sound the way he wants them to sound, which is friendlier than the voices of the real people. Therefore you have to listen to all those voices, make notes of what they are saying and when he is using them, understand what he is doing and help him function without them.

10.   If your child behaves in a 'normal way' for let's say 20 minutes and then that ability disappears, then he is telling you through that behaviour that he is tired. Therefore he would be grateful if you could let him be until he recovers and can function again. His hearing system has become tired. (I have witnessed a friend of mine falling asleep in mid-sentence, waking up after ten minutes and continuing the conversation from where we left it!)

Exercise

Ask yourself:

- What is my child's behaviour trying to tell me?

- How can I help him?

When trying to reply to these questions, match his behaviour with the list above.

I will borrow the diagnosis format of CAPD and expand it to include the entire sensory system and some of the cognitive system. Therefore:

CAPD = Central Audio Processing Disorder

CTPD = Central Tactile Processing Disorder

CtPD = Central Taste Processing Disorder

COPD = Central Olfactory Processing Disorder

CVPD = Central Visual Processing Disorder

CPPD = Central Papillary Processing Disorder

These lead to what we might term:

CRPD = Central Reality Processing Disorder

CMPD = Central Memory Processing Disorder

CEPD = Central Emotion Processing Disorder

Hence unique thinking takes place. That in turn could be termed: CThPD = Central Thinking Processing Disorder. Therefore one could legitimately say that an autistic child who thinks differently and learns to behave 'normally' does so because he has developed his own Added Ability Processing Order.

AAPD = Added Ability Processing Order

I used the above model to explain the *multitude of ways in which autism presents itself.* It also explains the roots of your child's behaviour and shows you how hard it is for him to behave 'normally'. If faced with a child who behaves autistically, the non-autistic child seems to either avoid social interaction or bully the autistic child. That avoidance could translate in our autistic child's mind as 'social interaction is not something that I need to learn' and/or 'I must avoid other people' – protective reasoning.

Telling your child about his autism

Every behaviour mentioned in Amanda Baggs's article can be worked around and stems from the above-mentioned mock disorders. After you read the article, spend some time pondering over the following questions.

- *How does your child present his autism?* Does he know that his behaviour and way of being is what we call autism?

- *Can he voice his opinion about it?* If he can, encourage him to explain why he behaves in certain ways. Model that behaviour for him to help him visualise the meaning of your question. There will be times when he will be unable to explain the reasons for his behaviour. However, he might be able to talk about his needs as he perceives them.

- *Have you the courage to tell him?* Telling Alexander about autism, enlisting his help when I wrote this book and explaining to him that I don't always understand what goes on in his mind encouraged him to talk to me more. It also helped him understand why other children might pick on him.

- *Would you know how to tell him?* If you decide to discuss his autism, please describe it as 'a way of learning' and non-autism as a completely separate way of learning, not as a disability. (I have sheltered many adults who resorted to self-mutilation because autism was explained as a worthless way of being.)

Note

1. I call these 'learned responses'. If a non-autistic child learns to use them, he is praised. If an autistic child uses them during play, his speech is labelled as 'using stereotype phrases'. Why?

1 7

Self-exploratory exercises

Learning processes

The aim of these exercises is to direct your attention towards what you and your child have in common during any learning processes as well as where and why differences occur. *As a non-autistic child, addressing the person who cared for you and learning his/her name was a natural development.* Spare a few thoughts and try remembering how you learned to talk to your mother. Can you remember your first word or do you remember what you were told that your first word was?

If your mother brought you up, then your first word was Mummy or Mum. If your father played with you, then your second word was Dad or Daddy. If a nanny brought you up, then your first word was Nanny, Nan or her name. If your grandmother and grandfather looked after you, your first word was Gan, Gandad, Grand, Granddad, Nan, Nana, Pop, Poppy, Pappy, or other similar word.

Comparison

Some autistic people invent names for the carer. The child's intention is to communicate with you, not to upset you by using the wrong words. The child addresses you incorrectly because he doesn't allocate the same meaning to words as you do. You need to assist the child with the process of allocating the right meaning to the right words.

Example

Alexander was eight years old when I wrongly believed that he connected the meaning of the word 'mother' with both myself and with the concept of mother. Prior to that he called me:

- Girl

- Mummy-girl

- Mama-e-a

- Mama-e-a-mama-crowl-a-zee-zaa.

When he was extremely affectionate I became 'mam-e-a-mam-crol-a-zee-zaa-crowl-a-ziza-ziza'. He called his father 'man' and 'daddy-man'. All the girls in the world were called Francesca, after his sister, and all the boys were Sebastian, after his brother.

Buds of flexibility

After Alexander called me mother, he accepted that I could be called Mum and Mummy. He also accepted that I could be his mother, Sebastian's mother and Francesca's mother. He showed first signs of jealousy when a child other than my own called me mother. He insisted that I ask the child to stop calling me Mum because I wasn't that child's mother, *I was his mother!* However, he cried in desperation when I told him that my name was Florica.

I therefore concluded that 'mother' was only a 'label' that he used to get my attention (literal learning before flexibility). At that stage he probably believed that each object, person or action could only have one label. It took him one more year to accept that Florica is the name of the person that is his mother. All those problems disappeared after Alexander realised for himself that every word can have multiple meanings.

Alexander was four and a half years of age when his father and I divorced. After the divorce I chose not to mention their father unless they asked questions. The children, Alexander included, visited him on occasion and spent a few short/long holidays with their father and paternal grandparents. The children continued to call my ex-husband Daddy. Therefore Alexander's question (then seven years old) 'Mum, do I have a father?' took me completely by surprise.

Other examples

A child addressed his father as 'mykiss', his mother Cathy (after her name) and myself as Mum. Another child called his father 'Mum' and his mum by her Christian name. Two children believed that they were adopted and deliberately called their parents by their Christian names. The child who addressed his father as 'mykiss' did so because each day when his father returned home from work, he opened his arms wide and with a huge smile asked, 'Where is my kiss?' The child ran to him and a game of tickles filled with laughter followed. The child learned *by association* that 'mykiss' equals the guy that gives me a hug and makes me laugh.

Food for thought

Regardless of how your child addresses you, you know when he wants *mother's company* when going to bed and *father's company* when going for a walk. You know that the child means 'father' when he says 'mother' or whatever else the child might choose to call you. How did you learn? Dad, Mum, sister, names, etc. are all concepts.

Using words

As you grew older, you realised that saying words captures the attention of other people. You also realised that people react differently to different words and you modelled your language according to the reactions you were aiming for (not necessarily because you understood their meaning). Can you remember any words that triggered laughter around you? Can you remember deliberately using them because you liked the atmosphere filled with laughter?

Comparison

Compare your memories of using words with the behaviour and responsiveness of your child. Use the following questions to help you list which part of the statement applies to your child. Keep the answers as a profile of your child's ability to make sense of interaction. From time to time revisit these questions and observe how the answers to them have changed in line with his evolved understanding of spoken language and motivation to interact with you.

1. According to your perception, which word is your child using to catch your attention?

2. Are those words matching your expectations?

3. Do you understand the meaning of those words? How?

4. Did you try and then gave up teaching the right words? Why?

5. Do you feel offended/hurt by his choice of words? Why?

6. If your child is currently non-verbal, does he behave in a particular way to engage your attention?

7. Does the *attention-seeking behaviour* come across as friendly?

8. Is the attention-seeking behaviour disruptive?

9. Is the attention-seeking behaviour 'overly friendly'?

10. Does your child look bothered by your responses (runs to you, runs and hides, screams, gives up)?

11. Is your child modelling his behaviour according to the general mood of the house? (If he does that it is more than a sign that he wants to please you.)

12. Did you, at any moment in time, feel as if under given circumstances you can connect with your child?

13. Do you hold the motivation to recreate those circumstances?

14. Could you play repetitively in order to sustain shared attention, motivation and fun interaction?

15. Could you tickle your child during your favourite soap opera only to help him interact more?

Ability to please

You were born with the ability to want to please. Probably you exercised this ability in similar ways to the following examples. You recited the newly learned nursery rhyme and took pride in the praise. You left the nursery and proudly showed your painting to your parents. You took pride in your schoolwork or you wiped a tear from a friend's eye.

Comparison

Do you feel that your child exercises his ability to please you? How? Our children spend an enormous amount of time trying to figure out meanings. Therefore it may be some time before you can enjoy the benefits of an action directed at pleasing you. Alexander showed this ability after he was able to talk about his emotions, discovered what triggers them and how his behaviour is influenced by them, and after he understood that all people are driven by emotions. Here are a few examples:

- Washing dishes unprompted.

- Making paper flowers and a welcome sign when I returned from a long trip away.

- During an unsuccessful shopping hunt for a rare game he wanted, we found an equally difficult to find transformer for his sister. As soon as the shopkeeper told us that he had it, his face lit up with excitement and he said, 'Wait till Francesca gets to see this. I will make a special box for her.'

- Whilst waiting in the dentist surgery a little girl began crying. Alex made her a toy out of the building blocks and gave it to her. After we left the surgery he said, 'It was nice to help her smile.'

Curiosity

You were born with an inquisitive mind and the ability to figure out the power of a question. As soon as you realised what the question stands for you began using 'What is this?' in order to learn about the surrounding environment. When you first used the question you repeated something that you heard. You acquired the concept of a question (what a question means) after you connected the fact that every time you ask a question someone replies. This period in your life is known as 'the terrible twos'.

Even after you realised the link between you asking a question and people talking back, you could have experienced dilemmas. If your mother had time to reply she gave you a full, honest answer. If she was tired or fed up hearing you repeat the same question she might have shortened her answer or might have told you to stop asking questions.

Comparison

Because your child explores his environment in a spatial, tactile or olfactory way, you might be thinking that your child doesn't possess an inquisitive mind or that he is happier playing repetitively. In fact when playing repetitively the autistic child is learning.

As babies, we explore our environment the same way through touch, taste and smell as well as repetitive play. The repetitive play helped us formulate the concept of *cause and effect*. We learned cause and effect through repetitions. The difference between our autistic child and us is that he needs to repeat certain activities more often or for longer periods of time prior to linking cause with effect.

1. *Have you 'caught' the questioning face of your non-verbal child and guessed what he wanted?* A questioning face shows curiosity.

2. *Do you know how you were able to guess the right answer?* The body language associated with curiosity is the same in both autistics or non-autistics.

3. *Could you see yourself spending more time observing your child at play?* The more you observe him, the better your understanding of him.

4. *At the end of a repetitive activity does he share his findings?* If he doesn't, take the lead and show your curiosity.

5. *Is he asking you questions?* If he doesn't, prompt him and say 'Ask me "How can you help me mummy? What do you think about my toy?"'

6. *Does he debate your answer?* As soon as he debates your answer, you are in fact experiencing social communication.

7. *Do you debate the given answer?* If out of fear you modelled your interaction 'to keep the peace', it is likely that you don't debate his answer. Debate is useful because it can help you find out how your child is reasoning. Debate is not the same as arguing.

8. *If your child plays and replays certain parts of a video, is he able to tell you why?* Ask him to allow you to help him.

9. *If he is able to answer your question, are you satisfied with the reply?* If your child's answers are leaving you confused, ask him again and tell him that his reply doesn't make sense to you in the same way it makes sense to him. This way you don't walk away thinking 'This child has no idea about what he just said' and your child doesn't think 'My mum understood me but she acts as if she didn't, therefore she doesn't care about my opinion.'

10. *Do you 'dare' ask further questions?* Faced with an autistic child that is upset, most of us tend to stop asking questions for clarification purposes (possibly fearing a temper tantrum). I found that when upset an autistic person communicates better about his negative emotions in writing or through drawing. As a consequence, when exploring emotions I made sure that we had plenty of paper available and that I wrote my answer to their questions – as opposed to speaking my answer. My actions were always appreciated and more often than not we finished our conversation with laughter.

11. *When you ask questions, do you expect answers or are you assuming that he would not answer?* I have met the parents that stopped asking questions because they became used to receiving no reply. If that applies to you, then start asking questions again.

12. *Is your child repetitively asking you the same questions and behaving as if he did not hear the answers?* If he does, then your answer doesn't make sense to him. Therefore ask him to tell you what he thinks your answer means and then work your way forward from there.

Shared meanings

You were born with the ability to learn from a non-autistic system of shared meanings. Whether you liked watching your mother/father leaving for work you learned to wave goodbye and freely ran to greet them when they returned. Soon enough you learned embedded meaning. Thus 'dinner is ready' could also mean 'come and sit down for dinner'. According to your house and cultural rules you learned when you should talk and when not. You learned how to behave in public and how not to behave in public.

Observe

1. *Is your child smiling and waving goodbye when you are leaving?* If he does, it means that he is comfortable knowing that you will return.

2. *Is your child screaming when you are leaving?* If he does, it means that he is afraid that you might not return.

3. *Does your child look indifferent when you are leaving?* If he does, it could be that he is unaware of you leaving the house or that expressing emotions feels too painful for him.

4. *Does he run to the dinner table when you shout out 'dinner is ready'?* If he does, it means he understands the meaning of these words and feels comfortable sitting with you at the table (a mutually enjoyed social event). If he doesn't, it could mean any of the following:

    - He doesn't understand those words.
    - He is unable to distinguish between sounds that make up words from other ones.
    - He doesn't enjoy sitting at the table.
    - He doesn't want you looking at him when he is eating.

5. *Does he run to the door when you return home, welcoming you through his body language?* If he does, it is his way of welcoming you home. His choice of words or actions may be original but are irrelevant. *The fact that he runs to you matters.* Once you have his motivation, all you have to do is model the right social actions.

Reasoning

An intrinsic part of your mind is the power to reason, behave according to reason and figure out intent from intonation. If your mother addressed you with an angry voice, you ran and hid, apologised or asked for help. If she behaved in a 'half-half' way you might have chosen to 'push your luck'. No one had to teach you this. You knew. You were born with the ability to 'figure' things out. If your teacher told you off, you kept quiet because you knew that more trouble would follow. (See Chapters 9 and 18 for your child's perception of reasons.)

From a very young age you learned to exercise choice. If in your mind you believed that something was worth pursuing you asked and asked and asked for it. If words failed to get what you wanted, you used body language and an emotional display. Can you remember throwing a temper tantrum with the sole aim of reinforcing your demands, position in the matter or purely for the purpose of gaining sympathy? (For your child's perception here see Chapter 9, Violence means 'help me', p103.)

You understood the meaning of danger through generalisation skills. You stopped doing dangerous activities because your mother told you that 'touching hot water' is dangerous. I believe there are very few children who did not at some point experience something that was dangerous and as a consequence they felt the pain. You associated the word 'dangerous' with something that might lead towards you feeling pain/hurt. You felt it because your sensory system felt pain as pain. Your brain's feedback of such sensory input 'told' your body that what happened leads towards you feeling pain. Therefore you did not need to touch the burning candle, run into the road, jump out the window, or cut yourself with a knife just to check if your mother was right or not. (For your child's perception here see Chapter 8.)

As you can see, there are many similarities as well as many differences between the way you behaved and the way in which your autistic child behaves and learns.

A few pointers

If you travelled abroad and tried to talk with the local people in their own language you would notice the similarities and differences more easily. If you succeeded in learning a foreign language, it is highly likely that you were motivated not afraid. *Motivate your child to learn your language.*

Remember that you used body language when words failed you. *Your child uses body language to communicate with you. You also use body language to communicate back.*

Remember the expressions of the local people while they were listening to you? If they looked confused you tried to explain yourself again. *If your child doesn't understand what you are communicating he will look confused or walk away. Follow him and try conveying your message differently until he 'gets it'.*

Question your level of motivation and the reward – or lack of it. *If the local people looked down on you and laughed at your efforts, or even worse punished you for trying, you would have given up talking to them. If they were kind to you, you probably learned new words and shared a few laughs. The same applies to your child.*

When you first talk in a foreign language you are doing just that – talking. You hold a literal interpretation of that language. Because of that you might offend when translating and could offend others when addressing them. The motivation to learn a foreign language and the move from *spoken foreign language* to *spoken native foreign language* takes time, interaction, motivation and support from the natives. You are the native speaker and your child is the foreigner.

1 8

Reasons behind repetitive behaviour

Facilitating change

Most of our child's independent learning happens quietly. Therefore I cannot stop stressing how important it is for you to encourage him to talk. You will be amazed by what you find.

Repetitive behaviour was and unfortunately continues to be believed to represent a child's inability to play imaginatively with toys or purely as an obsessive behaviour (collecting Smarties lids or rewinding tapes are just two examples). Let us see what it really means.

How to deal with repetitive behaviour?

Making things different

Some of us were led to believe that 'repetitive play' symbolises our child's lack of imagination. You might have been advised to make things different for him each time with the aim of expanding his imagination. As a consequence you might interrupt his repetitive play with one toy by replacing that toy with another, or you might be trying to stop him from spinning or flapping his arms, etc.

Making 'things' different every time with *your hidden* aim of *expanding* his imagination confuses him and leads him to feel frustration and resentment.

Changing things, *with his knowledge and within his understanding of why you are changing things,* is a gift of unconditional love from you to him and good teaching practice. You are now laying the foundation for teaching the meaning of flexibility and are helping him exercise self-control that stems from self-reliance.

Your child holds the power of imagination. His repetitive play is a representation of his style of learning and does not mean that he lacks imagination.

Predictable environment

On the other hand you might have been told that because of autism your child thrives in a predictable environment. As a consequence you focused your efforts on creating predictable routines/environment etc. and made no changes to those routines.

A predictable environment aids your child to feel relaxed in general and to feel grateful and friendly towards you. A predictable environment is something that your child will seek constantly, even when he reaches the height of his development. He would be grateful if you provided it for him. Predictability translates as security and most people wish for it. However, a predictable environment with no changes can prevent him from developing flexibility of thought and flexibility in his reactions to changes. Therefore he becomes dependent on you and when he encounters change he panics and loses control. A predictable environment is only needed until your child has 'mapped' it and feels ready for new experiences. Then *you and he together* can make changes to it.

Playing autistically

Some of you might have been introduced to the idea that 'playing autistic' in moderation is good for your child. Therefore you were advised to allow him to play autistically for a few minutes and then stop him. You might have been told that if you don't stop him he would never develop imagination.

Experience taught me that the truth is somewhere in the middle and that the truth holds unique ground for each unique child.

The child plays autistically because it is his way of exploring the environment according to his sensory system. For *24 hours out of 24* his senses function the same way. Each time you allow him *five minutes* of autistic play you are acknowledging that he is learning differently. He cannot understand why he is only allowed to learn/explore autistically for five minutes and no more. As a consequence you are witnessing temper tantrums or complete withdrawal. Each time you are asking him to learn in a 'normal' way, you are asking him to *change his sensory and thinking system.* To the best of his intentions *he cannot* do that.

What he can do is to continue to learn *within his sensory ability* and you can help him learn faster by:

- adjusting the environment to meet his needs

- modelling your interactive games to suit his current and constantly changing understanding

- talking and behaving in a literal way until he is using questions.

Collecting Smarties tops

I asked a few autistic and non-autistic friends to tell me why they collected Smarties lids. The unanimous reply was that there are letters under the lids and they wanted to collect the whole alphabet. They believed that the manufacturers deliberately omitted some letters in order to increase sales. Wow! I fail to see the obsession in that.

Rewinding tapes

I know many children who would learn how to operate the video player and then rewind and play selected parts of a videotape. Such solitary and repetitive activity makes us think that our child must really like a particular part of the video or that the act of rewinding is an obsession.

The most likely explanation is that the part of the tape which they are replaying fails to make sense to them. If your child engages in such activity you can help by playing that part of the video sequence frame by frame for him. It works every time. As you do this you will notice your child's attentive face and in every case the child stops replaying that part of the video.

Exercise

Watch the parts of the video your child is interested in. Observe if those parts include a fast action sequence. For example, the visual image accompanying the nursery rhyme Humpty-Dumpty ('Humpty-Dumpty sat on the wall, Humpty-Dumpty had a great fall') shows Humpty-Dumpty on the wall. The next clip shows him broken. There is no visual image of him falling down. This is the part that the child rewinds.

On a Postman Pat video, Postman Pat's van disappears around the corner without showing the van driving towards the corner. This is the part that the child rewinds.

In Crazy-Cat, the mouse picks up a brick and then we see a shattered window. The video doesn't show the mouse throwing the brick or the brick hitting the window. This is the part that the child rewinds.

In every case the reason/cause for the effect is missing. Your job is to explain to your child the reason why the van disappeared, why Humpty-Dumpty fell off the wall and how the window was shattered.

I remember watching an interview with an 18-year-old child. He liked rewinding the part of a movie where people began to cry. To the best of his abilities he explained to the reporter that he couldn't understand what *makes tears fall out of other people's eyes* (a very literal description of crying). He was rewinding the tape because he hoped that one day he would understand what happens.

He also reported his awareness regarding his parents' 'feeling of anger' when he rewinds tapes. Therefore he only rewinds them in their absence. If someone were to explain emotions to this child and the link between tears and joy, anger and despair, he would stop rewinding those tapes.

Conclusions

Your child *will further develop* social communication and *derive enjoyment from social interaction* when he feels he can take his time to:

- hear you

- think about what he has heard

- form an opinion

- share that opinion.

He also needs to possess *flexibility of thought*. You can show him you are there to help him through in the way you choose to react to his various behaviours.

Imagination

As a matter of interest I asked my elder son to remember the first time he imagined something. After some time he replied, 'I think I was about five years old when I realised Alexander's love of trains. *I wished and imagined him happy* on the back of a miniature train that looked *exactly* like his train set (colours and the shape of the track) but bigger. In my imagination he was able to ride it as opposed to pushing it along.'

Imagination roots from something that we *have seen, understood what 'it' was and wished to make 'it' better.* Therefore we come up with a solution. We employ imagination to *create* something unique because we wish to solve a problem.

The autistic child will show you his imagination during peer play, conversations or creatively after:

- he can understand all the words being used

- he understands the purpose of that conversation

- he wants to participate

- he has something to contribute to it

- he feels proud to contribute to it

- he wants to share his creations.

Food for thought

An autistic child will play with his toys in an imaginative way when:

- he can *see* the whole toy (a car, not just wheels that he spins around endlessly)

- he *understands* that wheels keep the car in motion

- he *observes* that the car doesn't always end up where he wants it.

This might lead to him entering *temper tantrums* and he will push that car along the same track for hundreds of times.

Then one day he understands that the wheels take the car to an *unpredictable place.* He doesn't like that so he *invents* a way to get the car where he wants it, when he wants it, every time he wants it. He might move the furniture round, pull up the carpets, pour water on the floor – whatever it takes to make that car arrive at his desired destination. Without imagination he cannot solve what he perceives to be a problem.

Exercise

Ask yourself *what is imagination?* Ask your partner to share with you something that he is imagining and explore the reasons why he is imagining it. What are you imagining when daydreaming? Do you ever imagine a holiday in the sun or a holiday in the snow? As you are imagining it, can you feel the heat? Are you smiling at the imaginary sun? Can you experience the feeling of well-being even before you have booked the holiday?

Food for thought

Imagination is filtered through your sensory system.

If you and your partner share that sensory system one could say that you are able to feel the same way. A successfully shared holiday, social gathering or game happens because you both enjoy similar experiences.

Implications

Your child's sensory system is unlike yours. Therefore what you might imagine to be a perfect holiday set-up, he could perceive as his worst nightmare. Whilst you might have fun in a hot climate, your child might sweat and faint because his body is not equipped to regulate his temperature. Whilst you might enjoy the company of a few friends, your child could feel overwhelmed by the sounds and therefore seek refuge in the furthest room or cover his ears and scream every time your friends are laughing.

Literal interpretation

The observable 'repetitive play', or in other words the lack of ability to play imaginatively with toys, is sometimes blamed on 'the literal mind'. I doubted this statement and asked my non-autistic children to share examples of their literal interpretations and what they felt as a consequence.

The moth story

> My mum told me that moths eat clothes so I got scared because I thought that in one night one moth could eat a whole wardrobe full of clothes. I was scared for two years because of that.

Although my non-autistic daughter held the above belief, she did not develop autism, nor did she fail to play imaginatively.

Cured ham

> What is cured ham? A ham freed of a disease. [But it is actually ham with plenty of water and salt in it.]

> Although puzzled by his understanding of 'cured ham' my son did not refuse to eat it. He just kept this information quiet.

Computer chips

> I thought that computer chips were the shape of chips, and that the computer ate chips for memory. When it ran out of memory, it was because it ran out of food.

Although my son believed this, he didn't stop using the PC, nor did he 'serve' a plate full of chips to his PC.

Web surfing

> I took the words literally. I thought that you get a surfboard, and then connect to the internet, and download something to surf on from the web.

In this example I feel that his imagination ran riot! If I were never to ask my children about literal interpretations I would have never known. So ask your kid and have fun.

How common is literal interpretation?

Very common and all of us are guilty of it. Each time we don't get a joke it is because we interpret the words literally. How we react to 'not getting it' depends on how we feel about ourselves and on whether we allow our imagination to run riot. As you could see just from my children's accounts, 'literal interpretation' doesn't block the imagination. If anything it triggers new meanings. Stand-up comedy exploits the literal interpretation of words to make us laugh.

Before the autistic child comprehends a large vocabulary of shared meanings, *the lack of understanding* of what the memory logged on parrot fashion is responsible for repetitive reactions (e.g. asking the same question repetitively) and for unnatural reactions to the spoken word. Alexander's reaction to my comment 'You are frightened. The pigeon frightened you' was to reply screaming 'I am Alex!'

Flashback

David, the same volunteer friend who later moved on to playing with Pierce, came up with a solution that fitted the literal learning style. One day Alexander ran from the playroom into the kitchen and said, 'Mum, I am hungry.' David, who followed him, faced him and said, 'Alex, I am Thirsty, how do you do.' He shook Alexander's hand. Alexander paused for a minute and giggling said, 'Not that. I am Alex and I want to eat. I am not Hungry!'

I was over the moon. Alexander had cracked it for himself. He was ready to disassociate himself from the meaning of words as well as accepting that one word could mean more than one thing.

Repetitive behaviour, a sign of learning or confusion, can be separated from dangerous behaviour because the latter is governed by the sensory system.

Your call to action

1. Speak and behave literally with your child and thus expand his comprehension of words and interaction. This way repetitive behaviour stemming from lack of understanding vanishes.

2. Explain to the co-operative and inquisitive child the consequences of dangerous behaviours and they will vanish too.

In some cases, although some of the repetitive behaviour will not vanish, your child will understand why he should engage in those behaviours away from prying eyes.[1]

- *How do you implement this course of action?* Through prolonged interaction.

- *How do you know if this course of action is the right one?* You experience the difference.

Two examples of literal interpretation of language are extracted from Uta Frith's (1989) book *Autism: Explaining the Enigma*. A child is asked to pass the salt. The child fails to understand that something is wanted of him.

Q: Can you *pass* me the salt?

A: Yes. [But the child doesn't pass the salt, possibly thinking that he is asked if he is able to pass the salt because he cannot hear the intonation or doesn't understand the role of intonation.]

In a second example, a nurse wants to administer an injection into the arm of a child. The child responds to her request 'Give me your arm, it doesn't hurt' with a scream as well as becoming overly protective of his arm, possibly thinking that the nurse wanted to cut off his arm.

Unless we ask the child and until he can talk to us about his interpretations of words, we are left guessing and he will continue to live in fear.

Food for thought

The *literal interpretation* of words is responsible for miscommunication but *literal learning* is not an impediment to developing communication skills. Your child can overcome the confusions caused by literal interpretation of words and/or situations even if he continues to learn in a literal way.

The inability to readily figure out the *intent* is the main reason behind inappropriate reactions. Compensatory skills develop through communication.

If *you* were sitting at the table eating, you would naturally pass the salt when you heard the question 'Can you pass the salt?' If not you would say 'No!'

If you don't enjoy sitting at the table, if the words you are hearing are jumbled up noises and if intonation and body language have no meaning for you, then you will not behave in a co-operative way.

Example 1

I asked one of my visiting friends, 'Are you happy to go for a walk?' Instead of a verbal response, she threw herself on the floor crying. I was speechless. What had I done wrong? I sat there waiting for her to stop. Twenty minutes later she asked, 'Do you mean we have to go for a walk and laugh?' Imagine my dismay. Her autistic boyfriend told her that 'Are you happy to go for a walk?' meant 'Would you like to go for a walk?' After hearing his explanation her tears vanished. He was able to guess the source of misunderstanding. On the positive side, my friend acquired/experienced another visual interpretation of what 'Are you happy to go for a walk?' means and I learned not to take *shared meanings* of language for granted.

Every action taken by our children has a reason and a purpose. If your child reacts to your suggestions in an *unnatural* way, it is highly likely that he attributed different meanings to your suggestion. This is where your guessing game begins. Find out what he understood and then help him understand your intention.

Expose your child to various experiences and he will employ *literal learning* and *literal memory* to expand his 'database' of meanings. If you use a metaphor or a figure of speech, tell your child that you are going to use one and explain what it means. That way he will learn something new, you will not cause confusion and both of you can have fun.

Teach your child self-control. In other words that means making a written log of the words that made him feel panicky. If he cannot write, ask him to tell you about them. Teach him to conquer his fears:

- He can practise calming down, taking a deep breath and pausing to think.

- As soon as he feels confused because a verbal request doesn't make sense, teach him to remind himself about the figure of speech.

- Encourage him to ask for further clarification.

- If after being given further clarification he continues to feel confused, teach him the value of agreeing to disagree.

Example 2

My son and I bought some sweets and after he paid for them he placed them in his jacket's front pocket. I made a silly joke and called the pockets a 'kangaroo pocket'. Immediately he looked upset, gave me the sweets and said, 'I don't like that joke.'

I smiled and said, 'It was only a joke. It doesn't mean that you are a kangaroo you know.'

He replied, 'I know it was a joke but I don't like it.' So we left it at that. A few days later I asked if he could tell me why he felt upset when I made that joke. He replied, 'I don't want to talk about it.' So I left it at that. Seven days later we are watching a cartoon. A kangaroo is the star of the show. We both look at each other and giggle. Now I know why he didn't like my joke. From time to time he *has to hop over the cracks.* Using a kangaroo joke reminds him of his need to hop and he doesn't like that. *Helping your child feel at home when faced with jokes and metaphors takes time, trust and extensive interaction.*

Shaping your language

As well as opening your heart to your child's soul, in order to prevent possible confusions shape your language to suit literal learning. This process of shaping your language will remove misunderstandings between you and your child and help him relax. I feel as if I could rewrite the entire dictionary and my suggestion to you is to look for inspiration in the dictionary. The following list could form the subject of another book. Therefore I have included just a few pointers:

- *Time:* substitute 'soon' with 'in two minutes' or, if your child can't read the clock, 'after you've finished your breakfast'; 'later' with 'after your video is finished' or 'when the sun goes to bed'; and 'eventually' with 'after you have had a bath and gone to bed I will read you your favourite story'.

- *Quantity:* substitute 'a handful' with 'concrete numbers'. Same suggestion for a little, a lot, a huge amount.

- *Metaphor:* avoid using expressions such as 'pulling your leg' or 'until the cows come home' until your child has developed the ability to converse with you.

- *Biblical*: burning in hell – avoid using it. It could terrify your child.

- *Distance*: substitute 'near', 'far' and 'fairly near' with 'two houses away from our house', 'we must get in the car and drive for two hours' and 'ten houses away'.

- *Concepts*: once your child has the ability to talk with you, you can explain concepts, not before.

- *Emotion*: if your child smiles tell him that 'he looks happy'. If he cries tell him that he 'looks sad'. If he looks 'at peace' tell him that he 'looks content'. Avoid telling him you are sad before he has learned to understand the difference between being himself and feeling sad.

Note

1.   Such as talking to himself because he needs to hear his thoughts.

Exploring emotions

Mutual trust (emotion) as well as faster 'listen, think, express' process

Exercise

Keeping the following points in mind, analyse my conversation (further down) with my autistic friend Feather. When we perceive our children as being aloof they are in fact busy. They could be doing any of the following:

- gathering new visual images from the surrounding environment

- exploring new things (toys, objects, people's faces, situations)

- ascribing meaning to them

- re-ascribing meaning to something already learned[1]

- memorising more than one meaning to the same word, situation, etc.

- building a database of metaphoric meanings

- thinking about what was said to them

- wondering if they should reply or not

- wondering if it is safe to talk with you (you will not laugh or act angrily in response to his reply)

- wondering if he can trust you

- wondering if you really love him.

I met Feather in 1999 when she temporarily sheltered in America a young autistic man from the UK.[2] Our friendship has grown stronger over the years. She helped me understand many aspects of her emotional self that are unavailable to read in medical or therapy books. I understood why we don't read about such matters in these books after she helped me become more aware of *what I was doing wrong and what I was doing right* when interacting with *an autistic person*. One day she shared her dream of visiting a Native American reservation (she had First Nation ancestors) and confided her fear of travel. I offered to accompany her because I grew to love her and to value her friendship. I also found the idea of visiting a reservation very exciting. A day later she replied to my offer and this is a fragment of our conversation:

> *Feather:* I was thinking about something you said last night to me (as I often do during my editing stages, uh-uh). You said you loved me. (And that is why you would accompany me.) You asked me if I could feel that you did? You know… I don't believe I feel anyone's love. There are some people who I know love me. But I tend not to actually feel it. Usually when I am faced with you sending me personalised emotion like that [*hugs over the internet*]…I smile, and my face gets warm…but I feel confused and nervous and on guard…It makes me feel like a caged animal…pacing around not knowing what to do with it. [*After five minutes she continued*] I do not want your sole reason for being my friend, or being interested in me, to be because you feel you can help me and care for the aspie in me. I don't want to feel you 'pity' me and wish to assist me… I want you to be a friend who helps me for the sake of friendship…

> *Florica:* I would like to spend some time with you alone…to try to interact with you. Perhaps seeing me in person will allow you to understand me better too.

> *Feather:* Not too many people have invested any interest or time in wanting to understand me…at least in person. Trying to understand my expressions, and knowing what to do and where to go and what to focus on and my tone of voice, causes problems in people wanting to know me. NTs[3] seem to know how to disengage when not interested…or they can come up with plausible responses that keep the flow going… I just go duh. [Duh was a state of being, not a literal verbal word.]

Florica: If I don't get to visit you in your country, perhaps you could come and visit me in London?

Feather : I wonder if Moon [*my nickname*] would still see me as sweet if she were stuck with me in real time. I either have a joint topic with someone. Or I overwhelm with my thoughts. Or I do not know what to say. I have not spent much time in the presence of others in the past two years or so. I have lost a great deal of my ability to put my thoughts into words. It is harder than ever for me to interact. I am almost at the stage of avoiding talking to people any more. Sometimes I cannot put a sentence together that makes sense verbally. My listen, think, express talk is fragmented greatly…and I am lonely as I want to be able to talk but have a hard time any more…Do you understand this?

Florica: I think I do.

Feather: You understand me because of others and I am similar?

Florica: I understand because you explain it well and because I met other people who expressed their emotions the same way.

Please take your time in reading and re-reading our conversation. It shows that Feather feels emotion and her reaction to it is no different from other people's reaction to love. I chose to share this part of our conversation because I want you to make a habit of observing your child's body language and help him label the observable emotions. Feather became *lonely* because over the years people around her lost the patience to listen. Her trust in other people suffered greatly too. Her verbal communication may not be as fluent as her writing, but her capacity to love and care for her children and other people is immense. She adopted a child.

As I spoke to her on the phone, I could 'hear' her thinking. She taught me that long silences don't mean 'I don't want to reply' or 'I don't understand you'. They mean 'I am thinking about what the speaker just said'. I could not hear the non-verbal fluency she referred to. She told me that talking without having to assess the body language[4] of a person helps her focus on what is being said. It is important therefore to say what you mean and to leave nothing to gestures.

The 'editing stages' mentioned by my friend represent the time needed by a person to make sense of previous interaction. The length of time needed by an autistic to edit social information varies from person to person. Perhaps you can recognise the 'editing trance' by the look in your child's eyes or by the sound of his voice while talking to himself. Assuming that your child is talking to himself, he is not talking to himself because he feels lonely or because he is aloof. Nor is talking to himself because he doesn't want to talk with you. He talks to himself because he needs to *re-hear* what was said in order to *fully understand the meaning* of what was said. In time, the 'talking to oneself' phenomenon disappears and/or can be replaced.

Your efforts during interaction should not be directed at stopping the 'talking to oneself' but towards finding out what would best help him speed up the process of understanding. Perhaps you identify those editing stages by the way in which your child is pacing up and down, or repeating the same passage from a video over and over again. You can help him relax. He can feed on your patience. Shadow him silently and offer your arms as shelter. Your child will accept it.

Further exercises

If your child's main activity revolves around repeating entire scripts that he has previously heard on TV or chunks of conversations:

- try listening to what he is talking about

- if he doesn't allow you, persuade him to let you listen

- record the conversation and then make a written record

- share the written version with him and turn it into a play where you read some and he reads some

- persevere at asking him to allow you to hear him and ask him to share his understanding of what he is telling you.

Food for thought

Do you need time to edit information if you find the amount of information overwhelming? Our children find information overwhelming more often than we do.

This way you are actively helping your child to make sense of what to him may seem *just a string of words* that he is repeating for reasons known only to him. Your intervention will help him build a meaningful vocabulary. This in turn will help him speed up the *listen, think, express* processes. Faster processing will allow him to take part in social communication and interaction.

I am lonely as I want to be able to talk but have a hard time

There isn't much to say other than autism doesn't cause the emotion of loneliness. An autistic person becomes lonely and depressed because of conduct towards them. Don't we become lonely because we feel unaccepted and misunderstood? Why shouldn't they?

One year after Feather and I had that conversation I received the following note from her. I want her note to bring you hope and to feel that *inner peace* is within your child's reach. Remember how she said that she could not 'feel' the love? Her pacing up and down and the feeling of warmth showed me that she felt it but either felt afraid or that no one helped her label these feelings as love.

> I feel a stress lifting off me (but it has started happening before today)... I feel good enough today to go out and mow two yards. ...been many things going better. Moon, it isn't just 'things' happening around me... I am starting to feel 'god' in my court again... I know that I may not make sense but I think he is taking care of me now and I didn't feel him before for a long time.

> I wanted to write to you and tell you about how I have been feeling and the things that have been going on in my life (and yes you play a role in it)...but I just don't know how to explain it... Something is different.

> I guess what I can say is...I feel less scared, less weary, more inviting, a bit closer... Is that love?

I guess I want you to see that one of your roles in your child's life is to shower him with your unconditional love. You can do that better than anyone else. *Your love* can prevent and cure *your child's* loneliness. *Your love can help him develop self-esteem and overcome his fears – whatever his fears might be.* It can also inspire him to talk about a range of emotions.

Emotions, self-esteem, editing time, expressive language and the pleasure of communication

Your child must feel confident with himself and use words with shared meanings during a conversation before he can truly enjoy social communication. How can you help? Help him label emotions as and when he feels them.

Examples

When Alexander asked me 'Why did you put a butterfly in my stomach?' I replied, 'We call this butterfly excitement. You are feeling excited because we are going on holiday. *I am not putting it* inside your stomach.'

Later, as his vocabulary grew, we watched drama together and talked about each character's emotions. *Passions*, an American soap, helped Alexander realise how different people have different emotions about the same action. After each programme we talked about what emotion motivated each character's actions.

In another example, I came to realise that one of my visiting autistic friends had fallen in love with someone. I made an innocent remark, 'You are in love.'

She replied, 'No I am not! I hate this thing called Love! How would you know anyhow?'

'From your body language, from the joy exuding from your eyes, from the amount of time you spend writing your emails and from the type of cards you are buying.'

'I see,' she replied. (She had her personal reasons to stay clear of the word 'love'. Prior to falling in love she associated the word love with the way in which she was cared for – and that wasn't autistic friendly.)

Suggestions

Watch video programmes with him (drama) and watch his body language. Is he hiding behind the sofa? Is his body shrivelling? If you can relate to his body language, pause the tapes and discuss what happened. Encourage him to ask you questions about what motivates each character's behaviour. Tell him that all the people are motivated by emotions. Explain that the source of one emotion could vary, yet the emotion itself is the same. For example, he is happy to receive a toy train; his sister is happy to receive a flower; Cinderella is happy to go to the ball. The happiness is equal. If his toy train broke, his feeling of upset is equal to his sister's feeling of upset when the flower dies or to Cinderella being locked in her room.

Explain that feeling upset doesn't mean that he is no longer Alex or that his name has changed from Alex to Upset. He is Alex (if his name is Alex); the emotion that he is feeling is what we call upset. You must explain this in detail because of the literal learning style.

On more than one occasion I made the mistake of saying to a friend 'You're funny' when she made me laugh. I expected her to laugh and take my remark as a compliment. She didn't. She plunged into a deep silence. She took my remark as an insult. She did this because for many years she was called 'funny' as in stupid.

As trivial as they may seem, these extended explanations freed my son and some of his friends from some terrifying emotions and helped them develop self-esteem. Be prepared to spend a considerable amount of time explaining the subtle differences in language.

Example

Weird is a name we use for an out of the ordinary behaviour. The word weird represents an individual's perception of an action. What one individual perceives as weird, another may not. Behaving *weirdly* is not the same as being weird because there is no such thing as being weird. Weird could mean running naked in the middle of a football pitch and to do that *you don't have to be autistic.*

I believe that you too can help your child learn enough meaningful language so that he and you can hold a pleasurable or insightful conversation. I also believe that you can develop mutual trust between you so that he could feel comfortable exploring his emotions. Autism does not cause damage to self-esteem – the way in which we constantly nag a child for his behaviour does that. The following three stories are here to illustrate what could be achieved in nine years through love.

15 December 1995

We are walking up and down the car park every night after 11pm. It is the only safe place I can take Alexander for a walk. A pigeon flew in front of him and startled him. His heart was pumping and he looked frightened. I approached him and said, 'The pigeon frightened you. You are frightened.' In a flash he replied shouting 'I am Alex not Frightened!' and he ran away. So much for social communication!

21 June 2001 – personal diary

(Please pay close attention to the bracketed words in italic. They are here to show you my intentions[5] and to illustrate how you could help your child develop expressive language by shaping your language.)

Alexander and his brother Sebastian had an argument over who was winning a game. Sebastian snaps at Alexander and Alexander calls him names. Both boys are upset and in need of pacifying. A compromise is reached and the boys shake hands. Alexander approaches me and wants to talk.

'I thought you were going to tell me off,' said Alexander with tears in his eyes. (*I chose not to; instead I was hoping to explore the argument and their perceptions.*)

'Why did you think that?'

'Because I called Sebastian names.'

'You were angry, that is why you called him names. However, it isn't right to call anyone names.' (*His answer showed me that he knew that he was wrong to call other people names. Good.*)

'I know that, but he is so good at this game now. I was the one that taught him how to play it. It *isn't fair* that he can beat me at it now! I asked him to give me a chance but he wouldn't. So *I got angry.*'

'We will have to ask him again to give a chance and find out what you consider a "chance".' (*I wanted Alexander to learn that there are more meanings to 'chance' and compromises besides turn taking.*)

At this point Sebastian joined in and said, 'It isn't my fault that I am good at these games.'

I replied, 'No it isn't a fault, but if you want all of you to have fun, then you have to find a compromise.' The boys found a compromise and later continued playing together. Before that, Alexander had more questions.

'Mum, how can *we make a kinder world?*' asked Alexander and wiped two more tears from the corner of his eyes.

'What brought this question?' (*I was curious to find out what he meant.*)

'Well, I was thinking about the global warming, and how we could stop it.'

'I don't know how to stop that Alexander.'

'Well I was thinking about inventing a "freeze cannon ball". Would that stop it?'

'I don't know; how would it work? You could join Greenpeace and share your ideas with other people who are concerned with global warming.' (*I was teaching him about the existence of other people who think on similar lines.*)

'Are those people autistic like me?' (*This was the first time Alexander had referred to himself as autistic. His statement also gave me an insight into how he perceived autism.*)

'I don't think that all the members of Greenpeace are autistic Alexander. Autism has nothing to do with the environment.'

'I have another question.'

'What question?'

'Do you think that all autistic people are like me?'

'What do you mean?' (*It is very easy to assume what he might say as opposed to asking what he means to say.*)

'You know, emotion… [*pause*]'

'Do you mean emotionally sensitive?' (*I chose the word sensitive because he had a few tears in his eyes and was genuinely concerned over the future of our planet.*)

'Yes, that one, think a lot about problems and the feelings of other people.'

'I think so. The people who I know are that way. So you are not alone.' (*I wanted him to feel that he belongs and that he is not alone. Also I wanted to teach him that people's actions are emotion driven.*)

Alexander smiled and paused. Then he continued, 'I have another question.'

'What is that?'

'Why were people afraid of Hitler?'

'I don't know.'

'What made other people become friends/allies with him if he was a bad man?' (*Once again I wanted to see how he reasons.*)

'What do you mean?'

'I heard you talking about a programme on the TV. It was about killing people who were different. Why didn't somebody stop him?'

'I don't know. Some people tried but they were really afraid.'

'How do you become a president?'

'People elect you. You could become a president if people elected you.' (*I wanted him to see that he can have any aspirations and that he would have to work towards achieving them.*)

'I could?' said Alexander as half a smile lit up his face.

'You could if you had solutions to problems.'

'What is the difference between a president and Dalai Lama?'

'A Dalai Lama is chosen for life and a president is elected for a few years.'

The conversation went on for another half-hour and ended with 'I love you Mummy.'

15 August 2001

We are having dinner in a Chinese restaurant. Whilst waiting for the food, Alexander continued our conversation which started on 21 June with 'Mum, why would somebody want to rule the world? And anyhow, after they get to rule the world then what? Did anyone think to tell Hitler this?' (Two months to finish a conversation!)

Personally I derive great pleasure from talking with Alexander. I never know what his next question will be. Also watching him reaching a compromise while playing with his brother and sister gives me hope that by the time he reaches adulthood he will be able to interact and compromise with society at large.

Not a miracle cure, just love and empathy

What changed between the time Alexander was diagnosed with autism and today? First of all, Alexander's autism is just as present today as it was the day he was born and he is no less autistic today than ever before. Because he learned to express himself verbally, he can teach us about his autism as well as present us with a new perspective on things in general. I can talk to him and he can talk to anyone. It is easy.

However, if we didn't help him communicate his personal perspective on life, his imagination, his kind words, his wisdom and his hurts would have remained unknown to us. He would have remained 'autistic, frustrated and lonely' instead of 'autistic cherished, belonging and proud'. By recognising his *wish to communicate and his right to an autistic-friendly environment for learning*, we created an approach that supported *his own quest* to develop:

- his ability to 'listen, think, express'

- flexibility of thought

- a larger vocabulary

- his ability to recognise how emotions govern social interaction and communication.

Hand in hand with those:

- his emotional security grew

- his sources of pleasure included social interaction (as opposed to solitary play)

- our tears were exchanged for joy

- our frustrations could be dealt with

- our emotions could be shared and enjoyed.

- life as a family unit began.

Alexander's topic of conversation is irrelevant. Your child will converse with you about whatever you talk about as a family or whatever he might be interested in. Your child's fluency of speech will reflect his understanding of words and desire to understand concepts. His *curiosity* reflects his desire to take part in a conversation. The length of time he is happy to take part in a conversation represents his current level of ability to cope with all the stimuli and his level of understanding of language. The current level changes with increased interaction.

Issues

If we deny the child the autistic-friendly environment, we are denying an opportunity to learn about our 'system of communication'. We are making him more dependent than he is already and deliberately ignoring his style of learning. If we place him into a non-autistic-friendly environment he stumbles like a drunk through a maze of meaningless and fragmented understandings.

Notes

1. See Chapter 3, A strict need for accuracy, p.34.

2. See 'Why the eighth colour of the rainbow?', p.12.

3. Jargon invented by autistic people to describe non-autistic people which reads neurologically typical.

4. If like me in the past you were taught to constantly ask your child 'Look at me when you talk to me', question your motives. Would you rather he looked at you but be unable to converse with you or vice versa?

5. Various examples of what I mean are in Chapter 18, Shaping your language, p. 185.

20

Autistic communication and pragmatic learning style

Imagine your child's learning style (not imagination) as that of a cartographer – or that of a pragmatic[1] learner. He must 'see' what he is about to learn, sometimes even experience it, before he can make a log about it, label it, store it and then understand it. Each time he learns something new, his map grows bigger and contains more finer details. His ability to relax and interact with others is closely linked to both the size *of* and the details *on* his map.

The following story should help you visualise what I mean by saying that the child will relax if you behave in a literal way, as well as how you can help him expand his understanding of words and thus help him create a 'detailed map'. I was serving dinner and I asked my autistic friend, 'How many peas would you like?'

He replied, 'About three.' I served him three peas and placed the plate in front of him. He looked at me and said with amusement, 'This is great! You are so literal!'

Sniggering I continued, 'There is no such thing as "about three" is there?'

He replied, 'Whenever I was asked before how many peas I would like I always said about three, hoping that the people would understand that I don't really like them. Regardless, I ended up with a huge spoonful, which I then left on my plate. This, what you just did, is so different. I like it!'

We then moved on to describe and 'map' subjective[2] interpretations of quantities such as a little, a lot, a huge amount and more than before. During one evening my friend learned the meaning of the transient[3] interpretation of quantity and his map of understanding grew. As a consequence, his ability to talk with other people, and not be confused by those words, also grew.

Dealing with change

The following examples are here to help you find a way to help your child relax when a change occurs and build a bigger map. All the solutions were designed to fit pragmatic learning through doing.

Action

Your child screams every time you move his toy without his prior knowledge and/or consent, when you move the furniture around, or when you enter the room in which he is already present.

Probable cause

Before the child left the room he took a mental picture of that room and is expecting to find it unaltered. Through your actions you are changing the look of a mapped and logged place in his mind. Inside that mapped place he knows where everything is and feels comfortable. When you change it he 'feels lost'.

Example 1

I met a young boy (we shall call him Richard) who screamed every time his mother moved his toy truck out of the way. Imagine Richard playing happily in the middle of the room with his truck until he remembered something else. Before he left the room, he carefully placed the truck on the carpet, per- fectly aligned with its pattern. Unfortunately the toy is in the middle of the room, causing other people to trip. Unknown to Richard, his mother moves it out of the way. Richard returns, looks at the *exact place where he left his toy*, pauses for a second and then throws himself on the floor screaming, 'My truuuuuck!'

SOLUTION

In Richard's case we involved him. We asked him to find a different place for his truck. As I placed my hands on his toy he screamed. I spoke softly and picked up the toy. 'Help me move it, it is so heavy!' He giggled and came over to help me. We placed it out of the way, so that *he knew where to find it* when he returned. As you can see, we worked with his learning style, not against it. We helped him make his 'map' bigger.

OBSERVATION

Puzzled by his behaviour, I remember thinking, 'If only he looked around first.' Then I remembered an episode between my son and me. As we walked along the supermarket aisles I moved two feet away from him. Alexander threw himself on the floor and screamed, 'Mummy girl!' I replied, 'I am right here.' Alexander continued, 'I can't see you! Where are you?' His voice was filled with desperation. Again I couldn't understand how he could fail to see me. Five years later, the above-mentioned behaviours made sense. The *natural ability 'to search'* was blocked by panic.

Hide and seek

Games such as 'Hide and Seek' can be used to model for your child the meaning of 'searching'.

- With his knowledge and involvement, 'hide' his favourite toy (perhaps the remote controller). Then ask, 'Where is the remote controller?'

- Next, uncover the remote controller and say 'We found it hiding under the pillow because we hid it under the pillow' – very literal. You are teaching only words matching your actions.

- Then, separately and on a different occasion, you hide it without his knowledge. Tell him that you hid it and offer to help him search for it.

- Your first *few* attempts will deliberately fail.

- The quantity of 'few' is determined by your child's mood. When you find it, make a big deal of it.

- The next step is to hide it and don't get involved (but supervise the search).

- With perseverance, your child will understand the meaning of search and will also learn to search, thus freeing himself from panic attacks.

What made the children panicky?

Richard expected to find his truck exactly where he left it. The truck was missing and he didn't think to search for it. Alexander expected to see me exactly where he last saw me. Perhaps he thought that I had vanished. Although he heard my voice, his fear that he had lost me was greater than *his ability to look around* and find me, or look towards the direction from which he could hear my voice. More likely I have moved out of his mapped place.

SOLUTION

In Alexander's case there was little that I could do at the time. If the same incident were to happen today, I would make sure to step towards him as soon as he panicked and reassure him that I am there.

However, I was able to use this knowledge during a shopping trip with a 21-year-old autistic friend. The shop was full of people and she became agitated. I remembered the incident with Alexander and realised that if we were to be separated she would panic. I knew about my friend's fascination with lights. I found a tin of beans with a hologram on it. In a friendly voice I said, 'I found a solution. You look at this hologram as we walk through the aisles and hold on to the trolley. That way you can ignore the people and have something fun to do until we finish.' It worked. She relaxed even more than I expected. We remained together and towards the end of our shopping trip she did not need the help of the hologram.

If your child finds shopping trips or journeys hard, take his favourite toy with him.

- Tell him why you are doing it.

- Ask him to take the toy that gives him most comfort.

This way, on the one hand, you are letting him know that you are aware of the fact that he doesn't feel comfortable taking part in the next activity, and on the other you are making it less scary for him as well as setting the foundation for teaching him the value of a compromise.

Example 2

For at least three years Alexander screamed every time a person opened the door and entered the room in which he was playing. I couldn't understand why.

SOLUTION

I can only guess that we physically changed *the look* of the room and he found that unsettling. If the same thing happened today, I would knock on the door until he came to open it to let me in.

Writing

The literal and the mapping style of learning doesn't stop with learning new meanings of words, learning to find toys or learning to relax in the outside environment. It can also be observed during academic exercises.

In Alexander's playroom and away from the dangers of the house we drew numbers together for hours on end. Before Alexander reached five years of age he could count and write all the numbers from 1 to 1000. Reluctantly, we too wrote numbers from 1 to 1000 hoping that Alexander would realise that we mirrored his behaviour in order to show him our love and acceptance. That was before I understood more about *autism and learning.*

We used his love of numbers in order to help him build language. We drew small numbers and big numbers, happy numbers and sad numbers, red numbers and blue numbers. From time to time Alexander expanded on our games. However, for most of the first year he was happier if left him to draw his numbers at his own pace. He derived much joy from his finished product. I had to accept that I didn't understand his fascination. Was his activity repetitive? Was it obsessive, or was he learning?

He was in fact learning – self-teaching himself to write. We didn't teach him. He copied words from toy boxes or video boxes exactly how he had seen them. For example, for 'Thomas the Tank' he wrote it exactly how it was written on the box.

As his writing incorporated other words, they too were reproduced as *he saw* them – colour included; for example, 'Woolworths' written in white on a red background.

I call this an example of literal or photographic learning. The problem with this learning style is that it creates confusion in our child's mind. Whilst we cannot change the learning style, we can work with it. Notice once again that we are not 'working with the unknown entity of autism', we are working within the parameters of that child's photographic learning style.

Example

Five years after I noticed Alexander's writing style, I witnessed it again whilst playing with Pierce. He loved Bob the Builder. Guess what? He also wrote the same way as he had seen it laid at on the box:

Bob

the

Builder

I suggested that the play helper make word puzzles and that they modelled for Pierce various photographic images of the phrase 'Bob the Builder', thus showing him that 'Bob the Builder' means the same as, for example, 'Bob the builder', 'BOB THE BUILDER' or 'Bob THE Builder'. After this exercise his flexibility grew.

A paper produced by a Swiss school for autistic children suggested that some of their students had a need to copy material from books exactly as they had seen it. For example, if a child was asked to copy the sentence 'I want an apple' and he was then asked to write one word on each line:

I

Want

An

Apple

the child either refused, threw a temper tantrum or looked confused. This could mean that:

- none of those words make sense
- the child believed that the string of words meant 'I want an apple'
- the child believed that only if he writes the words on one line do they mean 'I want an apple'.

So teaching the meaning of each individual word is the first call of action. This can be achieved through word puzzles. They can help him build a larger 'photographic' library of meaningful written words.

A story to ponder on

Once again I remember one parental heartfelt request: 'If only you could teach my child how to write I would be a happier parent.' I 'taught' that child the role of language and he spoke faster than any person I have ever encountered before. But my reply to his parent, before I had even begun to play with the child, was 'Imagine yourself as the richest person on earth. You have no relatives and you have no charitable cause. You have your love for your child and you have only your autistic child who you want me to teach to sign his name. After your death your entire fortune is left for your child to enjoy. But because he had learned to sign his name he signs it all away without even knowing that he "signed" a document. Would you still want me to teach him how to sign his name?' The parent paused and tearfully said, 'No.' Therefore we did more than teach the child to write, we set off to teach the child the power of meaningful speech.

Reading

Your child might be able to read very well, even if he doesn't comprehend what he is reading. How can you test his understanding of the written word?

You can talk to him about what he is reading, thus ensuring that he only memorises meaningful words.

One autistic friend tried to explain how he perceived words before they had meanings. He wrote 'Cat, tree, dog, run, hide'. Then showing me this paper, he asked, 'Can you read?'

Thinking that he asked me if I could read his writing I said, 'Yes I can read, you have beautiful handwriting.'

He continued, 'No, can you read the words?'

I read the words and my mind was trying to create sense from them. I asked him, 'Did you want to write "the cat was afraid of the dog and therefore ran to hide in the tree"?'

He replied, 'No, I wanted to show you that I was able to read words but that they meant nothing. Just like the sense is missing from the sentence that I just wrote, for many years I was unable to make sense out of anything that I read.' After a short pause he asked, 'If I learn all the words from the dictionary, do you think that people would understand me better?'

I shared this story with you because some of our children are able to read. You need to ensure that they also learn the meaning of the words that they read. Don't be fooled by his ability to pronounce and/or read a large number of words.

Can I teach my child to conform?

Yes, you can teach your child to conform after he has learned the meaning of concepts and rules. On more than one occasion I was asked to help a child 'conform' before that child even knew his own name. If conformity plays on your mind, take a few minutes to consider the reasons why we conform or not, as well as the many reasons behind why our children find it hard to conform in playgroup or school, a party, travelling on a bus, or just simply walking down the street.

We would be permanently unable to follow the unwritten social rules that govern multiple interactions if we didn't:

- understand the spoken word

- make ourselves understood verbally or through sign language

- ask questions and allow others to question us

- empathise with what the other person is trying to convey

- remember what we want to say even if we are interrupted in mid-sentence.

Without these, conforming will remain just a concept. Within an autistic-friendly environment you can help him understand social rules and the need to conform or not. It all starts with you attempting to unblock the communication blocks. The following list shows you the stages of development that your child will go through before he can understand concepts:

- acquire words

- learn the meaning of those words

- use meaningful words (e.g. drink, bed, TV, food, go)

- use words to make small, meaningful sentences

- speak out parrot fashion words or sentences that have no meaning yet

- ask questions, thus acquiring more meaningful language

- use that language in the context of a small conversation

- talk at you or talk to himself

- converse and talk with you

- talk with others

- talk in robot-like speech

- develop fluency and melodic speech

- communicate and develop communication skills.

Literal emotional communication

The physical changes made to your home cannot prevent or change your child's photographic style of learning or his 'original' way of expressing his emotions. (This is what I meant by a playroom not being a cure catalyst.) You can, however, decode and help him substitute his 'original' way of showing and acting on emotions with a recognisable and acceptable way. This way he begins to conform or not because he understands what conforming means.

My son was six years old when he watched *Hercules* – the cartoon version. After watching it at least 20 times he decided *to show me his affection.*

Appearing out of the blue, he charged towards my stomach, bashed his head into it and ran away before I could tell him that what he was doing hurt me.

One of my friends whom Alexander liked very much came to visit. Before I could warn Sue, Alexander approached her in the same fashion and crashed his head into her stomach. I realised that Alexander was showing her affection and called out to him, 'Are you showing Sue that you like her?'

'Yes,' replied Alexander in a loving and fun voice.

'Do you think you could hug her instead?'

'Why?' enquired Alexander in an innocent voice.

'Because it hurts! We would like it and enjoy it better if you showed us your affection through a hug.'

'I didn't know. The cartoons don't seem to hurt!' (He applied literal reasoning.)

Food for thought

Within a formal environment the above actions could have been easily misunderstood and punished. Alexander learned from cartoons and behaved with us as if we lived in a cartoon world.

It is highly likely that your child is copying similar behaviour from the TV. Find out which one by watching *his* TV programmes. Watch those cartoons with him. Find out what he is copying by matching his behaviour with that of the characters from the cartoon. What do you think he is trying to communicate to you?

Begin a parallel play session, where you play the same pretend game as your child. Then translate it for him and model what 'we' do in real life.

You cannot prevent your child's inability to use the support system that you fought to provide for him during school years. Before Alexander went to school he was able to communicate with 15 people and I believed that he had conquered generalisation in terms of communicating at least his basic needs to his teacher and paid assistants. Wrong assumption! Two years later I asked him if he knew that the assistants were there to help him and that he was meant to ask for help when he needed it. His answer 'I didn't know that Mum' took me completely by surprise. This incident happened just after I read Jim Sinclair's article and his words 'Make sure you check and double check that your translation of the situation matches the understanding of your child' made full sense.

The above example illustrates literal learning and the need for understanding and translations. In the comfort of your home you can check and double-check with your child to ensure that he understands what you want, what you are suggesting and that he feels able to use the provided help/support.

Food for thought

There are times when *you* and *I* as parents intuitively know what would be of help and benefit to our child. This is why we fought to ensure a support system for him in the first place.

All that remains for you to do is to talk with your child about it. Find out if he can use the support you provided or whether he thinks that something else is needed.

If a child cries before going to school, if he is biting your hands when you are taking him to a social place, then it is highly likely that he is not ready to go there.

What else stops a child from conforming?

A need for perfection and spatial thinking

Alexander's need for perfection[4] – as perceived by Alexander – caused him a great deal of frustration and upset during his school years. If asked to compose a story, most children would write the story as it comes to mind, perhaps stopping to think after each sentence, rubbing out a word they didn't like, and so on. Alexander had to think for 15 minutes first, formulate in his mind what he wanted to say and then write. I learned about this behaviour from his school assistant after she observed him writing.

Imagine an A4 blank piece of paper and Alexander in deep thought, staring at it for 20 minutes. Then watch Alexander writing the first word on the top left corner, a word in the middle of the page and the last word on the bottom right corner followed by a full stop, after which he filled in the rest of the story like a jigsaw puzzle. Every single word is the same height and the space between each word is equal in length. *That is what Alexander calls perfection.* This example also illustrates *photographic thinking.* However, this *need for perfection,* coupled with a photographic style of thinking, learning and producing written work, wrongly projects the image of a child that is perceived as *slow or disobedient* (e.g. refusing to start writing as soon as the teacher asked).

If your child is experiencing similar problems, consider which of the following questions carries most value:

- How can I influence this child's behaviour?

- How can I help him learn more?

- Why does he need to behave this way?

- What matters? *How* he learns or the fact that *he is learning?*

- Is he in the right environment for learning?

- If this is not the right environment, what makes the perfect environment?

Reasoning

I would like to help you scrutinise the area of our human development which we call reasoning. The subject of reasoning could be addressed in an entirely psychological book. It is not the purpose of this exercise. I wish to cover a common-sense approach to reasoning. Therefore I will address only three questions whose specifically tailored answers, I hope, will help you empathise with your child's actions and inspire you to teach him reasoning skills.

1.   Is the autistic child able to reason?

2.   How do we develop reasoning skills?

3.   How does reasoning influence our behaviour?

Is the autistic child able to reason?

In my experience I can reply with yes. He needs help to develop and/or expand his existing reasoning *skills.* You can do this by helping him master various reasonings described in the answer to the second question.

How do we develop reasoning skills?

We develop *reasoning skills* progressively and we use several forms of *reasoning*. A few examples of reasoning could be described as follows:

1. *Literal reasoning*: we copy someone else's behaviour without thinking about the other person's reaction. One example that comes to mind is a child who will empty a full bottle of milk into the sink because he wants to please his parents. This was an action he had previously witnessed but did not understand that the milk which the previous person emptied away had gone off.

2. *Protective reasoning*: employed for self-defence.

3. *Verbal reasoning*: talking with someone about the reasons that prompted us to do a certain action. The success of such reasoning depends on shared meanings.

4. *Pragmatic reasoning*: we acquire this from understanding cause and effect. This involves 'repetitive play' or hands-on interactive activities with a teacher.

5. *Positive emotional reasoning*: stems from empathy and a desire to please.

6. *Negative emotional reasoning*: stems from us wanting to make the other person feel bad.

7. *Inferred reasoning*: stems from our ability to rely on what we learned so far.

8. *Individual reasoning*: makes us unique and fuels our imagination.

How does reasoning influence our behaviour?

Our reasoning makes us behave in individual ways. It builds our character and personality, fuels our goals and motivates our actions. The list is endless. Our reasoning skills on the other hand will help us to achieve our goals and determine our course of actions when we set off to achieve our goals. How can this short lesson help you understand your child?

First of all *literal reasoning* is another aspect of your child's development that could spark a non-conforming behaviour. If your child is at a stage described in the following two examples,[5] your first call for action is to encourage him to express his thoughts so you can *identify* where he has learned his reasoning from (usually TV) and where the literal reasoning stops. I chose to 'label' the autistic social reasoning as literal reasoning. This type of reasoning precedes *pragmatic reasoning*, which you can teach through interaction and through explaining cause and effect, and gets the autistic person into trouble. More often than not, before you communicate, the only social reasoning skills that dictate your child's behaviour are literal. Punishing him for trying to make his needs understood in a way 'you don't approve of' or 'doesn't make sense to you' at this stage translates in his mind as more confusion.

One example that illustrates a combination of *literal reasoning* and *protective reasoning* comes from a personal account given by Temple Grandin. She tells how she threw her hat out of the car window, thinking that her mum would understand that she didn't want to wear a hat. She did not use *negative emotional reasoning*. I read this story in 1993 and found it both amusing and endearing, but didn't understand much about it. I did wonder why she didn't tell her mother, but that is where my thinking stopped. My thoughts were 'Well, some of Alexander's future behaviour might take me by surprise!' or 'I wish I had her courage to act on my emotions when I was made to wear something I did not like'. Years later I came across two more stories that substantiated my initial beliefs regarding reasoning skills.

PIERCE'S STORY

Pierce wanted to go and buy sweets with his dad. Minutes before their departure he dropped his shoes in the pool, drenching them. His father explained, 'Now that your shoes are wet we cannot go out and you cannot get sweets until the shoes dry out' (*pragmatic reasoning*).

A few days after the incident, my little friend's favourite visitor arrived at his house. After some time he announced his intention to depart. Pierce left the room for a few minutes and returned to tell his mum, 'I dropped X's shoes in the pool. Shoes are wet now. X can't go home now!' (His reasoning skills stemmed from a combination of 1, 2, 3 and 4 above.)

I chose to share this funny example because of its similarity with Grandin's story and because it shows reasoning. The difference between Pierce's and Grandin's examples are that Pierce explained his reasons whilst (at that time) Grandin didn't.

Your child's actions stemming from literal reasoning will seldom be the right ones. However, when your child feels free to talk about his reasons you will be able to find out *how he thinks, his motivation and intentions.* If your child remains non-verbal you are left guessing.

If you don't teach him about the importance of sharing his reasons with you, he might not know why sharing his reasons is important. If you don't inspire your child to share his reasoning with you, he could think that you can 'mind read his reasons'.

Without Pierce explaining his reasons for his actions, they could have been easily misinterpreted and labelled malicious or unruly. Pierce's intention was to keep his visitor and his action was motivated by the fact that he liked that visitor – social enjoyment. His choice of action stemmed from a past event – his shoes getting wet prevented him from going out. Therefore if he could get his visitor's shoes wet, the visitor would have to stay. There are two distinctive points to note:

- Pierce applied literal reasoning – copied an identical event.

- Pierce exercised generalisation skills. He applied the reasoning to prevent the other person from leaving because he wanted to *prolong (not avoid) social interaction.*

A similar aged non-autistic would have asked the visitor to stay longer. My little friend hadn't reached that stage yet because he didn't know that words could achieve the same desired effect.

By the same token, should your child engage in activities that end up with china being broken, it is highly likely that your child enjoys the sound of shattered glass. If your child understood that you are fond of a particular object, he would not deliberately or otherwise destroy it (*motivation and intention*). Assuming that the autistic child deliberately destroyed something, tells you about it and tells you why he did it, you can begin celebrating his *verbal reasoning.*

You are able to influence your child's line of thinking when you can hear it and identify where it 'goes in an unsafe direction'. How do you know if your plan of action works? You experience the difference.

BEXXY'S STORY

Strapping a non-verbal autistic child into the car is a battle for most of us parents. Taking a different route to school or to the shops could end up with our child screaming, biting or hitting. Why? This story illustrates just one possible reason as to why a child might scream during a car journey.

Told by her parents that they are going to visit her grandmother, Bexxy (then 14) stepped into the car. She is a photographic learner, which means that she knows the route even if she cannot read the map. As the car covered a few miles and she could not recognise the place, slightly alarmed she asked, 'Where are we going?' They replied, 'To visit grandma.' Unknown to her they had a surprise stop destination.

Bexxy began to panic and screamed her question, 'Where are we going?' The answer did not change so she demanded that her father stop the car. He ignored her request. She started to scream and opened the door, ready to jump out of the moving car. The parents, confused by her outburst, became concerned over their daughter's mental state.

Years later in my living room, Bexxy, her mother and I talked about this incident. This time we laughed. On the table there is a crude map of their house, grandmother's house, the usual route and the route they had taken that day. What made Bexxy want to jump out of the car? It wasn't her mental state. First, there was her need for preciseness. She knew of only one route. Therefore, the verbal statement of her parents did not match her knowledge of 'how we get to grandma'. Second, there was her fear of the unknown. This could have been prevented if the parents had told her that they were taking a different route and had drawn a map.

What reasoning did Bexxy use?

- *Literal reasoning* – she had seen people jumping out of cars on TV.

- *Protective reasoning* – she was afraid to a state of panic because she didn't know where they were going.

- *Verbal reasoning* – but not extensively enough as she had no means of explaining her fear and her parents were unaware of her fears.

- *Individual reasoning.*

Exercise

List a few of your child's activities that puzzle or exasperate you. In the light of what you have just learned about literal reasoning, try and figure out what he really wanted to communicate through those activities. Approach him and try talking to him about it. Model the right way of going about it. If you cannot find a solution, describe the activity and contact us via the website.

Notes

1. Practical, realistic, matter-of-fact, no-nonsense, down-to-earth, rational, plain speaking.

2. A personal perception of a little, e.g. if you like sweets, a little could mean 1 kg; if you don't like sweets, a little could mean one bite.

3. A meaning that changes and is dependent on context and on the individual's interpretation.

4. See Chapter 3, A strict need for accuracy, p.34.

5. For more examples, see Chapter 9, 'Other behaviours'.

2 1

Teaching to quantify

Money and numbers

I read that although a child might be very good at counting, he may never be able to understand money. Thus shopping independently would never be a viable option. I believed it and panicked. After a few days I came up with a strategy that was meant to keep Alexander motivated to interact, help him *quantify* numbers and understand money. Alexander loved trains and numbers. On a piece of paper I drew 17 circles the size of a £1 coin. Alexander needed £17 before he could buy his train. Every day he stuck £1 on the paper. Every day I asked him to count his money. On the first day I asked him, 'How much money do you have on your paper?'

Pointing at his first pound he counted aloud, '£1.'

The second day I asked, 'How many pounds do you have?'

Counting aloud, he replied, '£1, £1.'

'I see you have £2 there.' I tried to help him expand and invited him to count with me. Pointing at his paper I counted aloud, '£1, £2, you have £2, see!'

Alexander's reply remained unchanged, 'No £2, £1!' The same story happened every day until the tenth day. I began despairing, fearing that my child couldn't learn to understand money.

One of his play helpers decided to help him along and brought him five £1 coins. David told him, 'I know you really want this train so I thought I'd help you own it sooner. Where is your paper? Let's stick all these coins on it and see how much money you have.'

Eagerly, Alexander stuck on all the coins but wasn't impressed at all. According to his understanding, he had only £1. Up to 15 he counted, '£1, £1, £1, £1…' I decided to break my initial decision and gave him two more £1 coins. Alexander, David and I went to the toyshop, ready to purchase the train. Throughout our short trip, Alexander remained panicky, chanting in a desperate voice, 'I have only £1. I need £17!'

Reassuringly I repeated, 'You have all the money you need in your bag. Just give them to the lady and ask for the train.' In the shop, two minutes passed before Alexander gathered enough courage to approach the sales lady. In broken English he asked, 'I want that train, the red one!' The young lady knew about Alexander's autism and wanted to be as helpful as possible. Kindly she asked for his moneybag. Alexander was terrified but really, really wanted the train. *He had the motivation and I was exploiting it!*

As the lady emptied the coins from his bag and began counting, Alexander *echoed her.* This time his echoing sounded different. It had added intonation, an intonation filled with excitement *unlike* echolalia. When she finished counting he stared at me in dismay and exclaimed, 'Mum, I have £17. I can buy the train!' Joyful tears drenched my face. Alexander had clicked. I don't know how it happened but it did. Now Alexander has his own pocket money and no problems understanding money.

In this example the autistic-friendly environment meant:

- acknowledging that Alexander might have a problem understanding money

- using his interest and finding a way to overcome the problem

- acknowledging that just because one day he could not see that one plus one equals two, he might still comprehend the concept if we persevered.

As a matter of interest, Alexander and I have heated debates over the subject of taxation. His latest question is 'What does the taxman really do as in real work to earn his money?'

The difference between 'learned' and thought-out answers

It is very easy to test if your child understands the link between numbers and quantity. I have watched many children counting from one to ten whilst lifting their fingers. It was both amazing and insightful to see how a child up to the age of four would answer 'How old are you?' with the right number of years and the wrong number of fingers. What can we learn from this? Every child, autistic or not, needs time to understand quantification. If a child replies with 'I am three years old' but shows the wrong number of fingers, he is repeating a 'learned answer' – his speech is echolalic.

The difference between a non-autistic and an autistic child is that the autistic child's speech remains echolalic longer. An autistic child needs more time and/or visual prompts to comprehend the link between numbers and quantity.

Test

Ask your child to bring you, say, three Lego bricks or four grapes. If he brings you the exact amount, then he understands quantity and numbers. If he doesn't, then you can teach him the link. After he masters the concept of 'quantity', he can use it generally because *generalisation skills develop from understanding*.

How can you teach quantification? Each time you give him a piece of toast you might like to cut it into two, four or eight little squares. Make a big point of it and tell him 'I brought eight bits of toast' or if he wants a sweet you can say 'One sweet, two sweets or three sweets?' Offer him one sweet and say 'Here is one sweet, and here are two sweets' and so on.

Food for thought

Alexander loved his marble run. Before we developed a shared system of understandings, I tried asking him 'How many marbles would you like?' and showed him a fistful of marbles. He grabbed them all and left me staring. You can only ask and/or teach a child who is willing to listen.

Converging parallel realities

Pointing at a girl he said, 'That boy pushed me!'

At the end of Alexander's first day at school I was standing in the school grounds with my arms wide open. I hugged my smiling son as he ran to me and felt proud of him. Our hug and my thoughts were interrupted by his shouted-out words. Pointing at a girl he said, 'That boy pushed me!' My first thoughts were 'What on earth was my son doing? Couldn't he see that the child was a little girl?' I was faced with another hard reality. My son spoke, but his words did not reflect reality. I wondered why.

Many years later a 33-year-old friend let off steam and said, 'What is all this fuss about us autistics not knowing what you look like? Do you know that we don't know what we look like!' No, I did not know that. I felt over-whelmed once more. Two more years on from this short conversation, I asked one of my visiting friends, 'If we met on the street could you recognise me?'

'No.'

I had to find out why she didn't know what I looked like. She explained that a street filled with people equates with a visual bombardment too fast to decode. The next thing I asked was, 'If I close my eyes, will you look at my face? I promise not to open my eyes until you say it is OK.'

Eventually my friend agreed. After 20 minutes she said, 'You may open your eyes.' She continued looking at me and said, 'You have brown eyes.' My eyes were weeping tears of joy. She was able to see my face! Alexander also learned to recognise my face and the faces of other people. How did the transformation take place? Patience, empathy, the right environment for interaction and a road littered with trials and errors but never short of love.

Food for thought

This book is not meant to teach you how to 'cure' autism or how to 'behaviour modify' your child. It wants to show you how to connect with your child's soul, enjoy his love, make allowances and become his guide.

The message from my friends is 'I am not a *dog in need of training*. My soul needs the love of your soul. I would not point at a girl and call her a boy if I was equipped to distinguish the difference! *Help me, don't punish me!* If my words aren't quite right, model them for me so I can repeat them the right way. Don't give up on me.'

Are there any limitations to learning/teaching?

The only limitations to your child's unaided learning stem from the way in which he perceives the environment. The only limitations to your teaching stem from your understanding of his perception of the environment:

1. You can *guide* him towards seeing the differences but *cannot make* him see it.

2. You can *show* him what you consider fun but you *cannot make* him have fun. Your child likes having fun but at times noise, heat or other factors stop him.

3. You can make him *talk* but you cannot make him *communicate*. He talked before you tried to make him talk but he has not talked with you.

4. When you hear him crying during behavioural therapy he is hurting. He stops crying because he has surrendered, not because he made sense of it. You can give him reasons and motivate him to communicate.

5. You can talk to him but you cannot make him hear you. He needs you to help him hear you.

6. You can hug him but you cannot make him like it. You can find alternatives to hugs and he will like that.

7. You can explore your differences together and grow stronger together.

8. You don't have to teach him how to learn. He has been learning all his life. His learning is affected by his sensory system and you have to find out how.

Once you have helped him become a willing student and once you have begun working with his will, you can help him communicate and enjoy his love, but you cannot make him less autistic just as he cannot make you less non-autistic. Those who tell you that you can are preying on your despair.

Once your child communicates with you, you still cannot make him feel the pain if he cuts his wrists or if he cuts the inside of his mouth when for fun he chews sharp objects. What you can positively do is to teach him why he should stop. He will trust you, listen to reason and stop. *Autism is not an impediment to reason.*

What I hope for is that after he communicates with you, you will discover and enjoy his 'added' ability that only autism brought about. Until then, autism is cruel to both of you. Autism in itself doesn't hurt your child and it doesn't hurt you. The lack of meaningful communication, your guilt, your tiredness and his frustration do.

The issue of cure

I would like you to leave this book inspired to bring joy into your child's soul and not preoccupied to stop at all costs your child's behaviour. I hope you are inspired to remodel your everyday interaction into loving interaction aimed at discovering shared meanings. Millions of people live an autistic reality and are expressing it in millions of ways. Every personal account given by an autistic person is one possible way in which autism could manifest itself. The internet is filled with hundreds of personal accounts from which you can learn more.

The people who live the autistic reality are the true experts in the field of autism. Your role is to become the expert in communication whilst your child is the expert in his autism. The reason why interaction is not a therapy per se is because your child is not looking for you to provide him with a cure; nor is he aware of why you feel so much pain. Unlike cancer, autism doesn't hurt him. Therefore your child is not actively looking to you for a cure. Instead he is looking to you for love, acceptance, understanding, help and protection.

Lessons in empathy

One common description of how autism manifests in a person is described as 'the child lacks the ability to empathise with others'. My question is whether we empathise with them. If not, why don't we? What stops us? I believe that unless we are autistic ourselves there is no possible way of knowing *what it must feel like to be autistic.* We could blindfold ourselves for days on end and possibly feel what *it must be like* not being able to see, but there is no way of imagining what *it feels like.* Nor could we understand and empathise with the emotion of a person who once had the ability to see and then lost it. We cannot blindfold ourselves and thus feel our children's frustrations when we cannot understand what they want to communicate. We can open our hearts and minds and second-guess their wants until we guess them right. If you were your child, wouldn't you like your parents to try and understand you?

Loving interaction should be perceived as a lifelong way of living together in equanimity. In a moment of my deepest despair, I confessed my realisation and my pain to my autistic friend, Feather. I realised that, contrary to what I had been told, my non-judgemental love could not cure autism and that my child's autism would not miraculously disappear. Society wasn't prepared to make allowances for him and he couldn't catch up with normality to meet the demands that come with living in a 'rat race' social set-up. My despair was triggered by his newly developed depressed behaviour. Seven years after Alexander's diagnosis, I panicked and felt worse than the day when I was first told that he had autism. I resented my moment of weakness that led me to choose to believe in miracles. What a waste of time and emotion! That belief and the lack of understanding of autism clouded my judgement.

Patiently Feather heard my cries. I guess I found most of my hope for a better future without a cure from her. As an attempt to help me through this emotional time she sent me The Serenity Prayer. As a non-religious person I found it very calming and thought provoking. In essence it said, 'Give me the power to accept what I cannot change…and then love and hope.' My analytical self had a question. What exactly am I being asked to accept?

Example

Did I have to accept that my son needs to flood the bathroom or was I to accept that he loves water and that flooding the bathroom is not his agenda?

Was I to accept that he cannot talk to me or was it that he found it hard to talk and therefore I had to find a way to empower him?

Was I to accept that autism prevents him from joining the 'rat race' or to accept that not all of us were designed to join the 'rat race' and that it is not healthy anyway? She also asked:

- 'Does it bother you when you cannot understand me or your son?'

- 'Does it really bother you when you cannot understand autism?'

- 'Can you not just love him without understanding him?'

I answered her questions with a deep sigh and a yes. I was in tears and my heart was aching, but I lacked the words to describe why I was feeling that way. It took me two more years and the writing of a book to clearly separate autism from autism and to stop hurting. Without realising this clear distinction I would have never been able to:

- shelter my son from doing harmful things to himself

- teach him language so that he may talk to me about his problems

- provide him with comfort through a *hug*

- stop chasing this non-existent 'miraculous' cure.

Alexander did want a hug, but not the easy physical thing we all do. He needed a room; volunteer friends; a change of attitude on my part; my friendship and acknowledgement of his perception of reality; my knowledge about how his mind works and where my understanding failed me. He needed my acceptance.

Cherishing your child

Open your heart to *your* child and figure out for yourself *what your* child would want you to provide for him, so the communication bridge between your parallel worlds grows solid and long lasting. This book is dedicated to all the people who wish to befriend and feel the joy of friendship when fathering, mothering or befriending an autistic person. It is also dedicated to Alexander and my friends' efforts towards making themselves understood.

Just as there are Oscars for best performances, I wish there were thousands of mini-Oscars for every child who breaks his silence and speaks his mind and heart with you. Then, and equally, thousands of mini-Oscars should come to life to embrace the parents who made it possible for the child to speak his mind.

In Chapter 1 I asked you to imagine autism and autistic as a different culture. Remember that, but do forget it sometimes. Your child's soul, his unspoken love for you and his love for life are the same as yours. Your child is not an alien. He is a human being. His hugs feel just as reassuring as your hugs, his smile is just as powerful as yours and his tears convey just as much pain as yours. Remember that the next time the two of you cannot make sense of each other. No establishment could love your child more than you. Your child's present and future difficulties need not be those of Paradox's, Feather's, Bexxy's, Tom's, Pierce's, Alexander's or other Alexanders of this world. His path is unique. Who else can cherish and nurture him? *Only you.*

The following stories represent only a handful of possible outcomes for your child. Please try not to predict or identify your child's future development with any of the examples used. I believe that good parents do not behave like prophets or dictators. They are the embodiment of a protector and a mentor.

A bridge built on perseverance

I told a doctor friend of mine that I had played with a child for six months before he spoke his first word. To that she replied, 'You must be patient.' Then again if she were the mother of that child she would find the patience and the will within herself to do the same. This is where autism must become more than a subject we study and love plays an indescribable part.

Then, I told her that after he spoke this one word he plunged back into silence for another year. To that she said, 'It must have been a fluke, this sounds like science fiction.' On hearing this story you might think that there is no point in further trying, or on the contrary you might be inspired to continue trying. You might be curious to find out why he stopped talking. We used to run together up and down the room, tapping our chests, with me trying my level best to copy his sounds. At the end of each run I waved at him and said 'Hi'. We did this for about 15 minutes before for one moment he interrupted his running, looked towards me, his facial muscles showed him concentrating and thinking hard and five seconds later he said 'Hi'.

In my excitement I clapped my hands and praised him loudly, but I had scared him and sent him back into his 'silent bubble'. My voice sounded too loud for his sensitive hearing. Add to that the sound of my clapping and you have a child overwhelmed by sound alone. During my early learning years I did not know about the link between autism and audio processing disorder. I was completely unaware about some children's extreme sensitivity to sounds. Nor did I know how to identify the behaviour that helps me spot the child who doesn't hear speech as speech. I had not read about it or met the people who exposed me to this knowledge.

It follows that Jamie saying his first word was not a miracle and not a fluke. For one brief moment, he heard speech as speech and naturally copied it. I would have given any amount of money to repeat whatever it was that was right about that unique moment only to hear him talk again. But this isn't about money; it is about you adapting your interaction to suit your child's understanding of it and perseverance.

In 2000 I invited a group of healers into my playroom and brought them one child at a time, my little friend included. They were silently sitting in the four corners of the playroom. When he chose to approach them they played with him. They only wanted to see if their unconditional love could be helpful. After about half an hour my little friend felt something, stood up and said, 'I can hear.' I have learned from this group of healers (people who knew nothing about autism but knew plenty about unconditional love) that sitting silently around a child, *not doing* while keeping company, had its own value and that shared silences could lead to *a child talking unaided*.

If your child is non-verbal, you can help him say his first word and his second and third without being a miracle worker or believing in miracles. You can also help your talking child make sense of the words he is already using, and you can help your child grow wings of self-confidence. Be prepared to feel frustrated most of the time, but please don't give up.

One year went by before I went to revisit my little friend who had spoken the single word. Half an hour after my arrival he remembered who I was. He came to me, held my hand and smiling pulled me into the kitchen in front of the drinks cupboard. With his eyes focused on mine, he smiled and waited. As I reached for the drink his eyes followed my hands. Once I had the drink in my hand he pulled me towards the sink giggling.

He took his drink into the living room where he watched over and over the logo of a Walt Disney tape. I observed his body language as he was watching it. I took the remote controller in my hand. As soon as I could spot delight on his face I pressed the pause button. He looked at me, looked at the tape and rewound it once more. I again pressed the pause button so that he could see the frozen image of the half circle of light. He rewarded my efforts with a smile and left the room. A minute later he returned with another tape. His facial expression mirrored that of a 'man on an important mission'. I presumed that there was something on that new tape that either did not make sense or that he liked very much. We repeated the process of spotting what it was.

Silently, he approached me and sat on my lap. As I pressed the pause button he embraced me. Looking at the television and still embracing me, he smiled. A 'gurgle of sound' coming from the back of his throat warmed my heart. As if chained together in a long loving embrace, he pushed his body closer into mine and together we rocked back and forth as I whispered in his ear 'I love you so very much'. I remember wishing that he might just unleash his potential and talk to us. It did not happen that time. Instead, holding my hand, he guided me into another room towards a cupboard filled with tapes. My first thought was to wonder how much information is stored in his mind and when it will be unleashed.

The same day I delivered a box of Brio trains to Pierce. The once non-verbal child received my present with an explosion of sounds, a cuddle and a huge smile. He voiced his excitement in one long breath, 'Oh my God, look at all this Brio, you brought me the Brio, and the Sydney bridge, and the turning platform… Where are the curved tracks? And wow I can go upstairs and play, let's tip the box out.' As I am writing these words I feel my emotions choking me. In the introduction, I have said that there are no means of predicting how far and how fast a child can develop. This is what I meant.

I cannot become something that I am not

I left their homes and my thoughts returned to my son Alexander. I remembered modelling words for him hundreds of times, pausing tapes for him, drawing the missing parts, buying the Brio, hating the Brio, loving the Brio, teaching him the concept of money – all that effort just to hear him talk to me. In the end he talked for me, at me, to me and with me. Now, with the passing of each day, he talks more and more and expresses a perception of this world that I had not been ready for. That is: *I am different and will remain different. I love you and I need you to love me but don't ask me to be something that I am not. I am not asking you be like me. Don't make me do things that make no sense to me. Teach me 'sense', teach me how to relate to you but accept that what you think is fun I may not experience as fun. I love your company when you are kind to my differences and I am afraid of you when you are not.*

Affected by autism or not, your child is a child. Whether your child is verbal or not, whether he is two years old or 40 years old, for as long as you live your child is a child. Don't let your sorrow or your fears rule your actions. Try not to let reason alone block your vision of love. Whilst love cannot cure autism, interaction monitored by love and reason together can make you the best mentor he could wish for.

2 3

Are social interaction and communication possible without a cure?

Yes and yes – the issues are not about cure and independent[1] living as much as they are about:

- quality of life

- quality of interaction and help

- your ability to remain patient and resourceful when faced with his lack of responsiveness

- your efforts to teach your child interdependent skills

- your clear vision – that is, helping your child to find and pursue something he is good at, be it trains, buses, puzzles, dinosaurs, vacuum cleaners, etc.

The following questions were answered by an autistic friend of mine, when I was trying to find a common ground and shared understanding between my perceptions of what was needed and what she perceived that was needed. I was also trying to find out answers about 'cure/s'.

What would happen if I didn't help my child at all?

I don't know if I can even start to answer this question. No help is a very bad stand to take. I know that 'no help' impacts the life and self-esteem of the AC. Even stumbled attempts are better than blinding yourself to an AC's needs.

Educate yourself and listen to the AC. I would also seriously ask yourself your motives and thinking of 'helping'. Do you wish to help the AC or help yourself deal with them? There is a difference and those differences greatly impact the outcome of what your help will do.

Does an autistic person want to be cured?

I think that the issue of wanting to be cured differs from person to person, but I have found that most do not wish to be cured.

For an autistic person to be 'cured' would mean becoming a person unlike himself or herself. The very thought of curing translates in my mind as me being unacceptable as who I am.

That society wishes to change what *is* uniquely me for their own comfort with little regard to the identity of the person or people that they speak of.

Personally, I feel that this way of thinking is quite 'childish' on the part of society (i.e. if you do not play the game of life like I want I will just take my ball and go home…) and leaves me to believe that issues of other minorities in the world have little hope of being accepted either. As if to say to the black minority 'You will be accepted if we cure your skin colour', to say to the Jews 'You can be accepted if only you cure your religious beliefs', to say to women 'You will be accepted with equal pay and respect if you cure your gender', etc.

What a bunch of mixed messages I get from society! How can I stand individually as the differences in snowflakes, the beauty of the hues of the rainbow, the vast uniqueness in species of animals and then turn to look at the person sitting next to them and wish to make them a clone of themselves?

This whole world, autistic or otherwise, is screaming for acceptance and understanding for individuality. And their cries are answered with labels denoting them as lesser beings and their individual ideas never added to the collective thoughts that could make this world a better place.

Can an autistic person learn how to communicate?

My reply was:

> An autistic person communicates all the time. We may not like what he wants to say or how he is saying it. The way in which he communicates those wants may not make sense to all the people around him…but he does communicate.

Her answer was more insightful than mine:

> I would have to say I agree with your answer. The question isn't how can the AC be taught to communicate but more of how we can get them to communicate 'our way'. An AC tries to communicate and make sense of the world all the time. Some of your communication style doesn't always go through and make sense, thus leaving us in confusion. This confusion I believe leads to the oh so much disliked response of the AC repetitively asking the same questions over and over and being thought a moron for not understanding when it was already answered…but was it really answered? I have found it being my experience that NT [normal] communication to come across is incomplete thought patterns with emotional displays and gesture to fill in the rest.
>
> Then the AC is to be expected to gain answers from that display of gesture and emotion… Big whole guessing game it is! One I am not good at! As I am sure other AC would agree.
>
> Personally I would rather continually bounce a ball than communicate that way. A ball gives you the same response and doesn't hide it in anything other than what is there. You force a ball down and it comes back to your hand. Simple action reaction with a distant answer for the question of 'What will a ball do if you force it down on the ground?' It doesn't roll around, make faces, laugh, yell or give an open-ended explanation and then come to your hand and say 'See that is the answer!'

Her answer reminded me about something I had read before: 'Even if a person affected by autism talks, he doesn't know what he is saying.' It riddled me. So if the child doesn't know what he is saying, how can I help him know? How can we hold a meaningful conversation if the words we are using don't mean the same thing to both of us? To illustrate this statement an example of a girl 'browsing' through a magazine was used. The author[2] asked his patient if she liked reading. The patient replied, 'No, I am just looking at the pictures [browsing].' The author concluded that this girl doesn't know that browsing meant reading.

From what I have experienced when talking with adult autistics I can further the point. Some of our children feel a need for great 'preciseness' in order to avoid confusion. Therefore reading will always mean 'reading the words' and browsing will always mean browsing (as in looking at pictures) – literal and precise. The lesson to be learned here is for us to talk with our children in a literal and precise way until they don't misinterpret, offend or feel fearful of a figure of speech. You will know when your child realises the differences between literal language and metaphor when:

- he will speak in a mixture of literal language and metaphor as well as wait for your reaction to what he had just said (conversation – not just talking *at* people)

- he will not scream or withdraw when teased (not that I recommend teasing)

- he will ask you to explain a sentence which contains metaphor

- he will laugh at your joke or make his own jokes.

Alexander's cartoons are exploiting the literal interpretation[3] of language. None of this was possible prior to Alexander accepting the concept of *double meanings of one word* – flexibility of thought.

Can an autistic person talk about emotions?

Yes. The following extract comes from a 22-year-old autistic friend. Just as Alexander used to hide behind various toys (when talking about emotions), she used several nicknames, depending on the topic of conversation (Paradox, Enigma or Me). She also contributed the story entitled 'The Bridge'. She was the first adult autistic with whom I had a conversation. As our conversation developed, so did my excitement. I invited her to spend Christmas with me and bought the plane ticket. Given that her communication skills were better developed than those of my son, I was looking forward to our time together.

Although my son was more emotionally secure than she was he hadn't the communication skills to discuss them. She accepted my invitation because *she was curious*[4] to meet me. Also she was *in love* and I lived in the same country as her fiancé. She became one of my long-term adult autistic guides. Picture her as a child at heart from whom life experiences robbed self-esteem and inner peace. Together we explored many emotional issues; I was hoping to enlist her help, to further understand some of Alexander's behaviour by talking to me about her own. She did. Six months after she left my home in 1999 I asked her if she found it easy to talk with me:

> Talking to you was usually OK. Not always, but you know that now.

> I actually talk better, about personal stuff especially, and with less stress if I am doing something – especially building or 'stimming'[5] (like spinning that ball on the cookie tin lid) at the same time. Then I can trick myself in a way into not paying too much attention to the person I'm talking to or what I'm saying so it's actually easier to say stuff.

Your child too could find it easier to talk about emotions if he is busy doing something else at the same time. Therefore don't ask him to look at you when he talks about personal emotions unless he chooses to.

Does an autistic child want to play with you?

Yes he does. It seems to me that because our childen don't actively seek our company, we begin to believe that they don't want to be around us. However, here is one insightful answer that I was presented with:

> Did you know that there were times when you could have 'played' with me (would have been OK with me) but didn't? I don't know if you knew and decided not to or were trying not to get in my space.

> Sometimes you ask me for something or if you can touch or play with something and I say 'no' so you don't (which is good), but if you wait, then in a minute *I will say 'yes'* (maybe or maybe not in words).

> Wasn't fair for me to get upset when I knew very well that you were only trying to be helpful. I also thought you might do that [leave the room] but didn't/couldn't tell you not to in advance. My fault.

By 'her fault', my friend means that *her speed of expressing what she wanted* wasn't there. Something your child could experience as well. My *own* fault was not knowing to *wait that much longer*. What she calls a minute could have lasted anything between one minute and half an hour, as if time just flies and she is unaware of how many minutes go by, similar to daydreaming. Once again, this could be something your child is experiencing.

Prior to my friend visiting my home she had had little opportunity to interact with other people. Therefore 'time' and 'passing of time' carried little meaning to her. As soon as you begin to 'shadow' your child he will realise that you are seeking his company. Most communication is non-verbal anyhow. If your interactive activities are filled with respect and fun he will begin to follow you.

Since my friend wrote this letter her life has changed in many ways. I last visited her in 2001 at her flat, which she shares with her fiancé and daughter. I found in her the same child at heart whom I first met; the difference being that this child had self-esteem, inner peace, an incredible love for life and more stories to tell than we had time for.

Your call

I hope that Paradox's and Alexander's stories were able to illustrate that autism is not an impenetrable wall but a way of being, and that your child needs your support to help him develop:

- the ability to 'listen, think, express'

- flexibility of thought

- meaningful and precise vocabulary

- emotional security and self-esteem

- his personal method of translating his visual thinking into verbal expressions.

In doing so his sources of pleasure will include social interaction/communication as opposed to solitary play. Solitary play is not always bad. Through increased play/interactive times you will learn:

- to identify the times when your child uses solitary play as enjoyment and when he uses it as a defence mechanism (his body language lets you know).

- how to wait for your child to respond to your verbal requests (verbally or through body language)

- the various meanings of his silences.

In turn your child will use language and body language interactively. He will learn to adapt his language and body language. He will want to push his own communicative boundaries in his own time and at a pace that makes sense to him.

Notes

1. One autistic interpretation of our description of independent reads: 'Does it mean that people want me to live on my own? What if I want to live with a partner?' This interpretation illustrates once more the need to teach a child about various meanings of one word.

2. My personal observation: the author's native language was not English. When writing this book I had to consult the dictionary on numerous occasions to make sure that the information I am trying to convey reads as English. Please write to me if you find yourself confused by any term that I have used. As a matter of curiosity I looked up the word 'browsing': 1. not reading in detail, just browsing, scan, skim, and glance/look through. Thumb/leaf/flip through, dip in. 2. not buying anything, just browsing, look around, have a look, window shop, peruse. 3. cows browsing, graze, feed, eat, nibble, crop, pasture (*Oxford Paperback Thesaurus*). I think the autistic girl was right when she said that she wasn't reading.

3. See cartoons by Alexander Cowie in Appendix D.

4. See Chapter 12, Exploring social communication, p.126.

5. A self-comforting repetitive behaviour similar to twirling a strand of hair.

2 4

How to choose the right approach

One common statement that I came across was: 'There is no one universal way of treating autistic children. Each child is different and what therapy works for one child doesn't necessarily work for another.' With the risk of becoming more repetitive than an autistic person, I will say it again. *Interaction is not a therapy aimed at treating autism.* The concept of interaction describes our conduct during interactive moments with a child whose senses are sending mixed messages to his brain. These mixed messages make it harder for him to make sense of reality as perceived by us. Your role as a mentor is therefore very clearly defined. *You are there to help him relax. You want him to want to interact more and then during shared attentive moments you are teaching him shared meanings.*

Furthermore, for example, I the non-autistic have the ability to empathise with what it must feel like not to hear words or with the difficulty when trying to talk to someone over blasted-out music. The non-verbal autistic child has no idea what it must feel like hearing words, but he can already empathise with the irritation experienced by you when you cannot project your voice over loud sounds. Therefore I will motivate myself to create a silent environment for interaction to increase my child's chances of hearing me. At least this way he stands one chance as opposed to no chance.

My heart was left bleeding after I met the children who were exposed to behaviour modification techniques aimed at communication. Most 'helping' techniques are stripped of love and understanding, yet they are financed. They are financed by public money because scientific evidence proved that children learn words and the autistic behaviour can be modified to that end. I never understood why that was enough of an argument to win financial support. Call that 'my autism' if you like. It will not offend me. When the child grows old enough he runs away from places where those techniques are practised. He runs away searching for freedom, yet no one runs away from gathering more knowledge, from learning to make sense, from love or respect.

I met the child who knew 1000 words but never put a sentence together. During his programme all he had learned was to feel afraid of people. I have also sheltered people who ran away from those techniques and rubbed cream on their self-inflicted scars. I received phone calls from autistic people after an article that described autistic behaviour as 'manic' made the headlines. They shared their desire to phone the writer but they were afraid of being labelled 'manic' for phoning in. What a vicious circle, don't you think? There are children who continue to be tied to their beds, locked in solitary confinement or placed under heavy sedation – all that to teach them not to behave in an autistic way. It makes me wonder what happened to us, we the non-autistic people?

As further reading I strongly recommend Tony Attwood's (1998) book. Tony Attwood is a clinical psychologist and he approaches autistic people with respect and empathy.

Autism speaks a universal language

Riding through a Mexican village, I watched a boy walking out of his garden into the middle of a mud road. He was gazing at the sun through a McDonald's straw. Whilst he was showing his excitement through flapping his arms, our eyes met for a brief second. My elder son, who watched me from a distance, tapped my shoulder and reminded me that we were on holiday. I doubt that his parents knew that their 12-year-old child had what we call autism, or that they were worried over their child not being 'an active contributor to society'. I knew there was no school in the village and most people did not know how to read or write. I do believe however that his parents felt just as much pain as any parent in the world for not being able to talk to their son. Yet through love alone, they didn't lock him up to hide him from society. Instead they allowed him the freedom of smiling at the sun.

In December 1999, my children and I were sitting on the beach watching the sun go to bed into the Pacific Ocean. My gaze dropped to a little boy helping himself to a handful of sand. Silently he sat there studying it intently, and before long a second handful of sand made its way into his mouth, and soon the next, and the next. His face lit up with pleasure as if he tasted a rare gourmet dish. Parallel memories of Alexander eating sand with equal pleasure came back to mind – only now five years on, Alexander was busy talking to his brother and sister, choosing the restaurant for that night.

The little boy's mother came running and picked him up. I eavesdropped to hear her say in a half-scolding and half-desperate voice, 'How many times did I tell you that eating sand is bad for you?' The boy did not seem to listen and started wriggling in her arms. A scream followed and she had to let him down. As soon as his feet touched the ground he ran off with her chasing after him. It was like watching myself chasing after Alexander. I found myself wondering how this child would be taught to communicate. Will he be beaten? Will he be played with? How will his mother react when she finds out why her son loves eating sand? Will his father stay with them and be supportive or will the pain of having fathered a 'less than perfect child' make him leave?

A kinder world

How can we make a world that is kinder towards autistic people? Who would want to help the parent when he is tired? Would any charity in the world consider paying for a mother or father to stay at home and be on 'standby' for such a child? Would funds be available to train non-autistic people in the art of interacting with respect with autistic people?

For almost every other disability there is something mechanical to ease the difficulty. For autism there isn't. There is no white cane or guide dog, hearing aid, wheelchair, ramp, etc. For autism there is knowledge and love. There is education and a hope that the non-autistic would want to turn towards his inner kind self and befriend the autistic. In helping your child put thoughts into words, you cannot stop his life's ups and downs, but you can help him express them, share them and live a happier life.

'The bridge' by Kalen Molten

On numerous occasions Kalen (Paradox) was invited to talk about her autistic experiences at parent support group meetings. If your support group wishes to contact her she may be reached via e-mail (the address is prickle@softhome.net). This is how she describes her long-fought battle to make sense of our non-autistic demands unaided:

> I am sitting at the side of a wide, fast flowing river. My back is to the water. I am minding my own business, watching the trees and forest creatures. Suddenly a rope is around me, pulling me towards the water. I struggle as I am pulled in. The rope slips around my neck, continuing to pull me as the current carries me downstream. I manage to free myself from the rope and swim back to shore on my side of the river, nearly strangled, and completely exhausted.

> Again I sit down, wet and cold, my back to the river, and try to carry on enjoying the forest. But I am nervous. I look behind my back, but see nothing on the other side. Again I am suddenly interrupted, this time by something hitting me on the back of the head. I am knocked down and lay unconscious for some time.

> When I regain consciousness, I look around me, dazed and confused. I see a brick beside me, but do not understand its purpose or why it hit me. I run away from the riverbank into the forest. But eventually I return to my favourite spot to find a few more bricks lying there. I am more nervous now and will not turn my back to the river again. The forest is not the same peaceful place it was.

> Another brick flies at me. Again I am surprised, but this time I am a little more prepared and manage to dodge before it hits me. I begin to seriously wonder what this is about. I am angry and frightened.

> I stand, watching the other side of the river, ready to run. All enjoyment is lost. I am on the alert for unexpected attack. I want to run away, but I am intrigued by where the bricks are coming from and what the purpose of this activity is.

> Another brick. This time I throw it back, but I am not strong enough to get it to the other side. It splashes in the water. I yell loudly, in fear and anger. The forest animals are frightened away.

> There is no activity for a long time. I assume the attackers have given up. I lie down and fall into a light, fitful sleep. I am awakened by someone picking me up. They carry me into the water, towards the other side. I do not want to go to the side of the water where the bricks

come from. I struggle and bite and kick until they are forced to drop me. Again, I swim back to my side. They are forced to return to theirs.

More bricks come. I have grown stronger now. A few bricks reach the other side when I throw them. Occasionally I hear yells when one reaches its mark. I continue throwing them back one by one until I am too exhausted to fight back any more. I sit down, prepared to be killed by the next flying brick. I cannot run or hide or fight. Again, I fall asleep.

When I awaken, I find a paper aeroplane next to me. On it is scrawled some writing in a language I do not understand. I study it for some time. As I sit with the note, another brick comes at me. It is not thrown directly at me, so I needn't dodge. This time there is a rope from the other side of the river attached to the brick. Not understanding its purpose, I untie the rope.

Again there is peace for some time until another brick with a rope attached lands some distance downstream. I untie the rope, but this time I hold it. I sit and examine the rope and follow it with my eyes to its origin. Someone is there. I do not know if it is the same person who picked me up earlier. I am afraid, but hold onto the rope.

Soon there is a strong tug on the rope. A small boat is attached to the other end and pushed into the river. I pull it to my side of the river. In the boat are a saw, some more rope, a hammer, and some nails. Still confused, I study the items. Uncertain of what I am expected to do. I am left alone for a long time.

I have learned to use the saw to cut down trees on my side of the river, though I have no use for the logs. For the first time in many days, another item comes from the other side. This time it is diagrams of a bridge across the river. I have no idea why I would wish to cross such a dangerous river to what is obviously a dangerous and frightening place inhabited by aggressive people.

But I have a drive to build. I do not understand the written instructions with the diagrams, and in many cases the diagrams are wrong. I work for many weeks at deciphering the code and making corrections. Nothing more arrives from the other side.

Using the bricks that arrived first, I build a solid base for the bridge. Slowly, I begin to cut and assemble logs to create a fragile but functional bridge. Still nothing arrives.

At long last the bridge is complete. I gather my special treasures, the tools, and the small boat and begin the perilous walk across the bridge. I do not know what awaits me on the other side. I am very afraid; I consider turning back at every step. Yet I know I cannot return because my side of the river is no longer peaceful and safe. I am always afraid of being hit and the animals now fear me because of my yelling and brick throwing. I am also intrigued by the other side and the puzzling way the people who live there have chosen to invite me.

As the river rushes by under my feet, I consider jumping in just to be rid of the fear and dread of what I am about to face. I look ahead, but see nothing on the other side. I don't know where I am going or why I am going there. I fear I will not understand them nor they me. I fear they have forgotten me.

Several steps from the other side, I lose balance under my heavy load and fall into the water. As I am carried downstream, I do not struggle to swim. If I am wanted, I will be rescued. If I am not, I will die. Now it is up to them.

I am rescued. As I stand there, alien to this land I have struggled so hard to get to, my rescuers are praised. I am not. Everyone seems to forget that although they gave me the tools, *I* built the bridge.

Depression and social conventions

My chance meeting with Bexxy was emotional and educational. Over two months she taught me about depression[1] and social conventions. Our souls got as close as any two souls ever could without touching each other. On many occasions she challenged me and on others she reminded me to joke. I made numerous mistakes and wiped away hundreds of her tears. She asked me thousands of questions and these are just a few:

- 'What is there to prove that I am the autistic one and that you are not or vice versa?'

- 'What is the purpose of going through life without hope and happiness?'

- 'Why do we have to go to school if we cannot cope with the pressure?'

- 'How can we tell when the other person is truly happy?'

- 'If God loved all the people doesn't he love autistic people?'

- 'Are you a soul doctor?' (I liked that!)

Her life story helped me identify what was going on in my son's mind, even if he couldn't express his needs as well as her. She taught me that talking eloquently doesn't mean that autism has gone (because the sensory side remains unchanged and the working memory gets tired of talking or gets 'clogged up' by too many words). The inner fear of not being able to live up to someone else's expectations and the tiredness stemming from confusion can be surpassed only if the 'rat race' is taken away from the autistic person.

Bexxy, the girl who ran away from her country, her foster homes and boarding schools that failed to understand her way of being, finally found some peace. All along she wanted to be treated as a human being, not as a patient in need of a cure, and to be at home with her mother whom she loved dearly, or at least have a flat near the parental home. After 16 years of misunderstandings about what autism meant, and with as little as one week of intensive interaction between her mum and herself, her wish came true.

A letter from Bexxy

Soffle 00–03–14 (3 March 2000)

The flat has one living room…it's really big and has a huge balcony (orange wallpaper)…and the view overlooking a huge part of Arvika is so nice!!! 1 bedroom (blue paper) very nice…a kitchen with enough space and a bathroom…and my own TV!!!

You're very welcome to visit me. I'd love that and so would my mum – she really likes you. Mum and I had a few hectic weeks together. I think me moving out will do us both good…and hopefully we'll be able to communicate better in the near future, without her being annoyed with my social habits and without me being annoyed with her habits (includes nagging)…we're both annoying each other.

Please write back and tell me all the news and what is going on in your life. I hope your kids are happy, and Chris. I hope it's working out for Alex so that he can study at home if that's the best… Well my hand is hurting from writing so I will stop now. Take care and see you.

Love Bexxy xxxx

PS deep question…ehhhh
Why do we screw up? Why do we misunderstand each other?
Answer: Cuz we don't think alike.

Cherishing Alexander

I lived to witness the tiredness and confusion described by Bexxy first hand in Alexander, with my other two non-autistic children suffering from it too. Between 1991 and 2000 Alexander transformed from non-verbal and exclusive into an interactive and verbal child as well as a mainstream student. I really thought that he was overcoming his autism (a myth) until once more our world fell apart. At the end of living in the 'rat race' for three years, towards the end of year six in junior school he became unable to keep up with the pressures and became depressed.

Friday 11 May 2001

We left England a year ago. Once again Alexander and my other two children are happy. During this year he acquired many new words, walks taller and talks about his wants more often. His smile is back. He stopped spitting and coughing (me really pleased!).

I feel he is less confused because he interacts more. He would like to become an inventor and design the biggest and most fun waterpark in the world. Watch this space! As for his speed of 'listen, think, express', it increased. However, if you compare his speed of expressive language with that of his younger sister, she is twice as fast. When we talk he will interrupt to ask, 'What did you say? What was that? Say that again.' No teacher would repeat and re-repeat himself just to suit Alexander. The grammatical structure of his spoken language improved and continues to improve.

If the three children perform the same building task, Alexander is slower but his finished product is perfect and robust. The slowness arises from his need for perfection and manifests itself through his attention to detail.

Emotionally he is more aware – one could say extremely aware – to a point where he is afraid to say something in case he upsets the other person. We spoke of school and he voiced his main problems:

- He needed more time to finish a piece of work.

- He found some material 'repetitive and boring'.

- He was upset because they practised every day for the SATS exams. Because of that the school dropped the only subjects that he liked – technology and art.

I asked him if he could remember any of the 'stuff' he learned in school. He answered, 'Not really.' During the run-up to our decision to leave the UK, all the signs that my son was distressed were there but I did not know what to do. An e-mail from his school assistant read: 'Alexander's "autistic behaviour" is on the increase during school hours.' Soon after the e-mail, I had to deal with another problem. Alexander tried to strangle the child who bullied him. As I arrived to collect him from school, Alexander ran to me and in one long breath said, 'Mum you must help me! I need your help!'

Worried, I asked, 'What happened?'

In a disjointed voice Alexander continued, 'Well…I strangled child X… only for a second… I had enough! He kept picking on me. I told the dinner ladies but they told me to ignore him. I can't ignore him! Now I am being punished.'

'How are you being punished?'

'I was told that I cannot play tomorrow and that I must stay in the classroom when the other children are playing. That is not fair. You must help me! I beg you.'

'We will sort this out,' I promised. Holding his hand we went to his classroom. I approached his teacher to verify his story. It was correct. Alexander tried to strangle this child who was allegedly innocent.

The next task was my hardest task ever. I knew that, if punished, Alexander would continue taking revenge. I told him that he must not take such actions against any child. What I didn't know was what constituted a workable solution. I approached the teacher and asked for her help in the matter. After much thought the teacher decided to allow Alexander back into the playground accompanied by two bodyguards. The bodyguards were two children who cared for Alexander. Their mission was twofold: protecting Alexander from bullies and preventing Alexander from attacking others. Did this strategy work? For the following two weeks Alexander's visible behaviour seemed calmer and the teacher must be commended for her efforts. What went through Alexander's mind we found out much later whilst in Romania.

Alexander's increased autistic behaviour, described by his school assistant in an e-mail, continued in Romania for a further six months. During the first two months he ran after any member of our family who said a wrong word – not that we knew what the wrong word was. As he was running after us with the intention of hitting, he shouted, 'No, you can't get away with this! I do care! I will not ignore anything!'

During the first four months he made guttural noises that sounded like a mouse squeaking. We found out later that he was talking to himself. The squeaky sound was the sound of his breathing in the back of his throat. His head-shaking habit continued for a further five months. As he shook his head he walked past us, ignoring any of our spoken words. If we enquired 'What are you doing?' he answered 'I am not doing anything'. His style of walking around gained him the nickname 'whirlwind'. Because he shook his head for most of the day, he crashed into a tree with his bike. I remembered being told that because of autism Alexander would be unable to learn how to ride a bike. Never did I envisage him crashing into a tree whilst 'riding and daydreaming'.

I felt as if I had lost my son again and had no way to reach him. Eventually his anger levelled out and the communication channels opened once more. What he had to say, share, ask, tell and wish for is a story in its own right. What did I feel during these months when all this took place? Defeat, despair and inadequacy. The desire to find a cure mounted. The knowledge that I gathered kept my own depression at bay and continued to fuel a desire to protect and help my son grow further. My brother, my sister-in-law and my niece replaced me for a while. I needed that break so badly. They did a wonderful job and I shall forever remain grateful.

What was the best thing about our stay? My children and I regrouped as a family. My non-autistic children had the opportunity (and used it) to leave the house and socialise with other children, without having to look out for their brother and without being labelled 'the brother or the sister of the autistic child'. I learned from them that they continue to wish for Alexander to be like them ('normal'). This wish doesn't mean that they do not accept Alexander. It only means that they could bond easier, they could talk faster and use metaphors without upsetting Alexander as well as expanding the length of a game they are playing.

Whatever happened to Alexander may not happen to your child. You might find similarities between my son and yours, but your child is unique and *your relationship is what matters most to you and your child*. You too could experience highs and lows. If you find only one friend to support you, consider yourself lucky. If the family steps in, consider it heaven sent. No stranger will love you and your child as much as a family can, and no stranger's judgement will hurt you as much as a family's judgement. Your child might be equipped to deal with being bullied. Only the time and trials of integration will tell you that. What will you do when your child is bullied? You decide, but remember your child looks to you for help not judgement.

Is a journey of understanding worth it?

This question I believe is personal to you. Thus I can only answer it from my own perspective. Communication brought our family unit closer together. Emotions such as tiredness, exhaustion, depression, fear, frustration and pain have been laid to rest. One could say that we grew strong together. We realised one of life's paradoxes. We are all individuals, yet our unity and family wholeness stems from our love for each other, helping each other and enjoying our differences. The children stopped comparing themselves to each other. Instead they are looking at ways of helping each other and furthering their own individuality and interests. As a mother I can delight in watching the children laugh together and I laugh with them (including at the old days). Life tastes good again. We travel together and include in our plans the contingencies for what can go wrong. We are better prepared.

In one breath I was once asked, 'Are you glorifying autism? Don't you want a cure for it?' I am not glorifying autism and yes I did want a cure for all the things that were hurting my son. But autism is not hurting my son. The reaction of other people to his behaviour is. My son would not draw the way he does if he did not have autism. He would not be able to imagine the spirals that he does if he did not have autism. His jokes wouldn't be as funny as they are if he did not have autism. I never asked to give birth to a child who would be diagnosed with autism, but I did give birth to one. I love Alexander dearly. Trying to understand him was a long journey. Trying to get other people to understand Alexander's autistic needs was much harder and consumed much of my energy. For many years, I was depressed but did not know it. The day I lost my voice, a dear friend dared tell me, 'I think you are depressed.' I thought I was losing my voice through smoking too many cigarettes.

With hindsight, turning our home into a sanctuary and building communication bridges with my son was easier than providing an environment where he can continue to grow now. The challenge today, as I perceive it, arises from a mixture of misunderstanding regarding what autism is and social conventions. In my early years I believed that once my child talked the problems were over. In reality, once my child began to talk the 'problems' started. Before he spoke he was considered too autistic and no educational establishment wanted him. He was 'my problem'. With our help and due to his efforts he became a mainstream student. When he couldn't survive the pressure, the blame was once more placed on him.

In fact Alexander needs time to 'listen, think, understand, express' and to ask again if something doesn't make sense. Then the process of 'listen, think, understand, express' happens again. This affected his school performance. When that happened his behaviour became markedly different from that of the other children. One or two children also noticed it and then made fun of him. Alexander was hurt and took revenge. A vicious circle began.

Alexander needed more time to process input, not that he was unable to process it. I asked a team of doctors to review my son's needs. I told them about the problems and asked if they would recommend home tuition for Alexander. The answer was: 'We have successfully integrated many children with autism into mainstream schools; therefore we can't recommend home tuition. We must think about his social skills.' Whilst a team of strangers to us is thinking or worrying about Alexander's social skills, away from being bullied for being autistic, Alexander is developing them at a pace that makes sense to him.

The only person who can integrate Alexander is Alexander, not me, not someone else! I can *offer him the opportunity* to integrate, guide him through integration, but I *cannot make him* integrate. I put the phone down and thought, 'Checkmate Florica, now what? Send Alex back to school so that he can strangle another child when he bullies him? Wait for Alexander to be expelled for bad behaviour and meanwhile watch him become more and more depressed? Or start home education once again and only part-time integration?'

As it happens he studies art in mainstream school and hopes to study design technology soon. But that is not the point. The point is that we parents have to be on guard at all times.

Social convention and fears

The economy of the country in which a child is born determines an autistic child's *entitlement* to education. Regardless of what country the child is born in, that child learns in an autistic way and in our 'ignorance' we are trying to teach him in a non-autistic way. Where should the autistic child be educated? Should he be educated in a school, a special educational unit or at home?

Integration

Integration is a hard task and has nothing to do with a child not wanting to integrate. A child such as Alexander becomes an easy target for bullies. Keeping him at home means that a member of the family must be with him at all times. If I were to have been born a few years sooner and if I were to have lived in a society that decided to genetically cleanse its nation, my child would have died and my husband and I would have been sterilised. Out of fear, I would have complied or ran away. However, I gave birth to my child in a free and civilised society. I guess I should be grateful to life itself for delaying my birth. Equally, I did not ask for people to seek shelter in my home and to open their hearts. I only opened my heart to their needs and the rest followed. Without them coming to my home, I would have nothing to share with you.

I have shared with you the knowledge that will get you closer to understanding the meanings of some of your child's behaviour and, it is hoped, prevent him from loneliness and depression. My son's initial inability to communicate helped me scrutinise my own fears and my own need to comply with social conventions. I hope that this book is helping you face and overcome some of your own fears and allowing you to make decisions about what would be best for your child without the fear of social convention.

Later, Alexander's developed ability to communicate took me on one of life's very intense roller-coaster rides. When we finished riding it, we as a family grew wiser and learned to live each day at its fullest. One could say that we helped Alexander see the other seven colours of the rainbow and he helped us see the unseen one – the eighth colour of the rainbow. In his silence or through his violent behaviour, your child is asking you to become his prism of love, so that within the continuum of life he may enjoy with you the seven colours of the rainbow whilst living in the shadow of his own white light.

Note

1. More information in Tony Attwood's (1998) book *Asperger's Syndrome: A Guide for Parents and Professionals*, published by Jessica Kingsley Publishers.

25

Hope–TLC and the Year of Promise

In 1998 I founded Hope–TLC, a philanthropic organisation, because I believed that money alone should not prevent a child from experiencing an approach to autism that stems from love and understanding. With its limited funds it offered what money could buy. Money can help set up a playroom for a child; buy a PC to help communication or food for an adult autistic because income support is not enough, etc. However, I came to believe that we couldn't quantify in financial terms the support that parents need. That was equally true for my adult autistic friends.

Money cannot buy friends and understanding. Money cannot hurry time and it cannot change your child's spatial and literal learning style. Yet love can inspire you to try new ways of reaching your child and that doesn't cost a penny. What each family seems to need is 'people power' and tender loving care for themselves to cope with the extra demands brought on by the child's autism. The autistic child in turn needs the love and infinite patience of his parents. This is a full circle in its own right.

An autistic friend of mine said, 'I wish for a child, but should my child be born autistic and be a "screamer" during his early years, would you look after him for me, because I cannot cope with screaming?' I agreed because I learned to know that the screaming doesn't last forever. As a founder of

Hope–TLC, I have recruited and trained many volunteers who have helped other children improve the quality of their own lives.

However, *the call for action is always with the parent and the family.* If you decide to embark on this journey, you can decide how far you take your efforts and your child's sensory system will determine how far he can travel towards shared meanings. A good mentor needs to share love, dedication, patience, imagination and a sense of humour.

During the year 2000, the Year of Promise in the UK, Hope–TLC promised to further the understanding of each individual need of an autistic person and to offer loving support to his parents. This is how you can make the promises work for yourself without spending money:

1. Don't feel guilty because your child has autism and don't spend time blaming the cause of it on each other.

2. Decide to befriend your child and learn to decode the meaning of his autistic behaviour.

3. Don't be afraid of your child's autism and within your home create a space for him that he may call 'autistic space' (even if it is his own bedroom).

4. Enlist the help of volunteers who are willing to befriend a child who is different. You can do this by asking your local paper to run this small advertisement that time and time again has proved effective:

   > Hope–TLC – Imaginative, friendly volunteers needed to befriend autistic child. Age irrelevant. Patience and the will to share your love of life is. Training given. Phone [your number]

5. Don't give up trying to teach him the role of language. Treat him with respect and don't subject him to inhumane modification programmes.

6. Teach yourself *to speak and behave in a literal way* until he can communicate with you.

7. When feeling exhausted seek help from family or friends and rest. Take time out so you can offer tender loving care to a frustrating child.

8.   Don't allow guilt to run you into exhaustion.

9.   Write to your MP and tell him that your child deserves humane treatment. Write that autism is a lifelong condition and describe the way in which *your child* presents his autism. Thus help dispel stereotyping of autistic people.

10.   Believe in yourself, trust your intuition and become a better communicator. Don't allow misunderstandings to stop you from empathising with your child.

11.   Hold on to your hope and don't allow others to prey on your despair.

12.   Seek counsel with your own heart and soul and then decide what actions to take.

May all your actions be fuelled by love and not by fear and pain.

Thoughts from the heart

What do we have to accept?

Whilst the autistic style of learning cannot merge with non-autistics and vice versa, the two realities can converge through meaningful interaction and shared understandings. Each person can become a better communicator and each person can become more accepting. Just like Feather said, 'Autistic or not this world is screaming for acceptance.'

For as long as I believed it to be my fault that Alexander was autistic and that for some unknown reason I was being punished, it was difficult for me to accept and observe my son's behaviour. I wanted it stopped because it acted as a reminder of 'problems'. Yet that autistic behaviour was my guide towards how much he understood, how he felt, what he wanted and what he did not want. Your child's behaviour means the same and you can become very skilled at unscrambling it. It is that simple: *having the courage to observe your child's behaviour and using your judgement to translate it into meanings.*

I know that every parent is born with that intuition because prior to your child being diagnosed you managed to understand him. Now take it a step further. Teach him to understand you. You may not be able to offer the acceptance of the entire world, but your child is one citizen of this world and he will thrive on your acceptance and love. If you direct your efforts at behaviour modification without understanding the meaning of that behaviour, you are in fact removing his only communication tool.

Equally it is more important for you to accept your emotions as and when you feel them. You don't have to be happy with your child's autism and you don't have to blame yourself for feeling pain, but don't allow others to manipulate you because of it. Making an environment in which your child can thrive and you can rest will allow you to communicate with your child. Whilst this or any other book cannot stop others from laying claim to cures, it can protect you through knowledge from being emotionally exploited.

Should any person claim that he *can* cure autism, ask him: 'Did you ever give lessons to the wind on how to blow? Or have you the power to demand the wind not to blow?' Should he ask 'What do you mean?' then ask another question, 'Can you make the wind sing?' And should he answer yes, then tell him that you *want* him to teach laughter to your child, and that your child should learn to sing a joyful song of life. Then let him meet your child and as they play observe your child. Intuitively trust your soul to tell you if his silent soul is laughing joy, which his big eyes exude with inner peace and laughter, or, if through screaming or through deepest silences, he's crying, seeking your protection. But should the teacher tell you that the wind must only blow the way he wants it when he wants, then teach that teacher that your child is human, remind him that the strongest human bonds and freedom were born from love, humility or laughter; not through humiliation, submission or compliance. Embrace your child and search for other answers.

An open invitation to better the interaction process

If you know of any non-intrusive and non-painful ways in which we can help an autistic child with any of the following, I would love to hear from you. A collection of solutions could then be published to help other parents 'cut corners' if such a thing becomes possible. The areas of interest are:

- helping a child hear words when he cannot distinguish the sound made by words from the background sounds

- help protect a child's hearing if it is too sensitive

- helping a child overcome his tactile and olfactory sensitivity

- helping a child not to feel overloaded by too much visual input.

Appendix A

Frequently asked questions

The answers in this appendix stem from my own experiences with autistic children and adults and are provided to help you decide if the principles of loving interaction could guide you towards delivering meaningful help to your child. Since 1993 I have devoted my life to *understanding* autism and the aims of my work have been:

- the promotion of understanding and respect for any autistic person

- practising and advocating humane interaction between non-autistics and autistics

- to empower parents or carers to deliver loving and effective help to the autistic child so that he may reach a comfortable level of self-reliance, independence and interdependence.

1. Can autism be cured?

No. I believe that the genetic differences between an autistic person and a non-autistic will always remain. Autistic people dislike the fact that normal people (NTs) want autism cured. An autistic child can grow to develop communication skills, social skills and interdependent skills. This doesn't mean that we have cured his autism or that he is faking normality. It means that he is able to translate his visual thinking and learning style into words (cognition) and that he is able to contain various discomforts and confusions arising from his sensory perceptions of environmental stimuli.

He is a unique individual who is able to use the acquired communication skills to contribute his unique perceptions of our world to a pool of universal knowledge as well as develop relationships based on love with others (see Chapter 4).

2. Does that mean that they don't want to be cured?

The people whom I befriended wanted help to make sense of the world around them. They did not want to be punished for their behaviour when they did not understand why we consider it wrong. They ask of us to explain everything and they ask us to go with the autism, not against it.

Each person is unique – autistic or non-autistic. Autism gives a unique perspective on the world to a unique person. From this unique perspective a unique ability evolves. This ability can be discovered and nurtured effectively when the person who lives close to the autistic accepts that autism is a way of being, befriends the human being and teaches him how to make sense of the world around.

3. Does autism mean the same as autistic behaviour?

No. Autism has a significant impact on a person's capability to make sense of our linear and verbal world. The observable 'autistic' behaviour is unique to each individual and happens as a result of:

- a sensory system that functions differently from the norm
- memory (short term, long term and working)
- spatial thinking and learning.

What we see as unacceptable or repetitive behaviour is not the same as what they see and experience. What we call repetitive could be experienced as or mean:

- spinning because I can't get dizzy
- rocking for comfort or because I am feeling lonely or frightened
- flapping my arms because I am nervous
- looking at flashing lights because they are beautiful
- biting people because they are physically handling me and I want them to stop
- covering my ears because the sound of other people's voices is hurting me
- bumping into a wall because I am not spatially aware
- having a tantrum in the supermarket because the shelves have been rearranged
- hiding under the table because I feel overwhelmed.

4. Is repetitive behaviour a sign of obsessive behaviour?

No. The meaning of repetitive behaviours ranges from a sign of confusion or an expression of learning to an expression of enjoyment.

5. Can an autistic person live independently?

Yes, and there are many examples of people who manage to live an independent life. They are the ones to ask about how easy or how hard they find this experience. No one has a crystal ball to tell the future of any person. The same rule applies to a person with autism. Often this question is in the front of our minds because our child has little or no independence or communication skills. You can help him to develop skills yet only life will answer the question 'Will *my child* be able to live independently?'

6. Can an autistic person learn to communicate?

Yes. He communicates all the time. We may not like what he wants to say or how he is saying it. The way in which he communicates his wants may not make sense to all the people around him, but he does communicate.

7. How can I help an autistic person improve the quality of his communication skills?

First of all become his best friend. Trust is essential before any real change will take place. Inspire him to interact with you and the rest follows.

8. My child's behaviour can become violent. Why?

Most self-injurious or violent behaviour is born out of frustration. Removing the frustration is the tool to removing self-injurious and violent behaviour. Restricting a child's movements leads to more frustration. If he or she stops, it doesn't mean that he knows why he is not allowed to behave in a certain way. Creating a predictable and safe environment for your child together with the help of other people will help the child relax and will encourage him to engage in more constructive activities.

9. Should I ignore the repetitive behaviour?

Again to my knowledge, during a repetitive act or 'stim' the autistic person is busy 'stimming'. Whether you ignore it or not is of little relevance to him. However, accepting it as part of his personal need, allowing for this need and even joining in with him would contribute to him feeling more relaxed around you.

10. My child has no sense of danger. Why?

The meaning of danger and dangerous is filtered through our sensory system (see Chapter 12, p.123, sensory system). If he walks into the road, for example, it is because he is unaware of the danger of cars. The fact that a car could run him over and that he could get hurt or die is not something that he can imagine. Precautions to prevent accidents like this are essential. Again, if someone hurts himself it could be because his pain threshold is higher than yours. Best to keep knives and razors under control. My son chose to step on a lamp's lightbulb out of curiosity.

11. What makes a safe environment?

An environment where he cannot get hurt and you can relax. A safe playroom where everything goes and he can learn more and a house without ornaments that can break.

12. My child spends hours on end lining up bricks. Should I hide the bricks from him?

Taking away the bricks will only remove the sense of comfort your child has. Soon he will line up other things. Joining in, if he allows you, is more likely to lead to him wanting to become your friend. After you are his friend you can teach him how to build castles.

13. Am I encouraging autistic behaviour if I join in?

You did not teach your child to line up toys. He came up with the idea. It is his way to explore the world. By levelling with his way of exploring he is more likely to listen to you and trust you. If he could join in with you he would have done already.

14. When I call my child's name he runs past me, yet when he hears his favourite tune on TV he runs into the room. Why?

Perhaps his favourite tune gives him more comfort than being with people. Try singing the tune yourself and see if he runs to you the same way.

15. I was told that my child has no imagination. Is this true?

Without imagination he wouldn't be able to play at all. My autistic son has the most extensive imagination amongst us all.

16. Yes, but his play is repetitive.

That play is only repetitive to our perception. By playing together you will learn the role of repetition and get to invent games that are not repetitive (see Chapter 18). Also the more you play together, the more your chances are of helping him learn how to compromise.

17. I know he can say 'apple', but he will only say it sometimes and not all the time.

This could be why:

- The child doesn't know that 'apple' is the name of a fruit so he could say apple every time he wants to eat.

- The child is affected by something called auditory discrimination and he is unable to distinguish the sounds made by words from the rest of the sounds.

In the first example, learning that words have meanings and that they are an effective way to communicate is the first lesson your child needs to master.

In the second example, the child would benefit from a silent learning environment where only the spoken word is heard.

18. How do I do that?

Through loving interaction, communication, games and fun.

19. Yes, but real life is not only about fun. There are rules to follow.

Your child makes judgements on what is real life based on what his sensory system feeds as 'true' information about the surroundings. Therefore, some of our rules make no sense to him or remain unknown to him. Once you instil curiosity and he is ready to learn more, you can teach him rules and concepts even though he will never sense the environment in the same way you do.

20. Is my child too old to benefit from my autistic-friendly attitude and/or an interaction playroom?

It is never too late to begin and understand a person. It is never too late to accept and face autism for what it is. It is never too late to begin and ask for new things from your child. It is never too late to try and have fun. It is never too late to begin showing your love by creating an autistic space in your home for him.

21. Do I have what it takes to do this?

Every parent would love to die in peace. It is hard to think that way when our child is diagnosed with autism. We tend to think more about what would happen to our child after we die and live very little in the present.

By observing the child we have, not the child that was hoped for (see Chapter 2, Don't mourn for us, p.28), we can use our energies to help him and us. You have the motivation and some know-how. Changing the know-how a little could transform you into his best source of inspiration. Autism is with your child 24 hours a day. Change the way in which you are interacting with your child and interaction becomes a 24-hour approach to autism.

22. How long does it take before I see any changes?

On average a non-verbal child needs three years to manifest his genuine curiosity about language and communicate. It takes as little as five minutes for a child to notice that you have changed your attitude towards him and he will change for you too. Every change is a lasting change because it was the child who chose to change. You never drilled him to change. He understood why it was more fun to try and change the way he communicates.

It took me one year of communication to remove the fear of 'burning in hell' from a friend who took the words literally. She was able to let go of her fear after she understood metaphor or the role of a figure of speech.

23. How many hours a day do I have to do this?

As I said before, the more you play and interact, the easier your relationship becomes. The sooner you change your attitude, the sooner he will accept you as his mentor and learn from you. The more hours you choose to be respectful and curious about your child's needs, the sooner you will understand your child and your child will understand you. Getting people to come to your home and help you will make your life easier (see Chapter 10, Play helper friends, p.110).

24. What immediate changes can I see?

Any of the following:

- the first meaningful word that he used
- use of body language to indicate understanding of spoken language
- choosing to play with you as opposed to spinning a ball
- showing you how to spin a chair like he does
- a first goodbye wave
- the first blow-a-kiss gesture
- a first kiss
- a happy and relaxed face
- no self-injurious behaviour
- clear enunciation of words
- the very first sentence
- his first 'Mummy I love you'.

25. Are these changes long lasting?

If you continue to approach your child with the same attitude of respect, then they are long lasting and he will learn more. However, if the change means that he said his first word, and if that word made no sense to him and he repeated it in an echolalic way, you have a longer road ahead. When an autistic child talks for the first time he will speak in a mixture of echolalic and meaningful speech, sometimes only echolalic. This doesn't mean that he will never acquire meaningful speech. It means that he is able to hear words and he is repeating them. Your next job is to teach him their meanings.

26. What if my child will never talk?

I have not met a child without any speech or attempted speech. However, there are other ways of communication worth learning. Communication is not about speech alone. If your child makes sounds, try not to give up on trying to inspire him to copy words. Copying words is your starting point.

27. What would happen if I don't help him at all?

I don't know since I have no crystal ball. I know that these children find it hard to make sense of who we are and what we want. I was told many stories about the childhood experienced by the now adult autistic; wishing that they had had help to understand what is going on, wishing that the help was delivered in a kind way and hating the fact that autism is an invisible disability. I also know that a loving approach will lead to a child becoming relaxed and inquisitive and that from a platform of respect anything is possible.

28. What is autism?

I regard autism as a way of being. In Chapter 1 you can read various clinical definitions of this condition. This book is not about clinical definitions. Nor is it about miraculous cures or impossible recoveries. This book is about autism, your child and yourself in terms of your daily interaction.

29. What do you mean by a way of being?

A way of being quantifies a unique set of behaviours and a way of thinking that stems from a literal and spatial learning. This type of learning influences your child's behaviour to a certain degree. Therefore his interactive behaviour is visibly different from what we call 'normal'. A way of being also quantifies a set of unseen emotional states of being that are exactly the same as your own.

Example

At the age of five my tensed and confused autistic child ate earth, wore no clothes at all, drew on my walls, ran a mile from a cuddle and charged into my stomach to show his affection. At age 12 the same autistic child shares his affection through cuddles, gentle kisses, bright smiles, a good word and making presents for his brother or sister. He writes scripts that entertain us and finds literal interpretation of words most amusing and joins us for meals in restaurants.

30. Is autism the same thing as autistic behaviour?

No. Autism is a label or a diagnosis. Some autistic behaviour is explained in depth in various chapters.

31. Should I fear autistic/repetitive behaviour?

No. You should learn to observe it and find out what triggers it. Then create an environment that caters specifically for your child's needs.

Example

If your child is lining up toys he probably derives a sense of comfort from the order that he created. Should you take those toys away or prevent him from lining them up, he will find another activity just as repetitive if not even more so. What you can do is line them up for him and show him what you have done. If you are doing it out of love and compassion you will be amazed to observe that your child will smile at you with gratitude.

If your child bangs his head repetitively it could be that he has a headache but cannot tell you. Give him a massage if he allows you to and observe his reactions.

If he walks around the house repetitively chanting 'When is daddy coming home?' and 'ignores' your answer, it could be that he hasn't developed a concept of time yet, or that he repeats a learned set of words he heard from his brother or sister. He's not asking you the same question to annoy you; it's purely that he doesn't understand your answer. What you can do is to help him visualise your answer. Play a video and tell him that when this video is finished 'daddy is home' or tell him that when it's dark outside and the sun is not in the sky any more 'daddy is home'.

When daddy arrives home make sure to say it in words: 'Daddy is home' (see Chapter 20).

32. Is autism preventing my child from developing imagination?

No. Imagination is natural and comes to all of us. I will stick to an overused example stating that a non-autistic child will pick up a banana and pretend to talk into it as if it were a phone, but the autistic child will not do the same. It is wrong to conclude that the child lacks imagination because he doesn't engage in playing pretend games at the same age as his peers. Why? In the above example the non-autistic child is:

- talking or at least babbling
- comfortable in the company of others
- copying the adults or other children
- feeling at ease addressing other people
- able to decode body language.

The autistic child is:

- not talking to people, let alone talking into a banana
- not feeling at ease in the company of other people
- feeling overwhelmed by various sensory inputs
- unable to decode body language or copy body language
- happily spending numerous hours watching television, and after careful observation you will notice that he pretend plays the characters or animated objects which he has been watching all day.

For detailed information on social communication see Chapter 12.

33. Is autism preventing my child from playing with other children?

No. His sensitive hearing might prevent him from playing with loud children, his tactile sensitivity might prevent him from playing 'it', his lack of flexibility might make other children avoid him or he might not understand enough language to be able to keep up with the rules of a game.

34. How can I help my child join in?

Teach him flexibility of thought. Before your child can join in with other children, he needs your support and guidance. You can only offer support and guidance to a child who is willing to listen and willing to learn from you. Without those you might be able to 'enforce' a certain behaviour but you cannot teach – in the true spirit of teaching – anything. Your greatest gift to your child would be:

- to create an environment in your home in which he can feel safe enough to relax and learn from you
- to learn to observe him and make allowances for his style of learning
- to discover his sensitivities and help him compensate

- to develop a friendship and a close relationship so that you can teach anything (good behaviour, language, respect, acceptance, trust).

35. Can a non-verbal child learn language?

If a child is capable of making sounds he can:

- acquire words
- learn the meaning of those words
- use meaningful words (e.g. drink, bed, TV, food, go)
- use words to make small meaningful sentences
- speak out parrot fashion meaningless words or sentences
- ask questions, thus acquiring more meaningful language
- use that language in the context of a small conversation
- talk at you or talk to himself
- converse and talk with you
- talk with others
- talk in robot-like speech
- develop fluency and melodic speech
- communicate and develop communication skills.

This list is an attempt to show you how your child's language develops step by step. The process of learning communication skills takes both time and interaction.

36. My child bites me. Why?

He probably bites out of frustration. If he were able to express his frustration through language, you would understand his reasons and would be in a better position to deal with his frustration. Behaviour modification techniques may succeed in stopping him from biting you, but without communication you will never know what caused him to bite and he will never understand what is wrong about him biting you.

37. My child throws himself on the pavement. Why?

Some of the children whom I met threw themselves on the floor or pavement when they couldn't cope with the noise or with the demands that were placed on them. This behaviour vanishes in time.

38. Will my child ever learn social rules?

Your child will learn social rules when he begins actively to seek the company of other people. If a child is afraid to interact with other people, he cannot learn from them. If a child is interested in other people, he will learn from them. If he feels comfortable in their company or even more than that he enjoys their company, he will learn some of the social rules by himself whilst other rules will have to be explained. If you have his trust he will listen to your explanations. If he feels judged by you or by his peers, he will not seek explanations.

39. Will my child be able to go into mainstream school?

Some children will be able to *survive* mainstream education. Others are able to *thrive* within mainstream education. Others *cannot cope* with it. Mainstream teaching is aimed at linear learners. Even if an autistic child behaves impeccably and enjoys social interaction, he will continue to learn in a spatial way. Personal accounts from my adult autistic friends allowed me to understand their emotional trauma. This trauma stemmed from being bullied and called names such as 'weirdo', 'stupid', 'dumb', 'slow', etc. Although my friends were surrounded by role models of so-called normal behaviour, through no fault of their own the other students were unable to empathise with the autistic mind.

If you can find a mainstream school geared to providing a pastoral environment, then try sending your child to that school. If your child is happy to get out of bed in the morning and looking forward to the next day in school, then continue. If he is not happy and asks questions such as 'Why are you sending me to school? Do I have to go there? Why do people bully me? Why don't I have a friend? Why doesn't anybody like me?' then you might like to consider home schooling. Search for information on education other than at school. It is legal and you have that right.

40. What would help him adapt to a formal environment?

Flexibility of thought and self-esteem. Flexibility of thought comes after he finds a way to translate his visual thinking into meaningful words. The length of this process varies from child to child. Your role is to assist him with the development of this skill. Self-esteem stems from feeling appreciated as a human being and not being picked on for his style of learning.

41. Will my child marry?

Autism doesn't prevent a person from getting married, from falling in love or from wanting children. If you help your child understand himself better he will become a better husband/wife/mother/father. Whether his marriage will be successful or not depends on how in love they are with each other and on their ability to keep communication channels open. I believe the latter is needed in any marriage.

42. Can my child hold down full-time employment?

I already know of autistic people in full-time employment and I know people in part-time employment. I also know people who find it difficult to keep a job because of extreme tiredness or lack of allowances for autism. There is no way of guessing someone's future.

43. Can he become a parent?

Autism does not prevent a person from wanting or having a child. An autistic friend of mine has a non-autistic child whilst another autistic friend adopted a child and gave birth to two non-autistic children and one autistic. Another dear friend asked me: 'If I have a child and if my child is autistic and screams a lot, will you look after him until he stops screaming? Because I know I cannot cope with loud noises.' Therefore the questions are 'If your child did have an autistic child *will* you have the patience to help him with his parenting skills? Will you have enough inner strength to help your grandchild when your child cannot cope?'

44. What will happen to my child after I die?

This question played on my mind for many years. Therefore I would like to direct your energies towards the following question.

45. How can I help him while I am still alive?

- If your child is non-verbal you can help him speak and communicate.

- If over the years your child became violent you can help him reverse and exchange it for fun interaction.

- If your child was recently diagnosed and he is a teenager, you can learn more about the condition and learn more about how the condition affects him.

- You can campaign for a better understanding and humane treatment of autistic people. You can start this campaign by showing your child how much you love him as well as letting him know that there are times when you don't understand him.

- You can write to your MP and let him know about the difficulties that your family are experiencing/have experienced.

46. Is it my fault that my child has autism?

No it is not. The thing that really matters is how you can help him now that you know that your child has autism.

47. What is my role?

Your role is best described as translator and mentor. As you read the various examples and work your way through the exercises, I hope that you will understand that it *is in your power* to help your child, understand his reality and to empathise with him, thus helping him to communicate with you.

As his communications skills develop he will be in a position to explain what is in *his power to change* by telling you why he doesn't like being touched, why he doesn't eat soft foods, why he is afraid of a noise, or any other 'why' questions you might have.

You can cherish him so he may feel that he belongs, prevent him from feeling lonely, as well as help him develop a sense of self-worth and personal value. The rest is up to him.

48. How can I learn more?

If you feel you need more personal help, contact us via our website (http://hope-tlc.autistics.org).

Linguistic behaviour assessment table

Linguistic behaviour	Possible meaning
Non-verbal, only making sounds.	If the child makes sounds then he is able to pronounce words. He is not pronouncing them because: 1. He can't hear speech as speech so he doesn't know what to copy. 2. He doesn't know that language is a communication tool, which he is meant to use.
List sounds here: *Suggestions:* 1. Turn all sources of sounds off. 2. Wait for him to hear that you are repeating his sounds. 3. Once he hears you repeating them, expand on them and make words around those sounds. 4. Model their meaning if you can.	
When you call out his name, he doesn't respond.	1. He cannot hear you. 2. He cannot identify with that name – responding to a name is like responding to a concept.
Suggestion: Increasing the number of interactive games you play together will bring solutions to those problems. Playing in front of a mirror will help him form the concept of self and names. (Alexander was five years old when he wrote his name on his body and pointing at it told me 'I am Alex, see I am human too'.)	

Linguistic behaviour	Possible meaning
Delayed echolalic speech – repeats entire sentences over and over.	1. The entire sentence doesn't make sense. 2. Just one word doesn't make sense, therefore the whole meaning of the sentence is lost.

Your child's sentence:

Suggestions:

1. Observe his body language. When he repeats those sentences is he agitated? Does he look puzzled?

2. Offer to help him.

He calls you 'mother' or other invented names although you are his father and vice versa.	He doesn't understand the concept of mother or father.

Suggestions:

1. Increased interaction and play will bring solutions for this problem.

2. For more solutions see Chapter 14 on language.

Immediate echolalic speech: e.g. he responds to your question 'Do you want a drink?' with your question 'Do you want a drink?' even when he doesn't want a drink.	1. He can hear speech as speech and repeats it. 2. He could be repeating it because he likes the melody of the sentence or because it doesn't make sense. 3. When he repeats it he is memorising it.

Your child's examples:

Suggestions:

1. When you ask him if he wants a drink, take a drink in your hand, offer it to him and say 'Do you want a drink?' Label his body language in response to your offer, e.g. 'No you don't', and put the drink away, or 'Yes you do' as he takes it from you.

2. Replace 'you' with your child's name.

3. Replace 'me' with your name: e.g. 'Can Mum give Alex a drink?' 'Is Alex thirsty?'

Linguistic behaviour	Possible meaning
He engages in conversation but fails to ask questions.	He doesn't know what questions are for.
Suggestion: Encourage him to ask you questions and then give him the answers. This way you are modelling what a question is: e.g. encourage your child to say 'Ask me how was my day' (curiosity, bonding); 'Ask me to help you' (interactive tool); 'Ask me what is my favourite cartoon' (curiosity, pleasure, initiating a pleasurable conversation); 'Ask me what games I like and why I like them' (a tool to discover a person's reasons behind their actions and behaviour). Hopefully within days he will ask his own questions. As a consequence his vocabulary will grow and his behaviour will change.	
Talks to himself and doesn't like being interrupted.	1. He is trying to remember the whole sentence or the whole scenario that happened during the day. 2. He is trying to make sense of other conversations that took place earlier. 3. He is replacing the old meaning of a word with its new meaning.
Suggestion: Give him the space and the time he needs to finish talking to himself. Interrupting him will only delay his acquisition of meaningful language.	
He calls a boy a girl or a girl a boy, a female male and a male a female. He cannot remember the right names for the right people.	1. He may not be able to see the face of that person and therefore cannot distinguish between what a male or female looks like. 2. He could be unable to hear the differences in intonation between the male and female voice.
Your child's examples:	
Suggestions: Time and increased interaction will solve this. Show him photographs of the people he knows and teach him their names. Ask him to identify members of the family in a family picture.	

Linguistic behaviour	Possible meaning
If, during conversation, you interrupt him halfway through a sentence or just before he said the last word, he repeats the whole sentence.	1. He must hear himself saying the sentence from the beginning to the end. 2. If he doesn't he thinks that you don't know what he wants to say or he can't remember what he wanted to say and ask.

Suggestions:

Allow him to finish his sentence. Think up conversations that focus around his interests (e.g. Bob the Builder, Thomas the Tank Engine or Postman Pat). During conversations turn off all other sources of sound.

He talks to himself in numerous voices.	He developed different voices to help him cope with different situations and emotions.

List how many voices and what each voice is saying:

Suggestions:

1. First you need him to trust and befriend you.

2. Those voices are similar to the imaginary friends that some children develop during their childhood years.

3. With increased interaction and when surrounded by 'real friends' your child no longer needs to rely on them.

Your child doesn't say please and thank you.	Please and thank you are conceptual representations of two deep emotions. 'Please' means asking for a favour and 'Thank you' is an expression of gratitude. Your child will remember their meanings after he experiences the emotions.

Suggestion:

You can help him label those emotions when he feels them. I doubt a child will say 'Please stop me from lining up toys' or 'Thank you for restraining me'.

Linguistic behaviour	Possible meaning
He uses some words in context (drink, bed, walk, stop, video) and others are echolalic (e.g. if you ask him where his bed is he would say 'go to bed').	1. He realised that words have meanings. 2. He finds it easier to learn words by association but cannot understand concepts, hence fails to make a clear distinction between 'bed' and 'go to bed'.

Your child's example phrases:

Suggestions:

1. Increased interactive games will help his vocabulary acquisition.

2. After he acquires more language he will realise the distinction between 'bed' and 'go to bed'.

His intonation is too loud: e.g. he is shouting 'Please be quiet' when he is meaning to whisper.	He cannot regulate the tone of his voice because he cannot hear it whilst focused on talking.

Suggestions:

1. Model the intonation that matches his words by repeating his words using the right intonation. He will repeat the words and, in time, he will use them without you having to help him.

2. If you have his attention tell him the difference between whispering and shouting.

He talks in a robot-like speech.	1. He is developing spontaneous speech and needs time to formulate his sentence. 2. Robot-like speech becomes substituted with melodic speech after he acquires more language.

Suggestion:

Talk to him at every opportunity.

His speech sounds distorted.	He hears speech as distorted and therefore reproduces a distorted speech.

Suggestions:

1. Turn off all other sources of sound.

2. Whisper your words.

3. Experiment with your intonation.

Linguistic behaviour	Possible meaning
When you offer to help him he replies, 'I don't need help, don't help me.'	1. He associates the word help with him being unable to finish something alone. His pride feels hurt. 2. Your style of delivering help confuses him instead of helping him. Therefore the word help translates to him as 'interfere'.

Suggestions:

1. Find out what is his understanding of the word 'help'.

2. Model various meanings of the word help and get him to feel comfortable hearing it and using it (e.g. help with lifting, reading, cooking, kissing a hurt finger).

3. Ask him to help you lift something heavy and tell him that you could not have done it without his help. Then offer to help him with something that he can't finish alone (such as opening a bottle of soft drink).

4. Find other ways of illustrating the meaning of help. This way you are helping him to develop *interdependent skills.*

5. At the end of an activity, treat yourselves to something simple but enjoyable such as a chocolate bar that you *share* to celebrate your joint efforts.

He talks in invented language.	Because you responded to his invented language he believes that he is using the right words. Silently he accumulates words but he doesn't know that he should use them (see Chapter 18, p.175, silent learner).

Your child's invented language (e.g. he is asking you for a drink using the word 'red'):

Suggestions:

Every time you offer him the drink, tell him that what he calls 'red' we call 'drink'. Each day encourage him to say 'Can you say d-r-i-n-k for me?'

Linguistic behaviour	Possible meaning
He repeats your words hours or weeks after you said them: e.g. a young boy who did not use language at all repeated my words 'Open the window' five hours after I asked him to say those words. He wanted to throw plastic balls out of the window. I was happy for him to do that and each time he approached the window with a ball in his hand I asked him to say 'Open the window' and I will open the window faster.	1. He can hear the words. 2. He can repeat the words. 3. He cannot understand the cause and effect of those words. 4. He needs many hours to process the meaning of those words.

Suggestions:

1. He needs to speak more words before he can understand their meaning.

2. Interactive games will help him to do that.

Linguistic behaviour	Possible meaning
His intonation is made up of a hybrid between an 'American accent', a 'cartoon accent' and your family's accent.	1. He fully understands the words that sound normal. 2. It is possible that he doesn't understand all of the words that sound in 'different accents'. He learns them by rote and uses them to talk at you. You can help him understand them.

Suggestions:

1. Talk to him in different accents.

2. Test his understanding of those words by seeing if his behaviour matches his verbal instructions.

Linguistic behaviour	Possible meaning
He engages in conversation but doesn't finish his sentence. If you ask him to continue he says, 'Never mind, it wasn't important.'	He hasn't reached a comfortable level of verbal fluency and is self-aware.

Observation:

Time will solve this.

Linguistic behaviour	Possible meaning
He will only hold a conversation if he is initiating it. If you want to start one he tells you that he is not in a talking mood.	Not being in a talking mood means that he is in thinking mood and that he can't think and talk at the same time.

Suggestions:

1. By respecting his wishes and not talking to him when he is not in a talking mood you are passing control to him.

2. Over longer periods of time you can say to him, 'I know you are not in a talking mood, but this is important for both of us.'

3. 'Could we talk now?'

4. You might be pleasantly surprised by his co-operation.

He is repetitively asking you the same question: e.g. 'When are we getting to the swimming pool?'	1. He doesn't understand or like your answer. 2. He doesn't understand the concept of time.

His question(s):

Suggestions:

1. Ask him to tell you what he understood from your answer.

2. Draw a map from your house to the swimming pool. Explain the journey.

3. Tell him that you don't like the fact that it takes time to get there.

He tells you that you are his adoptive parents.	1. He can notice the differences in behaviour between you. 2. He notices that his brothers and sisters behave differently around him. 3. He doesn't know what those differences mean. 4. He is looking for reassurance and understanding. 5. He believes that you are his adoptive parents because you don't understand his needs.

Suggestions:

1. Tell him that you are his real parents.

2. Tell him that you don't understand all his needs and ask him to help you understand them.

Linguistic behaviour	Possible meaning
You can hold full conversations but they seem to end with an argument each time: e.g. if you loved me you would not send me to boarding school; you would not make me go to this party; you would let me use the internet all night.	This problem is not dependent on language alone. However, his understanding of it influences his emotional behaviour. 1. He believes that you sent him there because you don't love him. 2. He believes that you sent him there because he was adopted. 3. He can't understand how his behaviour is different. 4. He doesn't think that his school helps him. 5. Although you want him to go to parties so he may socialise, he doesn't like them because he can't follow the social rules or simply doesn't feel comfortable in noisy rooms.

Argument:

Suggestions:

1. Ask him to write about 'One Day in My School'.

2. Ask him to write why he thinks that he is going to boarding school.

3. Give him your reasons why he is enrolled in a boarding school.

4. Ask him to write a list of social activities he enjoys and one for those he doesn't.

Linguistic behaviour	Possible meaning
As soon as your conversation becomes emotional he loses his ability to talk. The conversation stops when you are using an *alert word*.	1. He feels overwhelmed. 2. He feels confused and needs help to understand the sources of his and your emotions.

Your child's alert words:

Alert words are words that your child doesn't understand or which trigger negative emotions in him. Those words could be any of the following: understand, autism, autistic, weird, help, different, change, learn, school, love, friends, behave, normal, question, no.

Suggestions:

1. Offer him a piece of paper so that he may continue the train of thought in writing.

2. Write your answers and your reasons for the answers.

3. Allow your child to read them in his own time.

4. Answer every question truthfully.

5. Encourage him to write and share his reasons with you, not just the answers.

6. Check and double check that your answers make sense to him.

7. Make a note of the *alert words*.

8. Work out a compromise.

Pierce's vocabulary after eight months of play

Numbers

One to ten and more

Books, Toys, Games and Amusements

ball
Bambi
Barney (red car driver)
Beast (Beauty and the)
boat
ook (book)
bridge
bubbles
bus
car
Dig and Dug
draw
Dum-Dum (Dumbo)
Dumpty (Humpty-Dumpty)
house

Noddy
Pat (Postman Pat)
pens
plane
puzzle
see-saw marjorie daw
slide
No-White (Snow White)
string
tractor
train
truck
wheel(s)
Woody (cowboy)

Adjectives/Senses

all wet
roken (broken)
cold

finished
hot
yummy

To Eat and Drink

apple
nana (banana)
cheese
nisps (crisps)
dinner
drink

ham
lunch
sandwich
seetie (sweetie)
toast
yoghurt

Family and Friends

Daddy
Mummy
Sames (James)
Matty

David
Kay
Baby

The Body

ears
eyes
feet
hair
hand

head
mouth
nose
toes
tongue

Exclamations

All gone!
Oh dear!
Oh no!

Ouch!
Whoops!

Commands

again off (same for on)
bite it
blow up (me up)
catch me
cay-ull (careful)
come back
come in
come on
cuggle (cuddle)
down (me down)
eedown (lie or sit down)
get up
go way
help me

piss (kiss)
ook (look)
ook out here I come
marks, get set, go
me want
more
open
pull
push
ready, steady, go
subbee (shut door)
tickle me
wait
wake up

Questions

ee are you?

where is he?

Animals/Birds/Nature

bear
birdie
cat
chicken
cow
doggie
donkey
duck
fish
flower

frog
horsey
fire (?lion)
mouse
rabbis (rabbits)
raining
eep (sheep)
spider
tree

Clothes, etc.

glasses
hat

shoe
zip

The House/Playroom

bath
bed
cock (clock)
door
keys
light
pushchair

sand
seet (sheet)
stairs
table
up the stairs
water
window

The autistic perception

In February 2000 I came across a new voice on the internet, Amanda Baggs. I reproduce here only two out of the many articles that she has written. For more articles written by autistic people visit the library (www.autistics.org). As you read 'Being a Spatial Thinker', try and understand why it is difficult for your child to learn from words alone as well as reinforce in your mind that it is not impossible for your child to learn and express his thoughts in words. In her article, Amanda Baggs describes a style of thinking which cannot be accurately described as visual or as verbal. This article, the one that follows and other articles by Amanda Baggs can be found at www.autistics.org Information Library.

Being a spatial thinker
by Amanda Baggs

I have been told I am very good at mathematical or verbal things, or alternatively that I am very bad at mathematical or verbal things. As if each is a category that cannot be divided. What I think is happening is that I am very good at spatial things, and that my spatial abilities (which are extremely pronounced) govern what I am good at within a broad category of ability. Spatial abilities are also not tied to any one sense, and are an internal way of functioning.

Spatial thinking is a way of organising things in my head. It is non-visual (though some people think visual and spatial are synonymous) but involves connections between things in a format like 3-D or more – dimensional space. Sometimes there is no connection but just a spatial relation. This is not the only level of thought for me, because there is another level of thought which does not involve representation of anything. However, this is my form of symbolic thought. I do not think with language. Sometimes I add in pictures sounds, smells, and other sensory things to each 'point' or 'area' of spatial thought in my head, that these things are not necessary but enhance it.

My senses have always sent me information that is to some degree or another garbled. Particularly, this is true for vision, hearing, and touch, with vision and hearing being the worst. However, I can count on the hand the number of times I have gotten lost in my life.

I talked to someone once who told me that by people's eye movements and speech patterns he could tell whether someone was a visual, auditory, or kinaesthetic learner. I said, 'What if they are equal in all three?' He said this was impossible.

They say that a visual learner says 'I see what you mean'. An auditory learner would say 'I hear what you mean'. A kinaesthetic learner would say 'I feel what you mean'. This is oversimplified, but the idea is that people use language idioms based on what kind of learner and thinker they are.

I use many of those idioms, crossing all the senses. Depending on which I am using at the time, people make assumptions. It would be more helpful in my case to look at the nature of idioms I use to describe things in a non-sensory way. I talk about things being 'on different levels': some things are 'surface' levels, and others are 'core'. I want to know what is 'behind' something. Things are 'over' things and 'under' things and 'through' things. I describe many things in terms of geometric shapes and concepts. This, for me, is constant, not fluctuating like my use of sensory idioms. Sometimes, but not always, my own spatial idioms clash with spatial idioms other people are used to. People often interpret my spatial idioms in terms of their own preferred sense. My brother, before realising what he had said, said, 'Well visual and spatial are the same thing.' Some people automatically associate the spatial idioms with visual things, some with auditory things and others with kinaesthetic things. I often associate spatial things with olfactory things as do a few other people I have met. *I WOULD GUESS THAT MY DOG AND CAT WOULD BE THE SAME.* Given that for them smell is the more primary sense than in most humans. I experience spatial representation in all senses but most often in none.

My mathematical and verbal abilities are divided along the line of spatial and non-spatial, not mathematical and verbal. There are some words I have immense difficulty in remembering the meaning of. These are once that for whatever reason I cannot find a lasting spatial representation for. These are words like 'ontology' and many other words I have encountered in philosophy class. If I can 'spatial-ise' them then I can use them. If I cannot spatial-ise them I have a lot of trouble.

Mathematics is similar. Internal geometric visualisation is very fun for me and I do do it. I have been fascinated by the concepts of infinities; number lines, geometric shapes, multiple dimensions of various kinds and other spatial things. These things have always seemed intuitive and natural to me and I like to play with them as if they are a game. However, other areas of maths some considered simpler are things that have made me feel like I was beating my head up against the wall. These things I have had to learn more painstakingly and slowly and am now deliberately learning them in order to be able to describe the things I do spatially.

One of the things I work hardest at is learning to catch up my non-spatially related skills to my spatially related skills. This is because some of the non-spatial related ones are considered essential: for example, speaking, cooking, getting dressed, and other tasks that tend to be more sequential than spatial. Also my sensory skills are very weak in some areas and I have to work at integrating them with my spatial skills in order to function.

Basically being a spatial thinker has extreme advantages and extreme drawbacks. When you are representing things in your mind with a multidimensional model, it is easier to see certain patterns in the world and infer things from those patterns. However, it is also more difficult to do things that are more sequential, one-dimensional in a line, especially when such a task involves picking a one-dimensional line out of a multidimensional web of possibilities. This can look like a slowness or inability about doing certain things or a learning disability. It can also be puzzling from the outside if you don't understand spatial thought, especially when abilities seem varied; like being able to do complicated geometry but having trouble with arithmetic. To quote myself in a moment of amusement and frustration, 'Infinity not a problem, toothbrushes tie my mind in knots.'

The symbolic level of representation inside my mind is like a big dark non-visual collection of things in a multidimensional (sometimes two, sometimes three, sometimes four, and so on) space. These things have qualitative and quantitative differences within them. I have spatial maps of everything I do, from the internal workings to the external world. My map of my neighbourhood to us is an example of something that many people use maps for. It contains no pictures of houses, it is a dark 'no picture' and contains location in space. I can because of this go almost anywhere and be able to find my way back. If I am focused enough I can tell where the stars are in the daytime. I believe this is my spatial sense kicking in.

I have several internal maps of my mind, which vary according to the situation. Some of them involve mathematical concepts like fractals, and others involve layers of spherical things. There is the 'Russian Nesting Doll' model, with the innermost 'doll' being made of something very different than the layers on top of it. There is this 'cave' model where the 'Real Me' lives far back in the cave, with a passage at the front leading to the outside world. These models are all manifestations of one model that I have. However, it does not translate easily into a three-dimensional linguistic and it is almost like a four-dimensional (or more) object intersecting with three-dimensional space. The same thing, with different cross-sections, can appear as torus ('doughnut') shape, a sphere, or many other things. There are many things it can appear as, especially if it is not a regular shape such as a hyper sphere and/or hypercube. So any description I give is the intersection between my thoughts and the linguistic and the three-dimensional-spatial mode of communication that I have available.

My map of time is a spatial thing too. It is a big curving thing that wraps around the front of my head and turns back, and wraps around itself many times. It is difficult to describe easily, but it is similar to mental number lines. I find a lot of beauty in spatial things. I do not mean as much spatial things like the layout of a room. I mean spatial things that are not representable in sensory context (you have to imagine them) representation.

Copyright © 1999 Amanda Baggs

Autistic adults and adolescents
by Amanda Baggs

Autistic adolescents and adults are people you might encounter every day but not know it. There are many things you might think about us, but often they are not true. Some of us may appear selfish or self-absorbed or egotistical because we do not respond adequately when someone says something, or because we talk on and on about one subject with little regard to the rest of the conversation. We may look childish in some or all situations because we seem to overreact to things that other people would not react to at all. We may seem gullible and naive, and some people out there will take advantage of that. You may wonder why we never seem to learn that there are people in the world we can't trust.

Others may appear almost paranoid, trusting no one at all. Some might seem 'psychotic' because of our eccentric behaviours or suspiciousness. Some of us might talk to ourselves out loud. Some of us might seem changeable or 'fake'. This is because it is fairly common for autistic people to develop a coping mechanism of a 'normal' looking persona with which to interact. Some of us have more than one such persona, and hence seem changeable. Sometimes this persona is fairly convincing, and other times it looks false and 'put on'.

Some of us might appear like loners, or eccentric loners. Some of us might appear as the opposite – people who try hard to be social but don't know how. Some of us might appear 'eccentric', and others might appear, in the common language, 'retarded'. You might love us or hate us or like us or tolerate us or dislike us. You might keep your kids away from us because we might look like there is something 'wrong' with us. We might look heartless because we do not have the same emotions you do, or maybe just don't know how to show them. We might look too sensitive, or too insensitive, or both. We might seem too immature or too mature, or both. We might do things we have done since we were kids. When we were kids, adults might have thought of some of these things as 'cute', but we are now adolescents and adults who are too old for 'cute'. Now, such things might be irritating or annoying, at best.

We might have so much skill in one area that we seem to be deliberately trying not to understand another area. We might seem to be manipulative when at one moment we can do something 'complicated' like fix your computer, recite things, or do complex mathematics, and the next moment cannot see that you are upset, or what to do about it. We might seem to ignore you, or seem to ignore your feelings. We might not know when to stop talking, or when to start. We might not be able to talk, or might talk oddly or in short repeated phrases. We might talk what seems to be normally.

Some of us may have been diagnosed as children with autism. Some of us may have been diagnosed with attention deficit disorder. Some of us may not have been diagnosed with anything at all, or held other diagnoses. Some of us may have been called 'psychotic'. Some of us may have facial tics left over from decades of anti-psychotic medications that did us no good. Some of us may have facial and other tics for no reason other than our neurological make-up. We might now be undiagnosed, be diagnosed with autism, Asperger's Syndrome, atypical autism, or things that have nothing to do with developmental disorders. We may have additional diagnoses of depression, anxiety, psychosis, personality disorders, epilepsy, or many other things. We might think of ourselves as 'cured', or might look forward to 'cure', or might hate the idea of 'cure'. We might have 'a few autistic traits'.

We come from all different backgrounds, and have all different appearances. We are classified as high functioning, low functioning, anything in between, and any combination of functioning levels. We may obviously have something different about us, or might just appear odd in some ways. Some of us wouldn't appear different at all until you got to know us. We may have been lower functioning, or higher functioning, or the same level of functioning, as children. We present our autism in as many ways as there are autistic people, and have as many opinions about it.

We may have high-paying jobs, or low-paying jobs, or no jobs. We may live alone or with our parents or in a group home or with roommates or have families. We may be students or work in any of many fields. We may live in a house or apartment, or be homeless.

The thing we all have in common is that we are autistic. We may not always appear like the child that so many people have heard of, who rocks and bangs his head on the wall and does not make eye contact and is completely mute and will never speak and lives in an institution. We may not appear like the *Rainman* savant who does complex calculations in his head but is otherwise autistic. But we are autistic. We share some of the same difficulties and the same advantages in being autistic. We have differences, yes, but we do have that in common.

The next time you think of autistic children, remember that children grow up. The next time you think of someone who you get furious with because they just 'don't get' something simple even though they can do some things that are complicated, remember us. The next time you see someone walking down the street flapping their hands in front of their face and making odd noises, remember us. They may not be autistic, but you never know. Autistic children grow up into autistic adolescents and autistic adults. We do not appear always the same as autistic children, though we may have a lot in common with them that may or may not be visible. Autistic adults exist, and live in this society, but not necessarily connect to it, every day. We are out there, trying to live. Remember our existence.

Copyright © 1999 Amanda Baggs

Don't mourn for us

by Jim Sinclair

[This article was published in 1993 in *Our Voice*, the newsletter of Autism Network International. It is an outline of the presentation I gave at the 1993 International Conference on Autism in Toronto, and is addressed primarily to parents.]

Parents often report that learning their child is autistic was the most traumatic thing that ever happened to them. Non-autistic people see autism as a great tragedy, and parents experience continuing disappointment and grief at all stages of the child and family's life cycle.

But this grief does not stem from the child's autism in itself. It is grief over the loss of the normal child the parents had hoped and expected to have. Parents' attitudes and expectations, and the discrepancies between what parents expect of children at a particular age and their own child's actual development, cause more stress and anguish than the practical complexities of life with an autistic person.

Some amount of grief is natural as parents adjust to the fact that an event and a relationship they've been looking forward to aren't going to materialize. But this grief over a fantasized normal child needs to be separated from the parents' perceptions of the child they do have: the autistic child who needs the support of adult caretakers and who can form very meaningful relationships with those caretakers if given the opportunity. Continuing focus on the child's autism as a source of grief is damaging for both the parents and the child, and precludes the development of an accepting and authentic relationship between them. For their own sake and for the sake of their children, I urge parents to make radical changes in their perceptions of what autism means. I invite you to look at our autism, and look at your grief, from our perspective:

Autism is not an appendage

Autism isn't something a person has, or a 'shell' that a person is trapped inside. There's no normal child hidden behind the autism. Autism is a way of being. It is pervasive; it colours every experience, every sensation, perception, thought, emotion, and encounter, every aspect of existence. It is not possible to separate the autism from the person – and if it were possible, the person you'd have left would not be the same person you started with.

This is important, so take a moment to consider it: Autism is a way of being. It is not possible to separate the person from the autism.

Therefore, when parents say, 'I wish my child did not have autism', what they're really saying is, 'I wish the autistic child I have did not exist, and I had a different (non-autistic) child instead.'

Read that again. This is what we hear when you mourn over our existence. This is what we hear when you pray for a cure. This is what we know, when you tell us of your fondest hopes and dreams for us: that your greatest wish is that one day we will cease to be, and strangers you can love will move in behind our faces.

Autism is not an impenetrable wall

You try to relate to your autistic child, and the child doesn't respond. He doesn't see you; you can't reach her; there's no getting through. That's the hardest thing to deal with, isn't it? The only thing is, it isn't true.

Look at it again: You try to relate as parent to child, using your own understanding of normal children, your own feelings about parenthood, your own experiences and intuitions about relationships. And the child doesn't respond in any way you can recognize as being part of that system.

That does not mean the child is incapable of relating at all. It only means you're assuming a shared system, a shared understanding of signals and meanings, that the child in fact does not share. It's as if you tried to have an intimate conversation with someone who has no comprehension of your language. Of course the person won't understand what you're talking about, won't respond in the way you expect, and may well find the whole interaction confusing and unpleasant.

It takes more work to communicate with someone whose native language isn't the same as yours. And autism goes deeper than language and culture; autistic people are 'foreigners' in any society. You're going to have to give up your assumptions about shared meanings. You're going to have to learn to back up to levels more basic than you've probably thought about before, to translate, and to check to make sure your translations are understood. You're going to have to give up the certainty that comes of being on your own familiar territory, of knowing you're in charge, and let your child teach you a little of her language, guide you a little way into his world.

And the outcome, if you succeed, still will not be a normal parent–child relationship. Your autistic child may learn to talk, may attend regular classes in school, may go to college, drive a car, live independently, have a career – but will never relate to you as other children relate to their parents. Or your autistic child may never speak, may graduate from a self-contained special education classroom to a sheltered activity programme or a residential facility, may need lifelong full-time care and supervision – but is not completely beyond your reach. The ways we relate are different. Push for the things your expectations tell you are normal, and you'll find frustration, disappointment, resentment, maybe even rage and hatred. Approach respectfully, without preconceptions, and with openness to learning new things, and you'll find a world you could never have imagined.

Yes, that takes more work than relating to a non-autistic person. But it can be done – unless non-autistic people are far more limited than we are in their capacity to relate. We spend our entire lives doing it. Each of us who does learn to talk to you, each of us who manages to function at all in your society, each of us who manages to reach out and make a connection with you, is operating in alien territory, making contact with alien beings. We spend our entire lives doing this. And then you tell us that we can't relate.

Autism is not death

Granted, autism isn't what most parents expect or look forward to when they anticipate the arrival of a child. What they expect is a child who will be like them, who will share their world and relate to them without requiring intensive on-the-job training in alien contact. Even if their child has some disability other than autism, parents expect to be able to relate to that child on the terms that seem normal to them; and in most cases, even allowing for the limitations of various disabilities, it is possible to form the kind of bond the parents had been looking forward to.

But not when the child is autistic. Much of the grieving parents do is over the non-occurrence of the expected relationship with an expected normal child. This grief is very real, and it needs to be expected and worked through so people can get on with their lives – but it has nothing to do with autism.

What it comes down to is that you expected something that was tremendously important to you, and you looked forward to it with great joy and excitement, and maybe for a while you thought you actually had it – and then, perhaps gradually, perhaps abruptly, you had to recognize that the thing you looked forward to hasn't happened. It isn't going to happen. No matter how many other, normal children you have, nothing will change the fact that this time, the child you waited and hoped and planned and dreamed for didn't arrive.

This is the same thing that parents experience when a child is stillborn, or when they have their baby to hold for a short time, only to have it die in infancy. It isn't about autism; it's about shattered expectations. I suggest that the best place to address these issues is not in organizations devoted to autism, but in parental bereavement counselling and support groups. In those settings parents learn to come to terms with their loss – not to forget about it, but to let it be in the past, where the grief doesn't hit them in the face every waking moment of their lives. They learn to accept that their child is gone, forever, and won't be coming back. Most importantly, they learn not to take out their grief for the lost child on their surviving children. This is of critical importance when one of those surviving children arrived at the time the child being mourned for died.

You didn't lose a child to autism. You lost a child because the child you waited for never came into existence. That isn't the fault of the autistic child who does exist, and it shouldn't be our burden. We need and deserve families who can see us and value us for ourselves, not families whose vision of us is obscured by the ghosts of children who never lived. Grieve if you must, for your own lost dreams. But don't mourn for us. We are alive. We are real. And we're here waiting for you.

This is what I think autism societies should be about: not mourning for what never was, but exploration of what is. We need you. We need your help and your understanding. Your world is not very open to us, and we won't make it without your strong support. Yes, there is tragedy that comes with autism: not because of what we are, but because of the things that happen to us. Be sad about that, if you want to be sad about something. Better than being sad about it, though, get mad about it – and then do something about it. The tragedy is not that we're here, but that your world has no place for us to be. How can it be otherwise, as long as our own parents are still grieving over having brought us into the world?

Take a look at your autistic child sometime, and take a moment to tell yourself who that child is not. Think to yourself: 'This is not my child that I expected and planned for. This is not the child I waited for through all those months of pregnancy and all those hours of labour. This is not the child I made all those plans to share all those experiences with. That child never came. This is not that child.' Then go do whatever grieving you have to do – away from the autistic child – and start learning to let go.

After you've started that letting go, come back and look at your autistic child again, and say to yourself: 'This is not my child that I expected and planned for. This is an alien child who landed in my life by accident. I don't know who this child is or what it will become. But I know it's a child, stranded in an alien world, without parents of its own kind to care for it. It needs someone to care for it, to teach it, to interpret and to advocate for it. And because this alien child happened to drop into my life, that job is mine if I want it.'

If that prospect excites you, then come join us, in strength and determination, in hope and in joy. The adventure of a lifetime is ahead of you.

Copyright © 1993 Jim Sinclair

Open your eyes

By Treasa Granell

You puzzle me... there are times
When I can stand back
And simply be intrigued –
Then moments when I'm too close –
+ want to weep
My eyes beseech – yours turn away
The window to my soul
In their pleading,
Overwhelm you.
I'm in awe of your uniqueness –
Yet want to change you.
I am in conflict.
How dare I want to mould you
Into one of 'us'
When that very uniqueness makes you
Who you are?
How dare I? Because.
I want the world to make room for you...
Instead, shelter you
From eyes that stare,
And anger swells within me
As I meet their gaze,
'Let he who is above reproof –
pass judgment',
But then I chide myself,
For they see only a beautiful child.
Allowances are bestowed by mankind
If a fault is visible –
Not in the mind.
I know then what I must do –
But first I need your trust.
You understand the literal word
But expression; gestures, perplex you.

Let me be your teacher...
I'll help you de-code,
The silent language of 'normal' exchange,

In doing so –
I, too, shall learn.
Our perceptions are so different,
So in trying to understand,
I imagine myself plucked from this world –
Placed in a distant land…
Where people speak in a foreign tongue
And I live in a haze of confusion.
But in this dream the people show
By deed & gesture –
That I am accepted for who I am.
I feel loved.
So I, in my clumsy way,
Attempt to respond
And we learn to live…
In harmony,
You are my little alien –
& I want to befriend you.
I remember now the time we explored
Your beloved red, steam train.
Inspected daily; minutely by you
Each time-seemingly-anew.
I was baffled.
What could you see that I could not?
So I knelt beside you
And stared…stared…
Until the wonder of it
Stood out to me too!
I saw gilded handles on carriage doors;
Eight shiny spokes to each wheel;
Felt the smoothness of the funnel here;
Harsh angles of the cabin there –
& time stood still.
Like you, I studied it from the front;
The back; & side-ways too –
Each perspective stored
As a different image,
Is this what you must do then?
Study the finer details
In order to piece together
The whole?…
Then you stood – arms raised; mouth open
And jumped with delight!

This time. I too, stood & jumped!
I joined you – & meant it.
Of a sudden, you stopped…
Met my eyes – & smiled.
We connected…& I was
Overwhelmed.
From that moment I chose to believe
That your 'disability' was actually
An added ability that we
do not share.
I want to build a bridge –
From my world into yours.
Will you meet me half-way?
Maybe one day,
Can it really be that simple?!
To shower you in unconditional love –
Not leave you to flounder,
But inspire you to test the waters
Of this alien land.
The answer must be yes!
And yes, again!
For you grow daily…
And far from being your teacher,
You have opened my eyes.
Things I dared only dream of
Have become a reality…
So now, when you look over your shoulder
(A look of devilment in your eye!)
And shout 'Catch me, mummy!'…
My heart soars
You still puzzle me…
But I'm learning

Copyright © 2001 Treasa Granell

Cartoons by Alexander Cowie

These cartoons are just a selection of the many that Alexander has drawn. I hope that your child will learn enough vocabulary to enable him to share a joke with you.

Inspired by 'It's Raining Men'

Inspired by 'Scream If You Want To Go Faster'

Inspired by 'Clint Eastwood'

Inspired by 'Fire'

Glossary

autism. A way of being with which we can empathise even if we don't understand all its implications. Because I am a parent of a child diagnosed with autism I refused to think about my child's autism in terms of an illness or a disease (a very emotional perception I know). I wanted to hear my child speak to me, and he now does. My last conversation about autism with Alexander started when he asked me why I had chosen the two pictures on the back cover of the book. I told him that to my perception they represent the leap from being autistic, a screamer, misunderstood and non-interactive to being autistic, understood, happy and interactive. I continued with, 'Alexander, you are no more cured today than the day I wished I could find a cure.'

He investigated, 'Why did you want to find a cure?'

I replied, 'Because you could look at a train for five hours and fall asleep looking at it but could not say "Mum, I am hungry" or "Mum, I love you". Those trains were hard competition!'

'Did you hate my trains?'

'Yes and no. No, because I bought you hundreds of them because you liked them. Yes, because I really, really wanted us to enjoy each other's company, and now we do. I am happy. Are you?'

'Yes I am.'

My journey of reaching out ended and was substituted with a journey of 'Take it away Alexander!' It was all I wanted. Science can or is trying to cure most illnesses. A way of thinking and learning cannot be cured but it can be worked with.

autistic. An individual way of being. It describes the combination of a visual, spatial and literal learning style of a person. In this sense I compare it to left-handedness or dyslexia. I make a habit of keeping my mind on full alert when I communicate with my child. Reminding myself about the differences in thinking strategies between my autistic child and myself (or any other autistic person with whom I am trying to communicate) helps us both. As soon as my child begins to converse it is very easy to believe that there are no differences between us, when in fact there are. Therefore I will talk slower. I will check if we understand each other and leave nothing to assumption. I will expect a pause between my requesting something and his reply. I will watch his body language and look for clues that we understand each other. I will encourage him to tell me what he is thinking about. I will make it easy for him to relax around me. I will draw or write my answers if he seems tired of focusing on the spoken words. I will draw maps of meanings. I will stop interacting if I am asked to.

autistic communication. Describes the autistic's attempt to communicate his needs prior to having received help with building a system of shared meanings. Such was Alexander's screaming, pulling me to the fridge, being afraid that his name changed from Alex to Frightened, charging into my stomach to show me that he loves me, etc. This communication can be translated, explained to a willing student and transformed during meaningful interaction.

autistic friend. I have made many autistic friends. In my experience autistic people are capable of forming bonds of friendship. This allayed my greatest fear, instilled by one line from one book: 'The autistic child lacks the ability to empathize.' One of the physical markers of friendship, the ability to accept and extend body contact through touch, is highly dependent on the tactile sensory system of a person. Showing shyness stems from an understanding of self. Self-control stems from a willingness to please. If there is no one to please, there is no need for self-control. Self-esteem, another must for mutual friendship, stems from knowing that you are wanted. Autistic or not, if you were to be constantly told off, your chances of developing self-esteem would be next to nil.

generalise = generalisation skills. Common questions from parents like myself are 'Why can't my child learn from experience?' or 'Why can he not generalise?' The answer to the first question comes from understanding your child's sensory system (e.g. the sense of taste). One autistic person said to me, 'I didn't know that I could peel carrots and boil them the same way as I peel potatoes and boil them.'

I asked, 'Do you like carrots?'

She replied, 'No.'

'Do you like parsnips?'

She replied, 'I do.'

I asked, 'Did anyone teach you how to cook them?'

'No. I just did what I had done to the potatoes.'

I chose this example because it illustrates our motivation to learn generalisation skills when we want to pursue one of our likes or meet a need of ours. Any autistic person will learn generalisation skills when:

- he masters a shared system of meaning with you

- he has a need to resolve

- his sensory system warns him of danger.

The answer to 'Why isn't my child talking more?' or 'Why is he not talking more after he spoke his first word?' is because he didn't know that he spoke and how speaking will change his life for the better – in the literal sense of speaking.

high functioning autism (Attwood 1998, question 10): What is the difference between high functioning autism and Asperger's Syndrome? 'At present, the results [of studies] suggest there seems to be no meaningful differences between them. They are more the same than they are different.'

As I perceive it, the only common link between high functioning autism or not so high functioning autism (not that autism functions – the person does!) is the ability of the person to make sense of the spoken word and fit in accordingly. In October 2001 I was asked, 'Are you sure that your child doesn't have Asperger's Syndrome?' (because he could speak and make jokes). I was sure. My autistic child had one core 'problem'. He couldn't relate to the spoken word in the same way as my non-autistic children. The only way to overcome the communication problem was to ensure that each spoken word that he uses shares its meaning with the majority of the English-speaking (in his case) population. This process takes time and sheltering from the 'rat race'. When we set off to solve the communication problem we prioritise our action this way: (a) his quality of his life – therefore he is more co-operative; (b) social convention.

'I'. Describes the emotional and rational efforts invested in understanding and translating autistic communication. I (personally) chose to *understand* Alexander as opposed to modifying his behaviour. I wanted to enjoy his hug (a very selfish reason) and also wanted him to enjoy mine (this is more precise than an autistic need). I wanted him to exercise self-control and to develop self-esteem. My rational self realised that we cannot 'behaviour modify' a person into enjoying a hug or a joke, relax and feel at home or share thoughts and dreams. Furthermore, self-control and self-esteem are personal characteristics, which cannot be 'drilled' into someone. This book is addressing the emotional 'You' as well as the rational 'You'. Perhaps you are the same 'I' who wants to understand his or her child. If you are, perhaps one day you could add to this story and make it better and clearer for the next parent and the next. This was the best that 'I' could do for I chose to believe that *to love is more important than to be known.*

listen, think, express. One autistic friend introduced me to this term. It describes the amount of time a person needs to hear the verbal instruction/request, think about it and make sure that he understands the meaning of it, formulates a mental reply and then replies. This time span can vary from one minute to weeks or months.

syndrome. In medicine, a typical grouping of features of a physical or mental disease. Thus the syndrome of measles includes spots, a high temperature and photophobia (dislike or fear of bright lights). This raises the question: Is a disease more than its symptoms? The symptoms are what are apparent, and used for diagnosis. There is much that is hidden and causative in the disease, beyond the symptoms (1987, *The Oxford Companion to the Mind*). The word 'disease' translates in my mind as something that could be painful and/or catching and/or life threatening. Autism – described as a behavioural syndrome or as a genetic condition – is not catching, it doesn't hurt the person, cannot be transmitted (unless through genes) and doesn't kill.

tactile sensitivity. This involves more than not enjoying a hug. One friend told me that he preferred not wearing any clothes. However, if he did he would bump into walls because he doesn't know where his body ends.

References

Attwood, T. (1998) *Asperger's Syndrome: A Guide for Parents and Professionals.* London: Jessica Kingsley Publishers.

Baggs, A. (1999) 'Being a Spatial Thinker.' www.autistics.org Information Library. Accessed February 2000.

Frith, U. (1989) *Autism: Explaining the Enigma.* Cambridge, MA: Basil Blackwell.

Grandin, T. and Scariano, M.M. (1986) *Emergence: Labeled Autistic.* Novato, CA: Academic Therapy Publications.

Sinclair, J. (1993) 'Don't Mourn For Us.' *Our Voice 1*, 3, newsletter.

Stores, G. and Wiggs, L. (1998) 'Abnormal Sleep Patterns Associated with Autism: A Brief Review of Research Findings, Assessment Methods and Treatment Strategies.' *International Journal of Research and Practice 2*, 2, 157–169.

Williams, D. (1992) *Nobody Nowhere: The Remarkable Autobiography of an Autistic Girl.* London: Jessica Kingsley Publishers.

Wing, L. (1992) *Autistic Spectrum Disorders: An Aid to Diagnosis.* London: UK National Autistic Society.